THE BANKER'S DESK BOOK

RICHARD B. MILLER

PRENTICE HALL
Englewood Cliffs, New Jersey 07632

Prentice-Hall International (UK) Limited, *London*
Prentice-Hall of Australia Pty. Limited, *Sydney*
Prentice-Hall Canada, Inc., *Toronto*
Prentice-Hall Hispanoamericana, S.A., *Mexico*
Prentice-Hall of India Private Limited, *New Delhi*
Prentice-Hall of Japan, Inc., *Tokyo*
Simon & Schuster Asia Pte. Ltd., *Singapore*
Editora Prentice-Hall do Brasil, Ltda., *Rio de Janeiro*

© 1990 *by* PRENTICE HALL, Inc. Englewood Cliffs, NJ

*To Ruth
and our four
(grownup)
children*

10 9 8 7 6 5 4 3 2 1

Library of Congress Cataloging-in-Publication Data

Miller, Richard Bradford, 1927–
    The banker's desk book / Richard B. Miller.
        p.   cm.
    ISBN 0-13-058538-6
    1. Banks and banking—Handbooks, manuals, etc.   2. Bank management—Handbooks,
manuals, etc.   I. Title.
HG1611.M56   1990   89-16317
332.1—dc20   CIP

ISBN 0-13-058538-6

PRENTICE HALL
BUSINESS & PROFESSIONAL DIVISION
A division of Simon & Schuster
Englewood Cliffs, New Jersey 07632

Printed in the United States of America

ABOUT THE AUTHOR

Richard B. Miller is head of his own financial communications consulting firm, BanCom. For more than 20 years, he has written about banking and finance, and was formerly editor of two national banking publications: *The Bankers Magazine* and *Bankers Monthly*.

Mr. Miller, who is a frequent contributor to business journals, has authored several books, including *The Banking Jungle* (with Paul Nadler) and *Investing in Tax Havens*. His latest books are *The American Banking Crisis* and *Super Banking*.

Banking today is an industry in which the decisions made on the so-called minor problems make as much of an impact on viability and profitability as do the decisions made on major problems. Dick Miller's valuable book, *The Banker's Desk Book*, helps bankers deal with all decisions more efficiently and effectively.

We well recognize that the banks that have gambled on interest rate movements, and tried to make money by borrowing short and lending long, have had a bad time of it. I am reminded of the bank investment department with the sign "Good News and Bad News. First the bad news: We can't predict interest rates. Now the good news: We finally realized this."

Thus, banking cannot make its profits by guessing rate movements. They must try to use so-called "gap" management—making asset yields match liability yields, so that no unpleasant surprises show up.

But matching asset and liability yields over the course of the business cycle means that the wider the spread the higher the bank profit. This means that anything that can be done to augment noninterest income and cut noninterest expenses will be of tremendous value to the bank.

Here is where Dick Miller's handy desk book does its job.

Do you need part-time or temporary workers? Dos and don'ts of the practice are right here in the book.

Can petty cash be controlled? Can more be obtained from fringe benefits banks provide? Can good people be kept from being pirated away? These are the types of "minor" decisions that make or break a bank, and they are all here, presented in an easy-to-understand format that gives the bank executive a starting point for his or her analysis of how to handle the problem.

There will be times when the reader will want more information. However, a basic understanding of and the ability to deal with a problem certainly makes the banker's job of digging deeper through reading and questioning far easier. Miller provides the momentum. As with any motion, once the car, train, boat, or idea is started, it takes far less energy to keep it going than to start it up.

Dick Miller has had a high profile in banking for years. He had edited important banking magazines, written several books of his own and has edited literally thousands of banking articles written by others to make them more understandable and valuable. As a writer for several publications Dick Miller has edited, I can honestly say that he virtually always leaves an article he has touched more readable and useful than it was when I submitted it to him.

Bankers will keep this book on their desks, as the title indicates. I predict that the main lament of owners of this volume will be that they didn't have it available to them earlier.

Paul S. Nadler
Professor of Finance
Graduate School of Management
Rutgers University

WHAT THIS BOOK
WILL DO FOR YOU

Banking has become one of the most, if not *the* most, complex segments of American business, with an everwidening range of disciplines. As a consequence, it is impossible for an individual to know everything there is to know about banking—much less how to make the most of the potential that banking has to offer.

The Banker's Desk Book is designed as a ready reference, a source of ideas, procedures, forms, checklists, and other aids that will help make your job as a professional banker easier and your efforts more effective. Although this book does not discuss all aspects of banking in detail—that's impossible for any book— it will build upon and add to the skills, abilities, and knowledge you bring to your job. As it does this, the information included in this book will contribute to making your bank more successful and more profitable. Moreover, use of *The Banker's Desk Book* will make *you* a more successful banker.

In this introductory section, we look briefly at a few critical issues. Banking is an ethical business. If it were not, the industry would have faltered long ago. When unethical people and/or practices are discovered they are tossed out. Thus, it is appropriate to begin this book with the formulation of a written code of ethics.

A CODE OF CONDUCT FOR YOUR BANK

When a bank bribery law was passed in 1984, many bankers objected, particularly to the section dealing with gratuities to banks. Today, however, many banks have instituted codes of conduct which establish ethics for bank employees to follow. Such codes really do help banks stay clear of potential problems.

Taking a Stand. A formally approved code of conduct should establish a framework to which all bank directors, officers, and employees can adhere. Receipt of the institution's code should be acknowledged in writing by each employee. With employee acceptance of the code, it then becomes an instrument for termination of employment in the event of nonobservance by an employee.

Who in the institution should assume the responsibility of drafting and enforcing the code? Usually an ethics committee has been delegated the responsibility of developing and implementing a code of conduct.

Elements of the Code. Each institution's code of conduct should be adapted to that specific institution. However, there are several elements appropriate to every institution's code of conduct:

1. It should be written in clear and concise language that can be understood by all employees.

2. It should contain substantive ethical content sufficient to protect both the institution and the employee.

3. It should be presented in a manner which will not offend the employee.

With these considerations in mind, the additional points below might be considered for inclusion in a code of conduct for a financial institution:

• *Opening statement.* A preamble or opening statement to the code of conduct is necessary. It should set the tone for each employee's acceptance of the code.

• *False statements.* An employee must not make, or cause to be made, a materially false or misleading statement about the affairs of the company.

• *Omissions.* An employee must not make an omission, or cause another to make an omission, in any company record, financial or otherwise.

• *Conflicts of interest.* Employees are to observe the following procedures to avoid possible conflicts of interest.

1. An employee must not act as attorney, consultant, agent, broker, or employee for any person, firm, or corporation interested directly or indirectly in any manner whatsoever in business dealings with the company.

2. An employee is forbidden to have any official interest, direct or indirect, in any matter affecting real property in which the company has a direct or indirect interest.

3. A financial interest in real estate by the spouse of an employee or other immediate family member shall be deemed to constitute an interest of the employee.

4. An employee must not represent the company in any transaction if the personal interests of the employee might affect his or her ability to represent the company's interest fairly and impartially.

• *Compensation.* Employees are to comply with the following provisions regarding the giving or receiving of compensation:

1. No secret or illegal payments, bribes, or kickbacks in any form whatsoever are to be made under any circumstances to obtain a benefit for the company or the employee that would not otherwise be available.

2. All contractual placements of company business and acceptance of business by the company must be awarded purely upon business considerations.

• *Incompatible employment and other business affiliations.* An employee must obtain written approval before accepting outside employment or serving as a director, officer, owner, or partner of any other business or government organization with or without compensation.

• *Disclosure of confidential information.* An employee must not disclose to unauthorized persons confidential information or records pertaining to or concerning the affairs of the company of its customers. Within the company, disclosure of such information must be limited to those persons whose duties require and permit them to have access to it.

• *Investments.* An employee must not invest or hold any investment directly or indirectly in any financial, business, commercial, or private transaction that creates a conflict with his or her official duties. In addition, employees must not allow information that has not been made public to influence their own investment.

• *Awareness of illegal conduct.* If, in conducting business for the company, an employee becomes aware of any illegal conduct on the part of any person, the employee must inform his or her supervisor with a view to notifying the proper legal authorities. Such notification shall be made after considering the confidentiality of the information involved.

• *Obstruction of an investigation.* An employee must not refuse to answer questions concerning any matter related to the performance of his or her official duties or any person dealing with the company.

GUARDING AGAINST CONFLICTS OF INTEREST

One of the greatest concerns these days regarding members of the board of directors at a bank is to avoid conflicts of interest and the appearance of such conflicts. Some banks have even gone as far as eliminating all business relationships with their directors. This is both foolish and unnecessary.

There are steps a bank can take to ensure that its directors are not involved in conflicts, and at the same time, get the bulk of their banking business.

First, a bank must make sure no member of the board receives preferential treatment, including preferential rates. In this way, the directors know they are treated the same as all other customers. Among other benefits, this practice allows board members to experience how the bank deals with its customers and then push for changes if they are merited.

More specifically, a bank should have formal, written policies of the bank's procedures concerning business with members of its board of directors. These policies should include:

• How a board member may obtain a loan

• The responses of board members to requests from other board members for loans

• Rates and balances required for a member to borrow from the bank

> **NOTE:** Once these policies have been established, they should be checked with the examiners to make sure they are proper and in accordance with regulations. Only then will the bank and the members of the board of directors know that if the policies are followed, there will be no possible conflict of interest.

ACKNOWLEDGMENTS

A great many bankers, consultants, banks, and organizations have contributed information and insights to this book. I hesitate to mention them by name for fear of omitting any of them.

However, I do wish to express my thanks to my editor at Prentice Hall, Bette Schwartzberg, who put up with far more than she should have—and who helped much more than I can say.

RBM

CONTENTS

PART THREE   OPERATING THE BANK   *147*

PART ONE

BANK OWNERSHIP

A bank, like all corporate entities, is owned by its shareholders. Too often this fact is forgotten. Yet the owners, the management, and the employees of a bank can forge a partnership that can make a banking organization strong, prosperous, and dynamic.

Whether the shareholders are few or many or whether the bank is small or large, a bank's main objective must be to make a profit for its owners.

A bank's stock, even when a bank is profitable, does not always reflect its value. Sometimes it is necessary to "court" the investment community and take active steps to make the bank known and make its stock attractive. These steps are outlined in Chapter 1.

It is often necessary, particularly for banks with large numbers of stockholders, to communicate with the shareholders on a formal basis. This topic is detailed in Chapter 2.

The board of directors is elected by the bank's shareholders. Members of the board can be a positive resource in the management and growth of a bank. Some ideas for using this resource are covered in Chapter 3.

1

BANK STOCK

This chapter and the next one on bank shareholders are necessarily complementary. One objective—and probably the main objective—of the management of a bank (and this includes its board of directors) is to increase the value of the company's stock. Of course, much depends on the quality of management and the profitability of a bank. However, there are other aspects that can be brought into play to increase the value of the stock. This chapter discusses some of these aspects.

COURTING THE INVESTMENT COMMUNITY

One of the best ways to get bank stock analysts interested in a bank's stock is to have a high price-earnings (P/E) ratio. High P/E ratios are essential if banks are to expand, enabling them to take over other banks and businesses on a share-for-share exchange without diluting the equity value of current shareholders.

In addition, a high P/E ratio can be useful for rewarding bank employees enrolled in stock option progams. High ratios also tend to keep existing stockholders happy as well as attract new investors.

Noted stock analyst George Salem cautions bankers and boards of directors by pointing out the changes in banking which make the industry generally a more exciting investment opportunity than in earlier times. Mr. Salem notes that unless there is an unusual story to be told to an analyst, there is little a bank can gain from increasing investor relations efforts. For that matter, a bank with no story to tell, or a bank that has an ineffective management presentation, may do itself more harm than good.

> **NOTE:** According to George Salem, if your bank has no story to tell and it has not been a leader, a bank probably would be better off staying far away from security analysts— something banks used to do simply as a matter of course.

WHAT MAKES A BANK STOCK ATTRACTIVE?

A bank stock that is attractive to bank stock traders and to individual investors will increase in value. But what is it that makes the stock attractive? According to one senior analyst at a major bank stock house in New York, there are five criteria, which he considers to be the most important. If a bank doesn't make it on three or sometimes four of the criteria, this analyst says, "We just don't bother with it." The five criteria are:

1. The bank's demography. If this analyst wouldn't live in the area, he wouldn't bother with the stock. Or, as he put it rather succinctly, by using astro turf as an example: "If a horse won't eat it, I won't play on it."

2. How management handles the spread between interest paid and interest earned.

3. The relative strength of the bank's international earnings (if, of course, it is involved in international banking activities).

4. How diversified the bank is. Too many banks, the analyst says, are not sufficiently diversified.

5. The quality of the bank's management. This particular analyst likes aggressive and smart.

WHAT DIRECTORS CAN DO ABOUT THE BANK'S STOCK

The public often complains to banking regulators and members of the various legislatures that the bank stocks they either own or are trying to buy are closely held, that the top officers of the bank determine the market, and for all intents and purposes, determine its price.

The end result is that people who are forced to sell their bank stocks because of death, retirement, need for funds, or other purposes, are not given a fair opportunity to receive the stock's full worth. At the same time, those who are very willing to pay a premium over the stated price to obtain shares are denied this opportunity.

In some cases it is well known that "insiders" like this arrangement because, after all, it gives them the opportunity to buy all the shares that come to market at extremely low prices relative to those available on other banks' stocks—an extremely cheap way of building up ownership of the bank. In some cases the insiders take over stock at one price, and then sell out the entire bank to a holding company or branch system at a price several times that paid for each share even though the purchase and sale may have been only several months apart.

Doing Something Bank directors are liable for the failure of the bank to provide as good a market for stock as possible as well as other acts of neglect normally under the surveillance of the bank's board.

Bank board members should make every effort to see that their banks' executive staffs have done all they can to interest local, regional, and national securities firms in creating markets for their stock. In many cases banks should have their stock traded by at least three dealers in order to be listed on the NASDAQ, the recently established nationwide securities trading computer information network. They also should make sure that shareholders are given the opportunity to sell at the best possible price. This can be done by having the bank's officers refer all shareholders to these dealers when a sale is contemplated instead of making the trade by themselves for themselves or for certain favored friends at a price established by the officers.

Stock Auction. One possible step toward changing bank policy on stock sales and purchases, if a sweeping change is necessary, would be for the directors to recommend an auction. Under this procedure the bank notifies all its stockholders that they can auction any or all of their shares and that these shares will be awarded to the highest bidders (with an upset price established if desired so that the holders know that if the bid is below a certain level, the sale does not take place).

The bank can then announce the auction and let the free market determine who sells, who does not, and what the price of the bank's stock should actually be. When auctions have been held, many shareholders were delighted to learn that their stocks were worth far more than the quotes the bank had been publishing for years and that there was a real market for the stock, not just the sole price offered by the bank's executives.

> **NOTE:** The Bank directors have also been delighted with the results of auctions for two reasons:

• First, they are shareholders themselves and benefit from a higher market price on their stock, whether they contemplate selling some shares now or whether they only want to ensure that they get the best possible price when their shares are eventually sold as part of their estates.

• Second, as directors, they have fulfilled their responsibility to ensure shareholders and potential shareholders the best possible free market for the stock that they, as directors, are sworn to protect and foster.

SALE OF BANK STOCK

When stock is not closely held, directors should know they are subject to section 16 of the Securities and Exchange Act of 1934, which originally only applied to officers and holders of more than 10 percent of any class of stock.

Under this section, if a director, when buying and selling (or selling and buying) stock of his or her bank, realizes a profit, the profit belongs to the bank when the selling and buying transactions occur within six months of each other. This provision also applies to purchases made under an employee option plan. The purpose of this provision is quite clear: The removal of any short-term profits eliminates the likelihood of using any inside information to gain those profits. To further remove any possibility of profit, a director is held liable for giving up any profit from a short-term stock transaction. This liability holds regardless of whether the director actually possessed inside information and whether or not he or she intended to trade on the superior information.

The law also provides any stockholder of the bank with the right to sue a director on behalf of the bank for short-term profits if the bank refuses to so act. Moreover, if the directors permit the bank to take no action, they may be guilty of mismanagement.

To further prevent bank directors from keeping their short-term profits, the law requires directors to file with the appropriate federal agency a report on each sale or purchase of the bank's stock. These reports are open to the public for inspection.

> **OBSERVATION:** Bank directors must keep
> in mind that whenever they change their
> holdings of the bank's stock, they must file a
> report with the appropriate federal banking
> agency.

This report must be filed within ten days after the end of the calendar month in which the change takes place. Moreover, a report showing a director's holding of his or her bank's stock must be filed within ten days after he or she takes office. The appropriate banking agency will supply these forms on which directors report their initial holdings and any subsequent changes. The same rules apply to bank holding company directors except that such directors report to the Securities and Exchange Commission (SEC).

Directors have been held liable for their profitable short-term transactions even when they have actually suffered a net out-of-pocket loss.

> **RED FLAG:** Bank directors should be thoroughly warned that any short-term transactions in their own stock can lead to trouble no matter how innocent or unprofitable they may be.

> **NOTE:** Before any director purchases and sells (or sells and purchases) bank stock during any six-month period, he or she is well advised to check with his or her counsel or the bank's counsel.

2

BANK
SHAREHOLDERS

Shareholders of a bank's stock, although usually a benign factor in the running of a bank, can be a source of trouble if their concerns are not considered. They will certainly be mollified to a considerable degree if the bank is profitable and the stock is popular. However, they still want those profits to be built upon a strong base and also have their bank managed in an effective and enlightened manner.

Stockholders will also want to know what's going on; therefore, communication between management and stockholders is most important. Stockholders should be told about the plans of the bank on a regular basis, not just at an annual meeting, which is usually attended by a minute fraction of the total shareholders.

The management of a bank must always remember that the shareholders are the owners of the bank. This chapter will assist in dealing with this.

WHO ARE THE SHAREHOLDERS OF YOUR BANK?

A crucial dilemma now facing directors is adequate identification of their diverse shareholder base. The rapid pace of recent merger and acquisition activity has made bank directors more aware than ever of the need to know not only who their owners are but how to contact them quickly.

The often conflicting shareholder family now includes:

• *Small, traditional investors.* These are widely dispersed shareholders who are difficult and expensive to contact rapidly. However, they are very likely to vote management's way on major issues.

• *Significant, long-term investors.* These are substantial owners with long-term investment objectives. They are likely to follow the bank's progress closely and communicate regularly with management. They are often represented on the board.

• *Arbitrageurs.* They generally buy and sell stock quickly and often appear on shareholder lists at the beginning stages of takeovers. They disappear just as quickly after taking profits.

• *White knights and other friendly holders.* These are people or organizations that take substantial stock positions partly in support of current management. They represent important votes on which management can count in fending off raiders.

• *Institutional investors.* Their sheer size is forcing a reappraisal of corporate ownership. Since they may hold more than one-half of a bank's outstanding shares, they can often influence not only stock prices but management strategy as well. Institutional investors generally act as traders and not as traditional owners.

> **NOTE:** Because shareholders think—and act—in different ways, it is recommended that a bank's stockholders are analyzed to better gauge their reactions to any moves a bank might make.

HOW TO FIND OUT WHAT SHAREHOLDERS THINK

Bankers frequently bemoan the fact that they do not understand their shareholders. They do not know their shareholder's average income or why a particular shareholder has invested in the bank's stock. More shareholder information could help the bank's management to better plan its policies. Few banks, however, have even taken the trouble to send out a survey to see exactly what their shareholders are like and what they expect from the bank.

Asking Questions. One bank, however, has done just that. It has sent out a stockholder's survey, which takes only a short time to answer. The replies give the bank considerable information on its shareholder population.

The questions asked of the stockholder are:

• Are you an individual stockholder or an institutional stockholder?

• How did you originally acquire your common stock of _____ Bank? Gift, inheritance, purchase, the shareholder of a member bank?

• If you purchased your stock, who recommended it to you? A bank, a broker, a lawyer, a friend, someone else?

• What was the principal reason for investing in _____ Bank stock? Income, capital gross, safety of capital, other?

• How many shares of the stock do you own?

• If you were financially able, would you buy more stock?

• Do you own stock in other companies, and if so, how many?

• How thoroughly do you read stockholder mailings? Fully, glance over, don't read?

• If you read these reports, do you find them (a) easy to understand, (b) barely clear, (c) hard to understand?

• Are stockholder reports (a) fully informative, (b) partially informative, (c) not informative?

Finally, the bank asks questions about the individual's sex, age, marital status, and total family income. The survey also provides space for further suggestions about the bank and the company's relationship to its stockholders.

> **NOTE:** Most important, shareholders should feel that the bank really cares, that it is interested in them and their motives as

investors in the bank. Even if the questionnaire is merely received, glanced over, and filed, it will have accomplished a great deal in the way of goodwill by making shareholders realize that the bank knows there are human beings who are receiving those dividend checks.

IMPROVING BANK–STOCKHOLDER COMMUNICATIONS

Banks don't usually know the precise reason why a shareholder purchased bank stock, or which of the many documents the stockholder receives best provides the information a stockholder feels is necessary to follow the bank's progress. Thus, a communication gap often develops almost from the start.

Are your bank's communications with shareholders really effective and useful? One way to find out is to survey your shareholders. A recent example of a bank survey designed to enhance communication with shareholders was produced by a major eastern bank. The questions asked on the survey included the following.

1. How long have you been a stockholder of the bank?

2. What do you consider the primary investment objective of your portfolio? Is it to provide long-term growth; to provide maximum income; to maintain purchasing power; or to preserve capital?

3. How important is each of the following information sources to you: annual reports; quarterly reports; brokerage house stock reviews; stock prospectuses; the financial press; corporate advertising; an investment advisor?

4. How thoroughly do you read the bank's annual report? If you read it, which of the following sections of the report are most helpful to you: general narrative; developments during the year; management's analysis of operations; financial statements and schedules; the five-year statistical review?

5. Are there any sections in the annual report that are difficult to understand?

6. On an overall basis how would you rate the annual report on each of the following characteristics: informativeness; interest; clarity; attractiveness?

7. How thoroughly do you read the bank's quarterly reports? If you read them, which sections are most helpful to you?

8. Are there any sections in the quarterly report that are difficult to understand?

9. How would you rate the quarterly report?

10. Do you have any suggestions for improving either the annual or quarterly reports?

The bank questionnaire concludes by asking for demographic information on the shareholder such as age, marital status, profession, income, size of portfolio, and number of bank shares held.

> **NOTE:** A survey such as this one can provide you with the information you need to determine if you are communicating your bank's situation effectively to your shareholders. Even as questions are asked, you will effectively signal the bank's desire to keep those shareholders "in the know."

HOW TO KEEP SHAREHOLDERS HAPPY

Bank directors are just as much in the line of fire from irate shareholders as any of the bank's senior officers. All too often, bank directors have taken the goodwill of shareholders for granted and found out too late that investors are better enemies than friends.

Consumer-oriented agitation from shareholders or shareholder groups are not the only consequences directors and management have to fear. Foreign investors have been entering the scene in increasing numbers with juicy, tender offers that shareholders can hardly refuse, especially if they feel the bank's P/E ratio or market performance is not up to par.

Most shareholders also recognize that the banking industry is entering an era of concentrated activity in which large banks will be making very attractive offers to acquire smaller institutions.

Because bank directors are practical businesspeople, they cannot—and should not—leave the wooing of shareholders to the senior operating management of the bank. Although price action of the bank's stock is open to many influences which the bank cannot control, a bank can take these precautionary measures to nip shareholder dissatisfaction in the bud:

• Make sure an independent dealer sets the price of your stock. Avoid linking bank management and share–price action, even to the extent that demands for outstanding shares and new issues are handled by the dealer and not by the bank.

• Avoid having your bank buy up most of a new issue for itself. A dealer cannot create an accurate market based on bits and pieces of a bank's stock. Also, scarcity on the market does not always cause favorable price movement; it almost always causes a narrow public investment base.

• Encourage more than one dealer to create a market in your bank's stock. This not only goes a long way in assuring your stock will receive good market price "play," but it also assures your stock will receive added publicity in the investment community.

• Sharpen your public relations and press relations efforts. Make sure your bank is providing comprehensive, understandable performance information on a regular basis to the press and to shareholders. Do not give only a short statement at annual report time and expect to keep shareholders happy.

> **TIP:** One way of keeping shareholders informed and happy is to have stock quoted on a daily basis in your local newspaper even though price movement and trades may be infrequent.

• If your bank does not have a dividend reinvestment plan, consider one. Dealers like these plans and will trade your stock more aggressively because they know some buying interest of size is going to develop every dividend period. However, don't go ahead with a reinvestment plan without first consulting shareholders. Ask them whether they would prefer dividend growth or reinvestment for capital appreciation.

• Use the trust business or other business of your bank as an incentive for preferential dealer treatment. Support can be obtained, in many cases, by permitting a dealer to bid competitively with his or her peers on bank business.

> **NOTE:**   With the dawning era of concentrated banking activity through mergers and acquisitions and with the inroads of foreign investors in the industry, bankers need all the help they can get in keeping control of their individual institutions. Taking shareholders for granted can be disastrous; they may not be with you when you need them.

FIELDING QUESTIONS AT STOCKHOLDER MEETINGS

Annual stockholder meetings are often traumatic experiences for many bank managements. However, with a little advanced planning this can be avoided.

Some banks produce what is known as the "blackbook," a carefully prepared indexed manual with facts and statistics concerning every conceivable aspect of the bank's operations. The blackbook serves as a ready reference guide for senior management to answer any and all anticipated questions that may be put to the dais or podium.

The conduct of the meeting is determined as much by history as by senior management's own particular style. However, no matter what form the meeting takes, the focal point is that time of the meeting when the floor is open for stock-holders' questions because this is when senior management is most vulnerable. Some stockholders (including professionals) view this as open season, and fire away at senior management with probing, occasionally embarrassing, often inane, and sometimes ridiculous questions.

Bank management's vulnerability can be reduced signifi-cantly (especially from the standpoint of the serious inquiry) by adequate preparation beforehand.

> **THE KEY TO THIS PREPARATION:**
> Anticipate the many and varied potential questions to be asked. The answers to these questions can then be researched and documented adequately and reviewed by senior management well in advance of the meeting.

To guide you in anticipating stockholders' questions, be-low are some questions suggested by KPMB Peat Marwick Main. You can anticipate that these or similar questions may be asked at bank stockholders' meetings:

• What is the bank's policy on loans to borrowers in less developed countries?

• What is the bank's policy on overdrafts by officers, employees, and their families?

• What controls exist for trading account securities?

• In which foreign countries does the bank have signifi-cant loan exposure?

• What amount does the bank have invested in New York securities? What is the difference between the carrying amount and the market value of those securities?

• What is the amount of loans to real estate investment trusts? What amount of these loans is in default?

• Are large loans handled by one officer or a committee?

• Why is the loan provision in 1990 _____ percent of the portfolio, while in 1989 it was only _____ percent?

• How does the bank go about evaluating the adequacy of its allowance for loan losses?

• What is the bank's exposure to additional federal, state, and local taxes on loan revenues booked offshore?

• What impact has the Financial Accounting Standards Board's statement on troubled restructuring had on the bank's financial statements? What effects do you anticipate next year?

• How would the payment of interest on checking account balances affect the bank?

• Does the bank speculate in foreign currency? What procedures prevent unauthorized foreign exchange transactions?

• What controls exist to prevent misappropriation of funds in trust accounts?

• What problems were noted in latest examination by state of federal examiners? What has the bank done to correct any problems?

• Is the bank on any so-called problem bank lists?

• What is the trust department's policy with respect to voting shares held in trust accounts? How often has the trust department voted against management proposals and for shareholders' proposals?

• How much debt does the holding company have? How does it expect to retire such debt at maturity?

> **NOTE:** For a specific bank some of these questions may not be relevant, but the potential does exist for some variation which could make them germane. Furthermore, it is obvious from the tone of some of the questions that the answers may very well be found in the books and records of the bank.

3

HOW TO ACHIEVE
A MORE EFFECTIVE
BANK BOARD

Boards of directors are an important, as well as necessary, part of any corporate structure. This is particularly true in banking. Members of the board can either be a necessary evil or a valued resource, depending on the outlook and the objectives of the management of the bank. It seems foolish to let such a potentially useful resource stand idle. Yet many banks do just that.

The topics covered in this chapter will assist a bank's management in realizing the potential its board of directors has to offer.

HOW BANK BOARDS ARE DIFFERENT FROM OTHER BOARDS

According to a study by the consulting firm of Korn/Ferry International, banks and other financial institutions have the largest boards in the country, with an average size of nineteen. The average number of directors for all U.S. corporations is thirteen. Here are other comparisons shown in the survey.

• Outside directors dominate. Banks and financial institutions exhibit the strongest preference for outside director dominance. This year 90 percent of banks and financial institutions said they prefer a majority of the board to be composed of outside directors, compared with 83 percent among all other companies. Moreover, 60 percent of all financial institutions prefer that at least 75 percent of their boards be composed of outside directors. Only 36 percent of other respondents agreed. In practice, banks and financial institutions average four inside and fifteen outside directors.

• More meetings. Banks and financial institutions meet more frequently than other corporations, averaging nine meetings per year as compared to an average of eight for all other participants.

• Senior executives preferred. Financial participants also show the strongest preference for directors drawn from the ranks of senior executives of other companies. They average nine per board, nearly double the overall average. Seventy-two percent of financial participants cite corporate experience as the primary consideration when asking a prospective director to sit on the board.

• Women, minorities represented. Banks and financial institutions continue to have the highest percentage of women directors, who now sit on 72 percent of the boards surveyed, compared with 45 percent for all companies. Financial organizations also lead in the appointment of minority directors, who are represented on 53 percent of their boards (compared to 26 percent for all companies).

• Compensation lower than average. Financial respondents lag behind other groups in director compensation, but the gap has narrowed to 7 percent from 18 percent five years ago. Their average annual compensation now stands at $17,500.

• Committees. Ninety-nine percent of respondents report using the audit committee. Next in popularity are the executive and compensation committees. Banks and financial institutions lead all other groups in the use of public affairs committees.

• Issues. Financial results top the list of important issues facing the board today. However, projections as to the importance of various issues five years from now showed that strategic planning was rated equal in importance to financial results as the number one priority, each cited by 47 percent of financial participants.

WHAT BANK DIRECTORS DO

Most American banks include on their board both inside (or management) and outside directors. Although all directors are charged with the responsibility of adequately representing the banks' stockholders and safeguarding all depositors, these different categories do encompass different functions.

Outside directors normally come into banks once a month and review a mass of reports involving earnings, loans, investments, and problems. They are supposed to instantly spot weaknesses and make constructive, remedial suggestions without interfering with the inside directors who run the show. They also, according to a consensus of experts, are supposed to depart from monthly meetings "with their confidential reports left on the conference table and their lips zipped."

Inside directors are usually chosen from senior officer staffs and all such directors usually constitute a minority on the board. These management directors are responsible for providing the full board with current and accurate information necessary to the conduct of board business. Inside dirctors must wear two hats. One hat bears the policy objectives of the institutions as set down by the board; the other concerns itself with the daily operations of the bank itself. Thus, inside directors often play the role of double agent: looking after the wants and demands of the bank employees and at the same time carrying out the directives of the directors. The greatest contribution inside directors make is serving as a soothing agent between board policy and bank operations.

It should be noted that a new kind of director has been appearing on bank boards in recent years. This type of director may not be experienced enough in business to qualify for the post of outside director nor have sufficient experience to sit on the board as an inside director. Instead, this director, called a *special interest director,* joins the board to represent some special interest such as an ethnic group. His or her role will be limited strictly to cementing relations of the bank with special segments of the community.

> **NOTE:** Roles of bank directors differ according to type. However, the success of any bank really depends on the ability of the inside, or management directors, to make the bank operate profitably—and with a minimum of problems.

DO'S AND DON'T'S FOR DIRECTORS

What can bank directors do—and not do—to guard against complaints and even law suits by disgruntled stockholders and/or customers? Here are some points to consider:

1. *Avoid Any Conflicts of Interest.* First, read up on what conflict of interest involves as a director or bank officer, and make sure any activity of yours outside the bank will stand up in court if tested. One way to determine this is to go to the bank's lawyer, or your own, if there is any doubt that you may be engaged in any activity that might have the remotest connection with your bank directorship which is not absolutely above board and legal. If you don't have time to read up on conflicts of interest yourself, discuss it with a proper person who can outline the basic principles for you. Do not delay in doing this.

2. *Avoid Self-Serving Strategies.* As with conflict of interest, you should do some serious research on precisely what constitutes self-serving strategies. The best place to start is to ask either your lawyer, or the bank's lawyer, to xerox some cases illustrating various kinds of self-serving cases that have been detrimental to bank directors when it came to court decisions.

3. *Attend Board Meetings.* This seems rather obvious to any director, but it needs repeating. Ignorance of what is going on in the bank is no excuse for any outside director. He or she is usually as liable, in the eyes of the law, for negligence as an inside director. So if you are interested in the risks involved in being a bank director, you should attend board meetings as often as possible.

4. *Review the Bank Insurance Program.* Too many outside bank directors rely implictly on the officers to manage the affairs of the bank, and insurance falls under bank management and operations. Because of this, it would be wise to ascertain if the liability insurance carried by the bank is sufficient in the light of today's attitudes in the court. It probably would even pay to employ outside counsel to review the bank's insurance program. Or perhaps by joining with other directors, the insurance program could be assessed by a working committee that normally wouldn't be involved in such matters. A new look from unbiased minds not too deep in the woods of bank management might help here.

5. *Bank Audits.* How many bank directors actually know the ins and outs of bank audits, which financial statements to examine, and which rations to use? Ask the bank officer in charge of balancing the books to draw you up a checklist of items to examine so that you can be familiar with the financial workings of the bank you are a director of.

6. *Board Meeting Conduct.* When attending a board meeting, do not fill the role of a "rubber stamp." First, make sure that any exhibits containing dollar figures or amounts to be discussed in the boardroom are mimeographed or typed and presented to all directors in advance of appearing at the meeting so that they can intelligently follow what is going on with the numbers and also make the numbers seem meaningful. Make sure when you are at a board meeting to be fully informed about operations, and what you don't hear, ask about. Too many unmentionables that should be discussed at board meetings are left unsaid. Too many thinkable and unthinkable thoughts are also left unsaid because of various reasons, among them trying to be a "nice guy."

7. *Evaluation.* Unfortunately, in banks as well as in other businesses, the statistical gobbledegook prepared by economists and statisticians often prevents fair evaluations of anything more than the bottom line. But evaluation of a human kind is desperately needed, especially by directors. For example, a computer cannot print out the appearance or manner of a bank officer on the bank floor, or how he or she sits at a desk or acts toward customers. It is a good idea for bank directors to make a habit of popping in at the bank at intervals and just look around a bit. This kind of evaluation is qualitative not quantitative, but it may be quite meaningful on occasion.

8. *Retirement.* In many banks an age limit for active directors has been installed. If this applies to your bank it makes sense for the directors who are nearing the age of retirement to do something constructive about selecting and evaluating future directors. One method is to invite likely candidates to sit in on board meetings as observers and then discuss the meetings with them afterward. This method makes it possible to form some sensible conclusions as to the future capability and action capacity of the candidate before committing the bank to making him or her a director.

9. *Meeting Frequency.* Although most big banks hold directors' meetings at frequent intervals, this does not necessarily hold true for small ones although it should. Especially in light of current disturbances all over the country in connection with banking, it would be more than prudent to have regular board meetings, say on a monthly basis. A director who attends meetings held frequently normally becomes an informed director. Also, the more a director knows about what's going on in the bank, the better for all concerned.

10. *Bank Policy.* Make sure that the policy of the bank with respect to activities such as politics, volunteerism, charity, and so on are clearcut and in writing. If these and similar activities are clearly understood by the directors, it is relatively simple to set them down in the form of a booklet for bank officers and even stockholders. What does a stockholder have to do with a bank's policy if he or she isn't an officer or a board member? The answer is that directors are supposed to set the kind of policy beneficial to the stockholders of a bank or any corporation.

11. *Personal Conduct.* It goes without saying that a bank director represents the bank wherever he or she goes. In this regard, a director's personal conduct may give others a right (or wrong) concept of what the bank is and does. Directors must be careful of their personal conduct and of associating with people who may give the bank a bad image.

12. *Warning Signs.* These are functions no computer or statistical analysis can do without human reaction. What is a warning sign? Is it the absence of a key person on more than a rare occasion? Errors of a frequent nature in housekeeping at the bank? Poor judgment when it comes to granting loans? Investing in the wrong securities? Trouble with staff at the lower levels of management? A drop in business? Probably there are a number of warning signs you can think of. Irregularities, it should be noted, are not warning signs; they are danger signals.

13. *Risks Review.* Possibly this checkpoint should head the list. It simply means a genuine review of the risks entailed in being a bank director. Once you yourself know and understand each and every risk you may be exposed to as a bank director, you are in a better position to conduct yourself to avoid future problems and to better able monitor your fellow directors and key employees in this same vein. Ironically, a bank director is required to assume large amounts of risk without any evident concomitant benefits except prestige, a certain community status, and so on. Thus, so check today on the risks you are assuming.

14. *Capitalization.* Part of any successful business involves making money on other people's money. When it comes to banking, this is really the only stock in trade. Without advocating any concerted effort on the part of bank directors to provide impetus to the gradual rise of their stock in the marketplace, it does seem that banks should publicize, somewhat more, the fact that banking is a growth business and that depositors can become stockholders also. In this manner an increase in the number of shareholders provides a future pool of capital for the bank through the issuance of rights to subscribe for more stock.

15. *Decision-Making.* One of the attributes that seems to be a common denominator of most bank directors is that they are already business successes before they achieve the exalted status of attending bank board meetings. In this regard it would seem logical that these successful businesspeople should inject some of the acumen and common sense that helped make them successes into the board meeting when it comes to decision-making. However, the literature contains many instances where bank directors, especially outside ones, say very little when it ccomes to any major questions and permit the decisions that count to be made almost by default.

> **NOTE:** In addition to the points listed, bank directors might check the following to make sure they have most of the major risks covered:

> • Be diligent with director functions. Require reports from all committees in advance of the directors meetings.
> • Check relations of the bank with its correspondents.
> • Review duties of the bank directors.
> • Collect a file of law suit cases successfully pursued against bank directors in recent years.
> • Check legal aspects of such possibilities as failure to comply with state regulatory orders.

IMPORTANCE OF THE NOMINATING COMMITTEE

One way to ensure that an independent, objective board is assembled is through the use of a nominating committee made up exclusively of people with no connection to the bank, neither employees nor directors, as suggested by Arthur Young & Co. The American Bankers Association (ABA), SEC, the American Assembly for Bank Directors, and others, maintain that nominating committee members who do not owe their positions to the institution's CEO demonstrate sound judgment and a high degree of willingness and availability to serve and therefore garner more respect from fellow directors.

The Committee's Role. The primary purpose of the committee is to identify candidates for nomination to directorships.

Some nominating groups simply poll executive officers and directors and evaluate the persons they recommend. Others conduct ongoing screenings, and keep files on potential directors identified as board members, executive officers, stockholders, or depositors. The files contain such data as employment history, civic positions, other directorships, and awards and honors. This way, when vacancies occur or the board is being expanded, much of the preliminary work has been done.

When the field of candidates is narrowed down, the choices should be reviewed by the CEO, if he or she is not a member of the nominating committee, and the existing board of directors.

Defining Characteristics. Desirable traits for membership to the board of directors should be established. They may include an excellent personal reputation in the community; broad experience in business, finance, and administration; and an interest in the thrift industry.

The committee should avoid selecting candidates who may have potential conflicts of interest, such as large commercial borrowers, realtors, investment bankers, or legal counsel to the institution.

Other Responsibilities. Nominating committees may also be asked to review the institution's policies concerning:

• Composition, membership, and terms of each standing committee of the board

• Fee structure of the board and its committees

• Directors' retirement procedures

• Number and percentage of management representatives to the board

• Management serving on other boards of directors

• Compliance with the institution's policies concerning conflict of interest

• The role of advisory directors

Some banks also charge nominating committees with:

• Annual review of the number and makeup of the full board of directors

• Informal evaluation of each director's performance

• Reviewing stockholders' proxy statements that pertain to directors' activities so that responses can be prepared

• Monitoring developments and studies related to proper conduct of directors such as the U.S. Senate study of interlocking boards

• Monitoring management succession in conjunction with the compensation and personnel committees

Size of the Nominating Committee. Three to five members should make the group large enough to allow for different perspectives and experience and small enough to permit discussion and effective decision-making.

Length of Service. As on other committees, a balance should be maintained between continuity and consistency in the interest of having all members understand the issues and encouraging new ideas. One approach that works is three- to five-year terms with staggered rotation since it retains at least two experienced members at all times while new members join on a regular basis.

Staff Support. The availability of staff support to the nominating committee can significantly reduce the time the group must spend to accomplish a task. Large associations often have their in-house counsels serve as committee secretary for preparation of minutes; file maintenance; and monitoring appropriate hearings, legislation, regulations, and studies. Associations with no in-house counsel often use the finance department as a source of committee assistance. Where no bank staff support is available, the committee chairperson may assume these responsibilities or divide them among the members.

The agenda. Three meetings a year are usually sufficient to address ongoing issues; however, the number of meetings depends largely on the scope of the committee's responsibilities, size of the association and its board, and the turnover rate of senior officers and directors. The activities of each meeting are described below.

• First meeting. Consider the system of candidate selection and identify and monitor potential canddiates; conduct annual review of management-succession program.

• Second meeting. Review directors' performance, size, compensation, and composition; recommend candidates to any additional seats, and nominate a slate of directors to be voted in at the annual meeting.

• Third meeting. Review shareholders' comments concerning the board, as well as the continuing validity of, and compliance with, policies relating to the board and its membership.

> **NOTE:** One rule of thumb is that directors should be willing to devote the equivalent of twelve days a year to board responsibilities. Busy executives and other committee members may not have the time needed to search for new directors, no matter how faithful and dedicated they are to the association. Therefore, a diligent nominating committee made up of persons not on the board of directors can be an effective means of ensuring the accountability of the board to depositors, stockholders, and the public.

WHAT AN ADVISORY BOARD SHOULD DO

Appointing advisory boards to assist with specific banking activities, or in the case of branch systems, one community or geographic area, has become common in banking over recent years. Often the role of the advisory board member is misunderstood by both the individual involved and the institution he or she serves.

> **KEY FACT:** Members of the bank's policy-making board in particular should keep in mind that advisory board members are not

directors. They have none of the
responsibilities nor liabilities which the law
places on a bank director.

Yet, often banks allow advisory boards to function in a manner similar to that of a directorate, often hampering the work of the officers that the board is supposed to help.

The primary job of an advisory director is to aid the bank's sales effort, particularly in situations that may not come to the attention of one of the officers; for example, a real estate transaction, a business expansion, a leasing opportunity, and so on. The advisory board member should make referrals of loan applicants to the officers he or she works with. However, once he or she has suggested the bank to a potential borrower, he or she should immediately step out of the picture. There should be no suggestion to the borrower that "influence" is being brought to bear, nor should there be any pressure on the loan officer by the advisory member.

How Directors Can Help. Banks that have advisory boards can and should use their directors to formalize the relationships of the advisory members and the institution. Where there is a number of advisory groups, they should be invited to sit in at a regular board meeting on a rotating basis.

The board should set time aside to discuss problems and programs for the region or department that is the focus of the advisory group's interest. More important, the board meeting should be used to impress upon advisory members the difference between their role and that of the directors.

CAUTION: The most serious mistake
bankers make in delegating activities for
advisory boards is to allow the boards to pass
on information for loan applications.

Whether or not the group's judgment is accepted as final, the practice can only serve to undercut the loan officer. Each lending officer should fee that he or she is accountable only to top management and directors. There is no reason to impose an additional layer of supervision on lending officers; particularly when no responsibility is attached to the individuals making the judgment.

> **NOTE:** This does not mean that advisory directors should not be made to feel at liberty to pass along any information they may have on loan applicants. However, it should be emphasized that once the facts are made known, the advisory board member's function has been fulfilled, and he or she should let the matter rest with the bank officer responsible for the decision.

PART TWO

BANK MANAGEMENT

Management is one of the essential ingredients of any organization in any industry. For banking, management is perhaps broader in scope than in, say, a manufacturing company or a transportation firm.

In addition to the normal concerns of corporate management, a bank is concerned with the safety of and increasing the value of the funds entrusted to it, the regulations progulated by both the state and federal governments, the competitive forces at work (within banking and by nonbank organizations), and the very significant changes now taking place in the industry as a result of modern technology.

In years past, much of the above aspects of banking did not exist or were of only ordinary consequence. During those years the quality of management was not of such overriding importance as it is today.

How has banking changed, and how have the demands on its leadership multiplied? Management has always been important, of course, but today it is the key to a bank's growth and prosperity, and in some cases, even to its survival.

This part of the *The Banker's Desk Book* focuses on management and all its aspects.

4

BANK CAPITAL MANAGEMENT

Managing the capital resources of a bank is no easy task, particularly in these days of volatile monetary and investment values, not to mention the increasingly close monitoring of bank capital by the regulators.

Each of the topics discussed in this chapter should give the reader a better insight into the capital concerns of present day banking and the tools necessary for a strong capital base.

WHAT IS A BANK WORTH?

According to John Duffy, a vice president of Keefe, Bruyette and Woods, a brokerage firm specializing in bank stock, a bank is worth whatever someone will pay for it. In a talk before a meeting of the ABA, Duffy said that dilution analysis may be the most popular method of analyzing whether a transaction makes financial sense. This involves calculating what earnings or book value dilution the shareholders will incur if their bank purchases another. Some bankers prefer to analyze acquisitions from a rate of return analysis, especially in transactions that do not involve the issuance of common stock.

Although this method is a worthwhile exercise, the output or result is too sensitive to certain assumptions one has to make far into the future, Duffy noted. Changing some of the assumptions by a small amount can dramatically change the price one is willing to pay in an acquisition. Even if a rate of return analysis is used to determine what price one thinks a particular franchise is worth, the impact of paying that price on one's own shareholders should be analyzed.

> **KEY POINT:** Whatever method is used, there is no question that the key factor that will determine the price someone is willing to pay is the earning power of an institution, Duffy said.

The current level of earnings, the quality of earnings, and the future growth rate of earnings will have the greatest impact on the price paid. Obviously, acquirors will also be sensitive to how much capital the bank has, but capital is not as important as earnings. Acquirors are also looking for strong market share and good management.

A rise in bank stock prices has been the principal reason for the rise in acquisition prices in recent years. If the stock of a potential acquiror is valued more highly by the marketplace, that acquiror can offer more for a franchise. In addition, as state barriers have diminished, the universe of potential acquirors has increased.

An Interesting Example. Look at the experience of the banks in South Carolina. A few years ago South Caroina National (the largest in the state) acquired First Bankshares (the fourth largest) for approximately 12.8 times earnings and 172 percent of book value. In 1985 the second, third, and fourth largest banks in South Carolina agreed to be acquired by Georgia- and North Carolina-based holding companies. The average multiple of earnings paid was a little over 15 times, and prices paid as a percentage of book value were 236 percent on the average.

The next year, the banks sold for substantially higher prices than the price First Bankshares. Why did this occur? One of the reasons was probably that bank stock prices had risen because of the drop in interest rates and the acquirors had to raise the stakes to get a deal done. The fact that the laws of South Carolina had changed not only helped raise the prices paid for these South Carolina banks but, in fact, made the acquisitions possible. If, said John Duffy, the laws had not changed to permit out-of-state bank holding companies into South Carolina, the reality of the situation would have been that none of these institutions would have been able to sell to anyone.

Merging versus Remaining Independent.

As the geographic barriers are coming down around them, bank directors must decide which path to choose for their banks. Should they merge with another institution or should they remain independent?

Although some analysts have predicted a major contraction in the number of banks, Duffy disagrees: "Most of the community banks that exist today have shown they can compete reasonably well in a deregulated environment. Certainly the last few years have been the easiest, especially if [one operates] in the oil patch or the ag belt, but...most community banks have fared fairly well despite the volatile interest rates and other challenges with which they have had to cope. Most of these community banks have very little to worry about in terms of an unfriendly takeover, especially if they have a good operating history."

Most banks that are embarking on a major expansion or acquisition program are focusing on market share and size, says Duffy. If they have a choice between acquiring a $2 billion bank or a $200 million bank, all other things being equal, they will go for the larger. It requires the same effort for either bank. Many bankers, in fact, will not look at banks below a certain size, say, $100 million or so, because such banks will not have a meaningful impact on the company. Consequently, small community banks probably don't have much to worry about with regard to hostile takeovers.

GROWTH AND CAPITAL ADEQUACY

Growth, earnings, and dividends have a direct relationship to capital adequacy. More banks are planning for future growth, earnings, and dividends in order to avoid the possibility of raising new outside capital.

Planning for adequate capital involves planning for growth, earnings, and dividends. Planning for growth involves two issues: inflationary growth and real growth.

If a bank grows at the same rate as the rate of inflation, it basically has stood still. You will not need additional personnel or facilities because your bank has undergone a false growth. Real growth means that your bank has increased in size by increasing its market share. A real growth rate of 6 percent per year will result in doubling the size (real growth) of the bank in twelve years. (To determine how many years it takes your bank to double in size, divide your expected growth rate by 72.) This real growth of 6 percent may result in the need for additional personnel and facilities.

The main issue concerning planning for growth is to decide whether you want your bank to grow with inflation or increase your market share. Planning for profitability is a difficult task. You must look at historical return on assets and then project into the future how much you believe you can earn as a percentage of assets. The future demands of stockholders must be projected to determine a divided payout ratio to get income.

David L. Donahue of Conley, McDonald, Sprague & Co., certified public accountants in Milwaukee, made some projections for a bank with a 1.1 percent return in assets and a dividend payout ratio of 40 percent of net income: Assume management has determined it wants to maintain a 7.5 percent capital ratio. Total growth (inflationary and real) would be limited to 8.8 percent (see Table 1). If annual growth was projected at 10 percent, the capital-to-asset ratio would decline.

To maintain the capital-to-asset ratio at 7.5 percent, a bank must do one or more of the following:

- Increase profits
- Decrease dividend payout ratio
- Reduce growth rate
- Obtain additional capital

TABLE 1

Growth Rates That Can Be Sustained without External Financial if a Bank Maintains a 7.5% Capital-to-Assets Ratio						
Net Income as a Percent of Beginning Assets						
2.0	26.7	24.0	21.3	18.7	16.0	13.3
1.9	25.3	22.8	20.3	17.7	15.2	12.7
1.8	24.0	21.6	19.2	16.8	14.4	12.0
1.7	22.7	20.4	18.1	15.9	13.6	11.3
1.6	21.3	19.2	17.1	14.9	12.8	10.7
1.5	20.0	18.0	16.0	14.0	12.0	10.0
1.4	18.6	16.8	14.9	13.1	11.2	9.3
1.3	17.3	15.6	13.9	12.1	10.4	8.7
1.2	16.0	14.4	12.8	11.2	9.6	8.0
1.1	14.6	13.2	11.7	10.3	8.8	7.3
1.0	13.3	12.0	10.6	9.3	8.0	6.7
0.9	12.0	10.8	9.6	8.4	7.2	6.0
0.8	10.6	9.6	8.5	7.5	6.4	5.3
0.7	9.6	8.4	7.5	6.5	5.6	4.6
0.6	8.0	7.2	6.4	5.6	4.8	4.0
0.5	6.6	6.0	5.3	4.6	4.0	3.3
	0	10	20	30	40	50
Dividends Paid as a Percent of Net Income						

KEY POINT: You must consider the needs of the community and the stockholders. If the community is growing, or if your increase in market share is profitable growth (based on a return on stockholders equity), you may have little choice to maintain that growth.

CAPITAL ADEQUACY AND THE PRICE OF A BANK'S STOCK

One approach that has been used by some banks to generate additional capital to back loan and deposit growth is to set stock below book value. Advocates of this approach believe that a sound capital position reflects a sign of strength that is appealing to companies with loan and deposit business. Furthermore, a strong capital position gives added assurance to firms that they can borrow as needed.

Opponents to this concept argue that it is not sound policy to sell substantially below book value. A strong reason for this position is that they believe such an approach takes away part of the net worth of present shareholders and rewards the new investors.

A bank's book value reflects cash and marketable securities. Therefore, if new shareholders can buy stock below book value, the logical assumption is that there must have been a certain amount of bond depreciation—certainly not the cash value. Similarly, loans that are overvalued (that is, deemed fully collectible, when, in fact, they are not) have the same depreciating effect on book value.

Relative Capital Adequacy. There is no absolute level of capital adequacy. However, some of the qualitative measures that affect capital adequacy determination are:

1. Quality, liquidity, and maturity of the bank's loan portfolio

2. Market value of securities investment portfolio at a given point in time

3. True, disposable value of real property

The Ratio Approach. The real question to be answered, therefore, is: What constitutes relative capital adequacy? To gain some perspective into this question, try applying the ratio approach. Here are some of the more common ratios used by banks for this purpose:

Ratio	Interpretation
Percent earned on assets (net operating income divided by total assets)	Capital growth is measured in terms of profit. Also, investor purchases of equity/debt instruments look to this indicator for profit performance.
Loan income plus loan loss provision divided by loan charge-offs	Safety in loan earnings as measured against loan losses taken in a given year helps to determine the quality of assets.
Equity capital and reserves to total assets	Strength of your equity capital position is second to loan loss coverage in determining a bank's ability to withstand losses.

The equity capital and reserve ratio can be applied to any asset base in determining relative capital adequacy. The ratio of equity capital and reserves to total assets, for example, reflects the least protection to be expected. The ratio of equity capital and reserves to total loans would show the maximum protection.

> **NOTE:** Banking has reached a threshold in its expansion wherein depositors and investors are taking a serious look at the manner in which banks are approaching the equity/debt financing problem. If the market price of a bank's stock is too high, then the sale of new stock might set the shares of outstanding stock to a realistic level.

RISK-BASED CAPITAL GUIDELINES

The Federal Reserve Board has issued new regulations governing the capitalization of a bank, based on risk. These regulations became effective in 1989, and are phased in over a two-year period.

In summary, the new rules are:

• Tie a bank's capital requirements to the risk of its activities, and include off-balance sheet exposure.

• Operate initially with existing capital requirements of 3.5 percent primary capital to total assets.

• Begin to standardize capital requirements on a world-wide basis.

• Redefine primary capital by adding sources of funds deducting certain intangibles.

Details of the capital guidelines are provided in Table 2, 3, and 4 from the Federal Reserve.

TABLE 2
Definition of Primary Capital for U.S. Banking Organizations

I. Base primary capital—funds included *without* limit
  • Common stockholders' equity (including surplus and retained earnings)
  • Minority interest in equity accounts of consolidated subsidiaries
  • General loan loss reserves
II. Limited primary capital—items included in this category must not exceed 50% of base primary capital less intangible assets.
  • Perpetual preferred stock
  • Long-term (25 years or more) limited-life preferred stock (amount included in primary capital discounted as instrument approaches maturity)
  • Debt that is subordinated to deposits, that can only be redeemed with or converted into primary capital instruments, that can absorb losses, and on which interest can be deferred under certain circumstances. (Debt instruments that are currently included in primary capital but that do not meet these conditions, such as certain mandatory convertible securities, would be grandfathered.)
III.Adjustments to primary capital
  • Deduction of intangible assets (existing intangibles to be grandfathered)
  • Deduction of investments in unconsolidated subsidiaries, joint ventures, and certain consolidated subsidiaries
  • Monitoring and possible deduction on a case-by-case basis of holdings of capital instruments issued by other banking organizations

SOURCE: Federal Reserve

TABLE 3
Summary of Risk Weights and Major Risk Categories for U.S. Banking Organizations

0%
- Cash, domestic, and foreign
- Claims on Federal Reserve Banks

10%
- Short term (one year or less) claims on U.S. Government and its agencies

25%
- Cash items in process of collection
- Short-term claims on domestic depository institutions and foreign banks, including foreign central banks
- Long-term claims on U.S. Government and its agencies
- Claims (including repurchase agreements) collateralized by cash or U.S. Government or agency debt
- Claims guaranteed by the U.S. Government or its agencies
- Local currency claims on foreign central governments to the extent that bank has local currency liabilities
- Federal Reserve Bank stock

50%
- Claims on U.S. Government-sponsored agencies
- Claims (including repurchase agreements) collateralized by U.S Government-sponsored agency debt
- General obligation claims on states, counties, and municipalities
- Claims on multinational development institutions in which the United States is a shareholder or contributing member

100%
- All other assets not specified above, including:
  Claims on private entities and individuals
  Long-term claims on domestic and foreign banks
  Claims on foreign governments that involve transfer risk
  Claims on all foreign private sector borrowers

SOURCE: Federal Reserve

TABLE 4
Summary of Off-Balance Sheet Items and Conversions Factors for U.S.Banking Organizations

- Direct credit substitutes (financial guarantees and standby letters of credit serving the same purpose)—100% credit conversion factor
- Trade-related-contingencies (commercial letters of credit, bid and performance bonds, and performance standby letters of credit)—50% credit conversion factor
- Sale and repurchase agreements and asset sales with recourse, if not already included on the balance sheet—100% credit conversion factor
- Other commitments, including overdraft facilities, revolving underwriting facilities (RUFs/NIFs), underwriting commitments, commercial and consumer credit lines. The credit conversion factors are:

10%—one year and less original maturity (maturity is defined as the stated maturity date or the earliest possible time at which the bank may *unconditionally* cancel the commitment, whichever comes first).

25%—over one to five years original maturity

50%—over five years original maturity

SOURCE: Federal Reserve

5

BANK
FINANCIAL MANAGEMENT

There is hardly a banker around who cannot, legitimately, complain about the squeeze on profits. Financial management in the banking industry has rightly developed into a fine art in recent years. Several topics are discussed in this chapter that will help a banker better manage the bank's finances. Of special concern, and receiving increasing attention from the bank regulators, are off-balance-sheet activities. The suggestions in this chapter can assist every bank in maintaining better and proper control over such activities, and, not incidentally, satisfy the regulators. Additional ideas in financial management can be found in Chapter 14.

HOW TO DEVELOP A WORKABLE BUDGET

To develop a good budgeting system for a bank, all levels of the organization must participate, down to the cost–center level. The budget figures should not be finite simply because variances become meaningless at so low a level.

The budgeted figures should be reasonably attainable, and only exception budgeting, which operates under the concept that only variances above or below a predetermined dollar and/or percentage level are reported, should be brought to management's attention.

Budget Checklist. Although general in nature, this checkist does key in on vital issues that are so frequently overlooked.

• The bank's overall concepts, goals, and objectives must be clearly identified so that the budget staff and all participants know precisely what management wants and expects of the budget process. Also, the budget output must be assessed to determine how it will fit in with other management decisions. For example, the annual budget should fit in with the first year of a long-range plan that perhaps extends to a five-year term.

• Consider whether or not you want a formal or informal budgeting system. Can you afford it (in terms of both dollars and resource commitments)? If the system is not cost-justifiable, seek a less formal operation, but one that will still highlight important decision points for you.

• Identify the budget cycle you intend to follow—fiscal period, rolling budget, and so on. In this way you can compare apples with apples.

• Integrate the system with the data processing department (assuming, of course, it is an automated system).

• Your general ledger system is the data base for budgeted data. Therefore, be certain it is sufficiently detailed to give you the kind of financial information you want to know. For example, if you want detailed information budgeted for payroll, the general ledger should separate the various categories of payroll into such classifications as regular, part time, overtime, bonuses, officers, and so on. If you budget for payroll, only all of these classifications must be lumped into the one account.

• The bank's organization must be clearly identified in order for the budget to be effective. Only in this way can you pinpoint responsibility by organizational unit within your bank. Frequently, managers think they report through a given chain within the organization. However, a little investigation might prove that, in fact, they should be reporting elsewhere. Such discrepancies must be cleared before the budget system can be meaningful.

• Variance analysis (the process of reporting variances between what was budgeted and what was actually realized) is a difficult—and frequently misinterpreted—function. Only someone who is completely familiar with the entire process should have the responsibility for analyzing variances. Managers should have an opportunity to analyze their variances before they have to explain them to the upper echelons.

> **TIP:** This is best accomplished by distributing budgeted reports in a sequenced or stepped fashion so that senior levels of management are not requesting explanations of variances before the lower levels have had an opportunity to properly evaluate their reports.

• Final budgeted (and accepted) figures should be communicated to those who participated in the development effort. This creates a feeling of belonging to the team, and it lets all levels of management know precisely what is expected of them.

MEASURING AND MANAGING FLOAT

Perhaps the simplest method of reporting float is by making a list of your bank's large-float customers. It might be a listing of the top fifty commercial accounts or the top twenty. *The main consideration:* The number should be relevant to your bank's size, its controllable external float problem, and its dependence on commercial business accounts.

Analyzing this customer list may lead to a new evaluation of your bank's relationship with many of its commercial depositors. If, for example, some customers have a large float for which they are mainly responsible, then you may be faced with the management decision: Is this float worthwhile, in order to have the balances generated by the account? In other cases the information from the listing might call for a program to help commercial customers reduce float by instituting earlier deposit schedules or by contacting their customers who may be providing them with items comprising large dollar amounts of float.

Demand–deposit Ratio. One of the most common ways of reporting float is by comparing total float with demand deposits. To be a reasonably indicative measure of float, this report must take into consideration any drastic changes in your bank's deposit mix. To rely on a demand–deposit ratio, it is advisable for your bank to use a 13-month year so that it will be comparing float on Monday to float on Monday, and float on Tuesday to float on Tuesday, and so on.

> **CAUTION:** If this approach is not taken in the report, there will be distortions in float measurement when the first day of the month falls on a Monday in one month and on a Wednesday the following month.

This type of report can provide you with a relative index of float, providing your mix of deposits does not vary drastically. *For example:* If your bank suddenly acquired a large amount of float without a large compensating deposit, or if it had a large number of correspondent bank cash letters, these seasonal influences could affect the float index.

Total credit ratio. Another method, somewhat similar to demand–deposit measurement, is a report based on dividing total float by total credits. Again, like days must be compared to like days in the report. If your bank is heavily dependent on correspondent business, a measurement report relating totally to correspondent bank float might be included. The correspondent bank's float for a day would be divided by the correspondent bank's credits. A bank may or may not want to decrease or apportion the credits by internal factors affecting float, for example, wire transfers, federal funds, and so on.

Type of account report. An important consideration early on in float determination is to identify the type of account creating float, for example, correspondent bank accounts, lock-box accounts, commercial accounts, and so on. Generally, float on personal or individual accounts is too small to include on an account-by-account basis. If included, most banks measure it in total.

If your bank has the systems capability of doing so, you can break float by breaking it down on the deposit analysis spread, and very readily determine float on any specific account or groups of accounts. Particularly, a deposit analysis spread will give not only total float by each day such as immediate, one-day, two-day, and so on, but also a spread showing the various sending or in-points for items making up the deposit.

This type of report can be very useful for a customer-by-customer float analysis and also for determining types of accounts that are costing your bank money in float.

A final method of reporting float is to divide nondemand float by total float. This would establish the relationship of the float generated in other than demand deposits as a relative percentage of the total float. A report based on this comparison would reveal just how great a percentage of overall float is accounted for by internal float, such as payments on loans, real estate mortgages, credit cards, and so on. Often, internal float figures will come as an unwelcome surprise and call for new policy decisions by management as well as a change in long-term strategy.

> **NOTE:** Remember that the data contained in these reports are particular to your bank. If you want to compare these data to data generated by other banks the size of your own, go into enough detail in the figures to make certain you are making proper comparisons.

HOW TO CONTROL PETTY CASH

Petty cash isn't always petty, particularly if there are no controls. Usually petty cash is an amount of cash kept in an imprest fund which is maintained in various departments to pay for miscellaneous expenses that come up during day-today operations (car fare, meal money, and so on). At times one can be lulled into a false sense of security; the amount is small and so is the exposure of the bank.

There are, however, four matters that should be considered:

(1) The amount does represent cash and, as such, should be accorded a similar degree of security over its handling as is the bank's other cash.

(2) The petty cash fund should be reviewed for turnover. A relatively small amount can be translated into a relatively large amount by the multiplying effect.

(3) Items flowing through petty cash should be scrutinized for appropriateness. Are these transactions authorized to be paid out of petty cash? Should some items be better controlled by facilitating payment through another system (that is, payroll, accounts payable, voucher, and so on)?

(4) A petty cash fund can be the depository for some very unusual items. Example: A mortgage department petty cash fund was counted and was found to be $5,000 over its imprest amount of $50. Upon inspection it was determined that a check in the amount of $5,000 was received by the mortgage department and included in petty cash. At the same time the check was received, there was a notice that a court action was being commenced by the borrower against the bank for usury on the loan for which the $5,000 check was being paid as satisfaction. The mortgage department immediately called its outside legal counsel, who advised them by phone to hold the check pending further word because there might be a question of "constructive receipt." The mortgage department decided to put it into petty cash.

The check was basically overlooked, and the matter somehow fell between the chairs, and the check remained in petty cash for quite some time. *Result:* Senior management was not aware of its existence. The check was never placed under any safekeeping control. It was exposed daily to the normal activity of the fund, and the bank did not have use of the funds. The overall matter was not addressed on a timely basis. Admittedly, this is a rather unusual situation but occurrences such as these are not all that uncommon.

QUESTIONS TO ASK ABOUT PETTY CASH FUNDS

• Is the imprest fund system used? (If not, what system is used? Describe procedure, particularly where a bank account is part of a fund.)

• Is responsibility for each fund vested in only one person?

• Is the custodian independent of the cashier or other employees who handle remittances from customers and other receipts?

• Are the accounting records inaccessible to the custodian?

• Does the custodian obtain formal evidence of all disbursements made from the funds?

• Is supporting evidence

- executed in ink or in such a manner as to make alterations difficult?

- approved by a department head or other authorized person?

- canceled at, or immediately following, the signing of the reimbursement check to prevent reuse?

- audited internally before reimbursement is made?

• Are reimbursement checks drawn to the order of the custodian?

• Are funds restricted as to

- amount not exceeding requirements for disbursement for a period of one month or less?

- expenditures of a petty nature not exceeding a designated amount?

• Are funds audited by frequent and surprise counts by an independent employee or officer?

• Are records maintained of the existence of funds and are results made available of surprise cash counts?

• If personal checks are cashed, does control seem adequate?

BETTER MANAGEMENT OF NET INTEREST MARGINS

Interest rate volatility has been the order of the day for several years and shows no signs of diminishing. Bankers certainly cannot control all the variables affecting rates, but they can attempt to anticipate and manage their impact on bank profits.

> **KEY POINT:** Stable income, adequate in proportion to risk, can only be achieved by careful management of interest margins, overhead, liquidity, and capital.

Knowing what causes net interest margins to vary can give you the tools to guarantee profits despite rapidly changing economic conditions.

Net Interest Margin Versus Interest Rate Spread. The difference between gross yield (total tax-equivalent income divided by average earning assets) and gross funds cost rate (total interest expense divided by average earning assets) is the net interest margin (NIM). *The greatest advantage of NIM management:* Its simultaneous focus on both sides of the balance sheet. A rise or fall in NIM means that either liability cost has varied more than asset yield, or that asset yield has varied more than liability cost.

Also, while interest rate spread deals only with dollar differences, NIMs calculation as a percentage of earning assets leads a bank's management to concentrate on asset earning power from the liability side. After all, the cost rate is actually the breakeven yield because it shows the yield required on earning assets to cover interest expense.

NIM fluctuations within individual banks can be traced to different combinations of change of rate, volume, and mix affecting each institution. Example: A large money center bank with assets and liabilities of like interest sensitivity would find margin fluctuations due mostly to volume changes over the business cycle. On the other hand, a suburban retail bank with a portfolio of fixed rate installment loans, retail credit, and mortgages funded by interest-sensitive liabilities would find its margin greatly affected by rate.

Necessary Systems. To evaluate and isolate these fluctuations and choose between possible management strategies, certain systems must be present in the bank's operating structure. They are:

- A formalized budgeting and planning process.
- A planning model in which budget assumptions can be varied.
- A method of maintaining both historical and forecast data for reference and comparison.
- Analytical tools to manipulate data.
- A timely reporting system to present alternatives to management, along with historical versus plan performance data.

This method presumes an integrated accounting system capable of producing an average daily balance sheet on a full accrual basis. This and the data manipulation and reporting tasks are best handled by electronic data processing techniques. Although the process may seem formidable, banks lacking such capabilities should move ahead to install a complete management information system to ensure that bank management has the most accurate and current information possible.

Objectives. NIM management seeks to establish causal relationships between NIM fluctuations and changes in:

- *Volume*—changes in overall levels of assets and liabilities.
- *Mix*—proportional changes in interest-earning assets and interest-bearing liabilities.
- *Rate*—changes in interest earned on assets and paid on liabilities.

Compare past operating results noting margin changes as a function of the interest (business) cycle. Segregate balance sheet items by variable or fixed rate funds, and look for relationships between NIM and rising and falling rates. This disaggregation of assets and liabilities should disclose interest sensitivities over time intervals of 1 to 30 days, 31 to 90 days, 91 to 365 days, and four consecutive one-year periods. It is an integral part of the NIM, management process.

Key Variables Ahead. What key variables will affect NIM in the future? This is management's considered opinion on future conditions based, in part, on key factors discovered to have influenced NIM in the past. Some possibilities are:

- Growth interest rate levels
- Inflation rate
- Growth rates of loans and deposits
- Ability to purchase funds
- Liquidity requirements
- Loan quality
- Capital formation rate

A CONSOLIDATED PROFIT PLAN

All departments should submit plans based on management's key variables and ratio goals (ROE, ROA, etc.) Balance sheets and income statements should reflect the disaggregation format showing interest-rate sensitivities.

"What if?" kinds of questions should be asked:

- What will happen to NIM as the prime rate changes above and below the plan rate?
- What if rates remain constant at a relatively high level and mix changes from commercial loans at variable rates to installment loans at interest rates set by state usury laws?
- What if loan volume drops, requiring increased purchases of bonds?

NOTE: These techniques will give you the information to draw up a detailed profit plan based on assumptions that have been quantified and tested in a profit model. Knowing what conditions have the greatest impact on margins lets you design the profit plan to capitalize on known strengths while shoring up weak areas.

Another important advantage of this planning process is that you can develop "hedging" plans allowing for quick, sure reaction, rather than improvised responses to crisis situations. This can provide a significant competitive edge in increasingly competitive markets.

OFF-BALANCE SHEET ACTIVITIES

The apparent growth in the use of off-balance sheet items has worried some bankers and many bank regulators. In fact, the Federal Reserve has included them in its new (1988) risk capital guidelines (see Chapter 4).

What are considered to be off-balance sheet items? Here are the definitions used by the Federal Reserve Board:

• Direct credit substitutes (financial guarantees and standby letters of credit serving the same purpose)—100% credit conversion factor.

• Trade-related contingencies (commercial letters of credit, bid and performance bonds, and performance standby letters of credit)—50% credit conversion factor.

• Sale and repurchase agreements and asset sales with recourse, if not already included on the balance sheet—100% credit conversion factor.

• Other commitments, including overdraft facilities, revolving underwriting facilities (RUFs), underwriting commitments, commercial and consumer credit lines.

KEEPING OFF-BALANCE SHEET ACTIVITIES UNDER CONTROL

Here are some policy suggestions from Robert Morris Associates, the national association of bank lenders:

• In each off-balance sheet transaction, there must be an account party who is well-known to the bank, who represents sufficient substance, and from whom the bank may reasonably expect any required reimbursement over the term of the facility.

• The risk analysis, credit approval, and grading processes employed should be the same as those used in other credit requests.

• The bank's senior credit policy officer should develop and recommend to the board appropriate and prudent policies for determining the levels of credit risks undertaken. Where applicable, the recommendations may incorporate distinctions in the terms and purposes for which the contingent liabilities are employed.

• The board should ensure that the CEO and other responsible executives have established policies and procedures to ensure that effective controls are in place to address the following issues:

1. Individual approvals in excess of an amount established by the board and related to the bank's capital must be reported to the senior lending officer, credit review, the CEO, or other specified parties.

2. Relationships involving such commitments must be taken into account in establishing the adequacy of the Allowance for Loan and Lease Losses. One agency already requires such a procedure.

3. An appropriate tracking unit, generally credit review, must maintain a historical record of the occasions on which the bank had to fund these commitments. This record should include sufficient data which, together with other information, will satisfy management that it can properly assess its liquidity and credit risks.

6

BANK PORTFOLIO MANAGEMENT

One mark of a well-managed bank is the condition of its own portfolio of stocks and bonds. It is one thing to manage other people's money; it is quite another to properly manage one's own resources.

This chapter provides some suggestions that any bank can use in handling its portfolio—not the least of which is the selection of the best possible security dealer.

HAVE YOU LOOKED AT YOUR BANK'S INVESTMENT PORTFOLIO LATELY?

The management of a bank's own investment portfolio, can, as you well know, impact greatly on the bottom line. However, for some unfathomable reason, many banks do not put in nearly the amount of scrutiny in their investments as they do their loan portfolio. Yet the investment objectives of a bank should be reviewed and updated and changed where necessary. After all, the volatile financial markets promise to remain in that state for the foreseeable future.

DEVELOPING AN INVESTMENT STRATEGY

The first step in developing an investment strategy for your bank is to review the current situation. There are three areas that should be covered:

1. *Liquidity.* In most cases, there is no specific distinction between those very liquid assets which serve as so-called secondary reserves and those which are part of the investment account. Selling bonds at a loss in order to meet a surge in loan demand is a sign of poor liquidity management. Regular forecasting of interest rates and loan demand is an important element in liquidity management although, admittedly, one frought with risk and hardly precise.

2. *Income.* It is important to achieve some degree of balance which can reasonably serve the needs for liquidity, safety, and income. High levels of safety and liquidity usually work against the goal of high income, although periods of low money may somewhat distort this. Actually, a case can be made for offsetting an aggressive loan portfolio with a more cautious investment tack. Also, a low-risk loan policy may be countered by an aggressive investment strategy.

3. *Diversification.* Your loan investment portfolio quality is usually dependent to a degree on the local economy. Municipals offer many banks the only opportunity for geographical diversification. However, placing a substantial portion of the investment account in bonds in a city several states away doesn't really achieve that much diversification. Certainly the diversification of maturities is a desirable objective. However, a concentration in long-term securities presents considerable risk on the interest rate side. How long-term should long-term be? In most instances, it is advisable not to exceed ten years, and then there could still be problems.

Investment Income. About 20 percent of the average bank's gross income is generated by its investments. The lower costs associated with this revenue, compared to loan income, probably makes the contribution even higher than 20 percent.

IMPORTANT POINT: Only a modest increase in investment return can provide a considerable difference in the bottom line.

NOTE: Traditionally, portfolio management calls for lengthening maturities when rates are expected to decline and shortening maturities when rates are expected to increase. However, with the volatility of rates and loan demand in banking nowadays, this approach merits some modification.

BETTER MANAGEMENT OF THE BANK'S BOND PORTFOLIO

The general procedure for investment of funds in bank portfolios in the past has been to find a good quality investment at a reasonable price with a reasonable maturity, buy it, put it in the portfolio, forget it, and at maturity reinvest it in the same manner. Enlightened portfolio managers have recognized the need to adopt a more rational, all-inclusive investment policy based on research and analysis, not on specific investment needs per se, but more on the nature of the bank's needs. Only then have they sought the appropriate security.

More recently some portfolio managers have recognized a new factor which is of paramount importance in today's banking world.

> **KEY POINT:** Conditions permit repricing of the bond account, perhaps more readily than many other segments of the asset base.

Consequently, the fixed-rate, long-term bond portfolio has become an important tool in the rapidly emerging field of asset-liability management. Now, for example, when bankers describe their ratio of rate-sensitive assets RSA to rate-sensitive liabilities RSL, bonds maturing in the next ninety days are considered part of the numerator of the RSA-to-RSL ratio.

MAINTAINING LIQUIDITY

The primary function of the bond account is liquidity. Liquidity must support the loan portfolio and provide a ready source of funds to ameliorate deposit fluctuations.

> **REMEMBER:** The determination of a bank's deposit volatility is one of the key factors in establishing appropriate liquidity balance, and, in turn, bond account composition.

Although an actual distribution of maturing deposits is useful in making such a determination, this is an overly simplistic approach.

A degree of deposit stability, in terms of net balances that remain in the bank, exists beyond straight maturity considerations. Given today's economic conditions, this "stability" can be reasonably anticipated, using management's own experience in the bank's service area as well as conservative local and national statistical studies. Correspondingly, a comparison of rate-sensitive assets, including short-term investments due within ninety days and assets that are revalued on a regular basis, to liabilities sensitive to rate changes can often illustrate unrealized investment opportunity or earnings vulnerability.

Such analysis, combined with liquidity studies, offers a working definition of liquidity and income needs in what has often been an uncomfortably imprecise aspect of asset management.

MORE INCOME

Once liquidity and rate-sensitivity aspects are properly understood, the balance of the portfolio can, and properly should, be viewed as a primary source of earnings. When discussing yield, however, there are two dimensions to bear in mind:

1. Yield that is achieved by reducing taxes payable

2. Yield that is possible through intelligent upgrading and trading within the bond account itself

If liability to the full corporate tax rate exists, or, if significant taxes have been paid over the last ten years that are available for recovery, the most attractive investment vehicle for preservation of earnings is likely to be tax-exempt bonds.

Although a tax-free return of 10 percent is no longer uncommon, capturing yields this high may well involve excessive maturity and/or minimal quality. Any investment, of course, provides return based on risk and maturity. The tax-exempt market, however, offers substantial yield opportunities with a sharp yield curve that rewards the more permanent commitment of funds in this area.

Banks with little or no federal tax liability, will find that tax-free state and municipal bonds have little appeal. Of greater benefit is the taxable income-producing investment, as long as the pretax income can be fully or at least largely retained. In addition to the traditional media (U.S. treasury and agency securities), corporate bonds can play a most important role. After all, if one is willing to make a loan to a company, why avoid its securities? In addition to offering a competitive yield with loans, they enjoy the added dimension of marketability.

LESS TAXES

The management of the bond portfolio is an ongoing activity subject to the changing needs of the bank. Tax exposure and liquidity needs fluctuate. Investment emphasis in the bond portfolio between tax-exempt and taxable income-producing securities can be shifted to satisfy these demands by virtue of the marketability of the investments.

In addition, tax programming within or across portfolio sectors can be considered.

> **EXAMPLE:** Significant tax exposure can
> often be offset by incurring losses on sale in
> the bond portfolio with reinvestment in higher
> net yielding securities. The gross loss on sale is
> used to offset taxable income, at the applicable
> tax rate, and reinvestment at higher net yields
> accelerates the recovery of the net loss on sale.
> Having thus repriced this aspect of
> investments, reduced tax payments, and

recovered the loss on sale, the increased net
return on investment builds in increased
future net earnings.

Programming within the bond portfolio can also be
pursued to increase taxable income using profits on sale, to
bolster liquidity, or some combination thereof.

CAUTION: Such programming should, of
course, be reviewed with tax counsel to verify
tax implications.
The structuring of reinvestment must take into
account current and future impact on
earnings, liquidity needs, and market
conditions.

NOTE: The old rules no longer apply. New,
more complex, strategic issues come into play.
The successful portfolio manager will form a
portfolio strategy based on an understanding
of these issues.

GUIDELINES FOR SELECTING SECURITY DEALERS

The federal banking regulators: the Federal Reserve Board,
the office of the Comptroller of the Currency, and the Federal
Deposit Insurance Corporation, issued guidelines in 1988 for
banks and bank holding companies to use in the selection of
securities dealers. According to the regulators, the guidelines
were issued because institutions were increasingly turning to
the securities markets for portfolio investments and relying on
advice from securities dealers.
    In selecting a securities dealer the regulators suggest that
bank portfolio managers should know the securities firm and
the personnel advising the bank.

CAUTION: Managers should not do business
with dealers that refuse to provide "complete

and timely" disclosure of their financial condition.

Also management should review a dealer's financial statements and make a judgment about the ability of the dealer to honor its commitments. Moreover, the bank should inquire into the reputation of the securities dealer.

The selection process should include:

• An inquiry with appropriate regulators and self-regulatory associations regarding any enforcement actions against the dealer

• An inquiry into the background of the sales representative to determine his or her experience and expertise

• A determination about whether the depository institution has appropriate procedures in place to establish or control of the securities purchased

> **SUGGESTION:** As part of the institution's code of conduct, an institution's board of directors may want to establish a rule that employees engaged in securities dealings may not trade securities for their own account with the same company used by the bank.

The guidelines also cover the type of investments made by depository institutions and their treatment for purposes of calculating an institution's capital. They require that investments made for the purpose of short-term gains rather than long-term investment should be placed in the institution's trading account. Securities in the trading account should be marked to market and reevaluated periodically to reflect an institution's unrealized gains or losses in capital.

Certain investments and investment practices deemed unsuitable for financial institutions include:

• Gains trading—that is, trading for short-term gain

• "When issued" trading, or buying in the interim between the time an offer is announced and the issue is actually made

• "Pair-offs," in which a transaction is closed out before the actual settlement date

The guidelines also state that the following practices are *not* proper:

• Using the corporate settlement method (that is, settling five days after the transaction date) instead of the government securities settlement method (settling the day after the transaction date) when dealing in government securities

• Repositioning repurchase agreements

• Short sales

7

HUMAN
RESOURCE MANAGEMENT

Although technological advances have automated a number of
banking functions and have reduced the reliance by banks on
people in certain areas, banking is still a labor-intensive
industry. This is because many of the skills required in banking
have changed and multiplied.

Too many banks focus on the running of the banks, its
operations, and its services. They overlook or pay little attention to the fact that a well-run bank begins with the effective
management of its personnel. Problems such as absenteeism
and unhappy employees can undermine efforts in the other
aspects of banking. They must be addressed before irrepair-
able harm is done.

Chapters 7, 8 and 9 all relate to the human resources
aspects of banking.

IDENTIFYING AND CORRECTING
PERFORMANCE PROBLEMS

One of the more difficult tasks a bank executive faces is to
evaluate the performance of subordinates. The most difficult
part of the process is to analyze performance problems and
determine appropriate solutions. Below is a method that can
help—regardless of any specific rating system (if any) your
bank has in place.

Describe Performance Discrepancy. The first step in analyzing a performance problem is to describe the performance

discrepancy. This kind of discrepancy occurs between an employee's *actual* performance and his or her *desired* performance.

> **IMPORTANT:** Note that the word "discrepancy" is used instead of the word "deficiency." Discrepancy means that there is only a difference, a lack of balance between the actual and the desired. Deficiency means that a value judgment has been made about a discrepancy and that the discrepancy is bad or in some way unacceptable. Using discrepancy avoids jumping to conclusions about whether a discrepancy is good or bad.

Importance of Discrepancy. The second step is to determine if the discrepancy is important or if it is worth changing. The consequence of the discrepancy can be evaluated by asking, "What would happen if I left it alone?" Many discrepancies are found to be simply personal biases about what is "right" or a blind preference for "the way we've always done it."

Skill Knowledge Deficiency. At this point you should begin to determine the cause of the discrepancy so that an appropriate remedy can be selected. In this step you must decide if the performance discrepancy is due to a skill/knowledge deficiency. In essence, is the person not performing as described because he or she does not know how to perform the task? If the person's life depended on it, would he or she still not perform?

> **RECOMMENDATION:** If there is a genuine skill/knowledge deficiency, then the primary remedy must be to either change the employee's skill/knowledge level (that is, teach the employee how to do it) or change what is expected of him or her.

If, on the other hand, an employee is able to perform but doesn't, the solution lies beyond enhancing his or her skill/knowledge.

THE REMEDY: Change the conditions under which the employee is expected to perform what he already knows how to do.

Following is a list of factors you should consider when a skill/knowledge deficiency does exist.

Why is There a Deficiency? Determining whether a lack of skill/knowledge is due to a form of forgetting or to a lack of training is an important decision. If it is determined that an employee has a skill/knowledge deficiency and that he or she has never had the skill/knowledge, some sort of training will be required; however, the solution is not necessarily a formal training program.

Is the Skill Used Often? When a skill or knowledge fades or disappears, an appropriate remedy to consider is a skill/knowledge maintenance program. A maintenance program comes in two forms:

1. If the skill/knowledge is used infrequently, the level of performance is maintained by providing a regular schedule of practice.

2. If the skill/knowledge is used frequently, but has deteriorated despite regular use, the level of performance is maintained by providing periodic feedback. Without feedback, practice may serve merely to entrench poor or imperfect actions. Practice without feedback is of little value. Obviously, this is important in auditing, as the audit function should not be mechanical or in any way substandard.

Is There a Simpler Way? Depending on the conditions, three tentative solutions have been identifed:

• If an employee used to perform a task, but used the skill/knowledge only rarely, consider systematic practice.

• If an employee used to perform a task and still gets lots of practice, consider providing more feedback.

• If an employee has never performed the task, consider formal training.

Two Simpler Solutions. Before any of these solutions are selected, there might be a simpler and less expensive solution. One simple solution would be to change the job—that is, change the skill/knowledge requirements to meet the skill/knowledge available.

An easy way to change a job is to provide some kind of job aid. Examples include checklists, instruction sheets, labels, and signs. This allows the individual to refer to the job aid any time he or she wants to. the job aid should simplify the job and assist in decreasing skill/knowledge deficiencies.

Another simple solution is to provide on-the-job training rather than formal training.

It Is Not a Skill/Knowledge Deficiency. At this point all the solutions have been discussed when a determination has been made that a skill/knowledge deficiency exists.

The next step is to examine possible solutions when an employee does *not* have a skill/knowledge deficiency but an important performance discrepancy still exists. In this situation it is probably obvious that something other than instruction is needed. Rather than modifying the employee's skill or knowledge, you will have to modify the conditions associated with the performance. Rather than changing what an employee *can* do, change his or her surroundings so that doing it will be more attractive, or less repulsive, or less difficult.

MODIFYING CONDITIONS

There are four areas to examine:

1. *Is desired performance punishing?* One reason employees don't perform as expected is simply that the desired "doing" is punishing. When desired performance leads to undesirable results, employees have a way of finding other ways to go. It is not your view of the outcome that is important, it is the view of the employee whose performance you want to change. What might be a favorable consequence to *you* might be unfavorable to the *employee*.

> **THE REMEDY:**   Reduce or eliminate the
> negative effects and create or increase the
> strength of positive or desirable consequences.

2. *Is nonperformance rewarding?* The other side of unpleas-ant consequences for desired performance is the fact that performance might not be as expected because nonperfor-mance is rewarding. Despite whether or not desired perfor-mance has favorable consequences, these consequences are not as favorable as those of nonperformance.

Often, irresponsible behavior is inadvertently rewarded, while dependable behavior is overlooked. At other times more attention is given to misbehavior than behavior.

> **THE REMEDY:**   Arrange for positive
> consequences for the desired performance.
> Many times this will involve merely redirecting
> favorable consequences or rewards.

3. *Does performance matter?* Sometimes a performance dis-crepancy continues to exist not because the employee does not know how to perform or is not motivated, but because perfor-mance is not rewarded. When favorable performance is not followed at least periodically by an event considered beneficial to the employee, performance will tend to diminish.

> **THE REMEDY:**   Since there is no advantage
> for an employee to perform, arrange for one.

4. *Obstacles to performance.* If an employee knows how to perform but doesn't, look for obstacles. Obstacles to perfor-mance can be numerous. Some examples include:

- Not knowing what is expected or when these expectations are required
- Conflicting demands on time
- Lack of authority, time, proper tools, working conditions, or equipment

- Restrictions by current policies
- Competition among the job responsibilities (for example, phone calls, office emergencies); demands are less important but more immediate

> **THE REMEDY:** In all these situations, the obstacle will have to be removed in order for the employee to perform his or her job.

Implement Solution. After you have thoroughly analyzed a performance discrepancy and concentrated on finding solutions relating to the problem, you must decide which solution is most practical or feasible in your situation. As a result, one or more of the remedies you have generated might be inappropriate because it is beyond the available resources.

> **THE REMEDY:** Select the most practical, economical, and easiest-to-use remedy which is most likely to give the greatest result for the least effort.

TAKING A POSITIVE APPROACH TO CONTROLLING ABSENTEEISM

Excessive absenteeism is generally followed by another problem: rapid turnover. Many of the conditions that contribute to one also contribute to the other. Absenteeism from all causes is also on the increase, particularly from sickness, despite the advancements in medical technology and the improvements that have been made in working conditions and employee benefits.

Although difficult to compute, absenteeism does cost your bank money. The cost includes salaries plus fringe benefits, paid to employees who are not on the job, the cost of obtaining replacements, the added overtime which may be incurred, and the costs of lost efficiency. In certain situations and under certain conditions, the replacement worker, because of his or her inexperience and the temporary nature of the job, could hold up the efficiency of an entire group.

Negative–Positive Reinforcement. There are many types of absentee control programs that produce good results. These programs are variations of one another and incorporate the same general guidelines. Experts who design these programs are in general agreement that the key to any control program is supervision.

> **KEY POINT:** Every effective program needs supervisory support, which can be accomplished through proper communication, proper disciplinary procedures, and proper follow-through.

Many well-entrenched programs, however, are based on the negative reinforcement approach to controlling employee absenteeism. As odd as it may seem, most companies have a built-in inducement to absenteeism: salary continuance or sick pay. Thus, absenteeism, is rewarded in two ways: (1) the pleasure of a day off, and (2) the pleasure of being paid for it. In reality, your bank rewards nonattendance. This is negative reinforcement.

There is a relatively new approach to controlling excessive absenteeism that has gained recognition and acceptance in the last few years: the positive reinforcement approach to controlling employee absenteeism. It is a new variation of the old "carrot on the stick" in that it rewards perfect attendance and appeals to the gambling instinct present in each of us.

> **EXAMPLE:** A pilot study used a lottery in which every month a drawing was held. Only employees with perfect attendance for that month could participate in the lottery. The employee selected by the drawing received $10 in cash. All the names of the employees that participated were also posted on the company bulletin board. Each employee was thereby

rewarded with the possibility of a monetary
reward as well as social reinforcement
(provided by recognition on the list).

The results of the study revealed that through the use of
positive reinforcement, absenteeism and its attendant costs
decreased.

NOTE: The positive reinforcement approach
to combat absenteeism, taken in conjunction
with programs designed to increase job
satisfaction in the areas of working conditions,
salary, and job expectation can significantly
decrease excessive absenteeism and job
turnover.

ADDRESSING EMPLOYEE COMPLAINTS

Concerned about employee discontent and the specter of
unionization, many banks are creating formalized systems for
their employees to register complaints and grievances.

According to one business research firm, nearly half of
the 778 companies surveyed (including banks) now have complaint systems for their nonunion employees. Also, well over
two-thirds of the firms that do not deal with unions have these
systems. Although some complaint systems are being created in
response to recent laws and regulations while others are long-
standing company traditions, the major corporate motive is to
stave off unionization.

Complaint systems are found more often in companies
that describe their primary labor relations goal as keeping as
much of the company nonunion as possible, than in those
whose main objective is getting the best bargain possible with
the union.

Even companies that are already heavily unionized view
their complaint systems as a means to limit further unionization and achieve greater equality between union and nonunion

employees. Virtually all union contracts contain grievance and arbitration clauses.

According to the same business research organization, recent research would suggest that discontent in the work place has become a major concern of corporate management. Almost all companies want to resolve as many employee grievances as possible within their firms, minimizing the involvement of third parties, especially union. There apparently is a growing interest in complaint systems, which many companies believe are an effective way to pinpoint and resolve employee grievances.

> **NOTE:** Surveyed firms stated their complaint systems are succeeding, especially in dealing with the root causes of complaints and such "objectively verifiable" issues as overtime pay and faulty equipment. They have been less successful in dealing with firings, salaries, and promotions—issues which frequently require outside arbitration. These companies stated their complaint systems also have been successful in warding off unionization, although this cannot be wholly attributed to their complaint system.

AN EASY-TO-INSTALL GRIEVANCE PROCEDURE

With bank employees being seriously courted by union organizers these days, a bank would do well to have a formal grievance procedure in place to provide solutions to potentially disruptive employee-relations problems.

The number of steps in a grievance procedure will depend, to some extent, on the size of the bank. However, the procedure should generally follow these guidelines:

1. An employee with a grievance will first see his or her supervisor.

2. If not settled at this level, the grievance goes to the department or division head.

3. If not settled here, the grievance is moved up to the executive vice president or even presidential level.

To a considerable degree, how effective a grievance procedure is depends on what happens at the first step.

> **TIP:** Filing a grievance should be as easy as possible.

This will encourage an employee to present a grievance and not keep it bottled up. It also allows complaints to be made while they are still current. As a result, the chances of settlements at the first level will be improved.

Safeguards for the System. The following measures will help keep a grievance system under control:

• Keep records at each step. A form, similar to the one reproduced below, will record the grievance, action taken, and ensure that disputes are handled promptly.

• Don't make spot decisions. Response should be measured and should follow procedures.

• Notify employees of decisions promptly. The grieved employee should not be the last to hear about any decision made.

• Make sure supervisors in each department of the bank know all the details about the grievance procedure. Only then can they be expected to perform their duties in this area in the proper manner.

> **NOTE:** Employees must know and understand their rights under the grievance procedure. Suggestion: Post the rules on the bulletin boards.

Grievance Report

(Name of Bank)
Employee . . . .
Dept. . . . . Position . . . .
Foreman or immediate supervisor . . . . .Employee's statement of grievance: . . . .
. . . .
. . . .
. . . .
Date presented to supervisor . . . .
Signature of employee . . . .
Supervisor's answer: . . . .
. . . .
. . . .
. . . .
Date . . . . Signature of supervisor . . . .
Sent to division head (date): . . . .
Disposition of case: . . . .
. . . .

UNIONIZATION AND HOW SUPERVISORS FIT IN

From time to time banks have been targets for unionization. In the late 1960s banks were singled out by George Meany as a prime source of new union members. Yet very few banks have been unionized in the last two decades. To a large extent this can be attributed to the conscientious fashion in which banks deal with their employees.

Most banks have employment policies that reduce or eliminate the problems that lead to unionization. The majority of banks offer fair and competitive levels of compensation and have strong benefit programs. Many banks have job analysis systems that serve as a basis for compensation, merit increases, promotion, and performance appraisal.

> **CAUTION:** This body of sound management policies, however, will not prevent unionization if your bank's front-line defense is weak. That defense is the quality of your bank's supervisors.

Responsibilities of a Supervisor. A supervisor is a manager. According to the National Labor Relations Act, a supervisor has authority to do such managerial tasks as hire, transfer, suspend, and promote other employees. As a manager performs these tasks, he or she exercises independent judgment.

Supervisors are on the "front line" and work on a daily basis with clerical personnel. Their primary responsibility is to oversee the work of your bank's clerks.

> **KEY POINT:** They also must see that your
> bank's policies and procedures are uniformly
> and fairly administered.

They must also notify senior management if employees consider these policies unfair or unrealistic.

Thus, the supervisor is more than a productivity specialist. He or she must be able to discuss policy with clerks without losing their goodwill. If the supervisor fails at this, the attitudes that foster unionization will appear at the bank.

Good Communications. A supervisor can use an officious tone and sharp tongue to motivate clerks in his or her department. However if this approach is taken, it is unlikely that the supervisor will enjoy the respect and rapport which is the basis of good departmental communication. Each supervisor must develop his or her own style. However, that style cannot sacrifice long-term harmony for short-term achievements or for the temptation to bully.

Communication can be improved by training. Many banks conduct labor relations seminars for all managers, at which techniques and practices that promote good relations are discussed. Some suggestions:

• Schedule informal brief meetings with employees to assess attitudes toward work and the bank.

• Encourage employees to seek advice in handling work problems.

• Notify employees in advance of changes in work content, assignments, equipment, and bank policy.

• Respond expeditiously to employee dissatisfaction with appropriate action or information.

• Show an interest in each employee's career goals and self-development.

• Administer personnel policies in a fair and impartial manner.

> **NOTE:** Unionization is a threat to banks that suffer from widespread clerical discontent. If you pay and treat your clerks fairly, chances are they will not feel the need for union protection.

ACHIEVING BETTER PRODUCTIVITY THROUGH WORK SIMPLIFICATION

The quality of your supervision in a bank is directly reflected in the performance and productivity of the clerical staff that is subjected to that supvervision. Although there are innumerable techniques that, when properly used, provide a fairly exact measurement of clerical efficiency and management effectiveness, the most dynamic technique is work simplification.

It is a rare experience to come across an operation that cannot be simplified at least in some small way. However, it's important that efforts at work simplification be selective.

> **EXAMPLE:** In a bookkeeping procedure, each posting operation can take two minutes of a posting machine operator's time. However, each month-end reconciliation may take several hours. It may be easier to find ways of simplifying the reconciling operation rather than simplifying the posting operation. However, if 2,000 to 3,000 postings must be made each month, you should tend to disregard the month-end function and concentrate on the daily operation.

Here are eleven clues to help you identify areas where work simplification might be applicable:

1. Excessive talking may indicate a need for a better floor-plan arrangement, more partitions, or possibly better sight supervision.

2. Excessive walking may reflect a need for simplification of the work flow, or possibly a more efficient floor-plan layout. In most instances only your messengers are working and producing when they are walking.

3. Many private stenographers or a large volume of dictation frequently points the way to savings through the use of dictating machines and typing pools.

4. Excessive copying or retranscription volumes may indicate the need for photocopying equipment or an upgrading of your current configuration.

5. Many hours devoted to filing may indicate the need for a reorganization of the files or possibly the need for a central filing system. In larger institutions, microfilm studies should be undertaken to conserve space, as well as to provide an efficient filing system.

6. Improper scheduling reflected in peak loads, high unit costs, low individual productivity, unequal individual output, and idle machines are usually clear signs that improved scheduling is needed.

7. Low typing and key punching production can lead to forms analysis and redesign that results in substantial savings.

8. High volume in unit record files, such as punched cards, can lead to savings through the acquisition of automatic files.

9. High-volume jobs in tabulating departments often indicate the need for machine load records, putting wheels on card file cabinets, and assigning tasks of transporting cards between machines.

10. Poor housekeeping, as evidenced by dust on furniture and equipment, waste paper on the floor, food and sodas placed on equipment, records and papers of value piled on tables, and disks and file cabinets open, are usually good indications of poor-quality work, reduced productivity, and a feeling of indifference among the employees.

11. Poor work station layouts, where frequently used supplies and materials are not within easy reach, cause wasted time and effort that often can be eliminated through a sensible rearrangement of the work station, based on the principles of motion economy.

8

DEALING WITH
EMPLOYMENT ISSUES
IN THE BANK

The right person in the right job is certainly desirable, although not easily attainable. In fact, the hiring process is a complex, difficult function, often made even more difficult by the vagaries of the labor market at any given time.

The topics included in this chapter will assist in making the employment process go smoothly. Although it may seem out of place here, the final item, the exit interview, has the potential of providing great help, both in hiring activities and in the utilization and treatment of employees during their working careers with the bank.

STEPS TOWARD SATISFACTORY STAFF SELECTION

Staffing the bank is one of management's most important functions. It includes planning, acquisition, and the assignment of labor power. Its importance can be seen in the cost of labor power for today's banking environment. In any given year, a bank can spend a large percentage of its revenue dollar for employee salaries and fringe benefits.

> **NOTE:** With these costs in mind, it is mandatory that managers select employees carefully.

Your bank makes a considerable investment in each employee. A great portion of the employee's time is spent in training, development, and familiarization with the job.

> **CAUTION:** As such, inappropriate assignment results in nonproductive training and development investment.

The loss of trained employees, of course, means a loss of the bank's investment.

Staffing is costly because recruitment and relocation expenses account for a major portion of a personnel department's budget. These are the expenses incurred in making a productive employee.

Equally important is consideration for the growth of the employee. It is imperative that the employee be properly placed because his or her career plays a primary role in the employee's life.

Preventing Employee Turnover To prevent employee turnover, transfers, and minimum job productivity, staffing decisions must be selective. You can avoid mistakes that result in turnover by:

• Selecting candidates best suited to the bank's needs

• Placing employees in assignments that provide job satisfaction

• Sensing indications of employee dissatisfaction with assignments

Basically, the staffing function in the bank consists of matching people to jobs. Your goal should be to obtain an effective interface between the requirements of the job on one hand, and the qualifications and needs of the individual on the other. This involves three steps:

1. The specific requirements of specifications of the job itself must be determined. This step is possibly the most neglected aspect of staffing, but in some ways the most critical.

It is obvious that to effectively match people to jobs, you must first know what the job is.

2. Evaluate the individual in terms of job requirements. Individual dimensions that must be evaluated include such things as work experience, training, aptitudes, physical capacity, and applicant preferences.

3. Weigh the accumulated information to arrive at a selection decision. The job specification must be weighed against individual traits to ensure a proper fit.

Whenever a manager hires certain applicants, he or she is, in effect, predicting that those hired will make better job performers than those not hired. This decision is based on information collected about the applicant which is then weighed in light of the job requirements.

> **NOTE:** The crucial question is whether the information the manager has collected is indeed predictive of latter job performance. This of course, can be followed up; hence, the need for keeping such records arises.

BETTER EMPLOYMENT INTERVIEWS

There are certain basics for effective interviewing:

- An effective interview occurs in a quiet place.
- It is free from interruption.
- It is controlled by the interviewer who first puts the job applicant at ease and then asks all relevant questions.
- Good questions are the machine that drives effective interviews.
- Good questions are specific when you need to clarify facts.
- They are general when you want to see how a job applicant handles a hypothetical situation.

• Questions can be leading or critical when you want to check the candidate's resilience or reaction to pressure.

• Good questions initiate a line of inquiry.

> **CAUTION:** Unless these questions are supported by other interview techniques, they will not thoroughly explore each candidate's attitudes and ambitions, and you may not choose the best candidate.

There are three effective tactics you can employ to control the line and breadth of an interview and to ensure that each job applicant gives a full and accurate impression. They are:

1. *The understanding nod.* Remarks such as "uh-huh," "hmm," and "I see" are invaluable interview tools. When used properly, they encourage the job applicant to expand upon his or her initial answers to your questions. Such remarks often elicit revealing statements or lead to information that strict adherence to set questions suppresses.

2. *Recapitulation.* A job candidate interprets the recapitulation of his or her remarks as an indication of interest and proof that you are listening. Restatement is often interpreted as agreement and leads naturally to expatiation. The candidate also will expand on his or her original remarks if you have tossed it back.

3. *Silence.* Don't feel compelled to fill every silence or pause with a question or statement. A pause gives the candidate the opportunity to direct the interview to topics that favors his or her abilities. It forces the candidate to focus on his or her strengths and selling points and to show you how he or she can take charge.

> **NOTE:** Good interviewers get the information they need. They listen carefully, giving job candidates room to maneuver.

QUESTIONS TO ASK APPLICANTS

Here are techniques to use during the interview process that will elicit honest answers from prospective employees.

Five Questions That Elicit Honest Answers.

Certain nondirective, simple questions can help you in the interview process, and they can also help the applicant to express his or her ideas and feelings fully. These questions permit the applicant to discuss subjects freely, and they also enable you to control the interview.

1. One of the things we want to talk about today is your work experience. Could you tell me about your present and past employment?

2. What do you feel were your major responsibilities in your last job?

3. In your last job, what were some of the things that you spent the most time on, and how much time on each?

4. What are some of the things on your last job you feel you have done particularly well or with which you have achieved the greatest success, and why do you feel this way?

5. What are some of the things you found difficult on your last job, and why do you feel this way about them?

Five Questions to Avoid.

To acquire good questioning skills, you should avoid the following questions:

1. Questions that can be answered by a simple yes or no.

2. Unimaginative, run-of-the-mill questions for which the astute applicant has prepared ready-made answers.

3. Leading questions that suggest the proper answer: "I suppose you left XYZ Bank for more money?" "You like close detail work, don't you?"

4. Questions or comments that reveal your attitudes: "That's a good reason to change jobs." "That wasn't a good reason to quit."

5. Questions already answered on the application form. They waste valuable time.

How Does the Applicant Feel about His or Her Present Job? It is important to know what the applicant's job responsibilities are and how he or she feels about the job. The response to the following questions may reveal the applicant's attitudes:

- How do you feel about your present job?

- What are some of the problems you encounter on your present job? Which frustrate you the most?

- How do you feel about the progress you have made with your present company?

- In what ways do you feel your present job has developed your ability to take on more responsibility?

- What would you say was the most or least promising job you ever had, and what are your reasons for feeling this way?

- What do you feel has been your greatest frustration or disappointment on your present job?

- What are some of the reasons you have for leaving your present job? (Always look for more than one reason for a voluntary resignation.)

- What is your general impression of the company for which you now work?

- What are some of the things you particularly like about your present job?

- Most jobs have pluses and minuses; what are some of the minuses in your present job?

- Do you consider your progress on the job representative of your ability?

- Where would you rank this job with others you have held?

• How many hours do you feel a person should devote to his or her job?

• What do you feel is a satisfactory attendance record?

How Does the Applicant Feel about Others? Feelings toward coworkers and supervisors are important to one's success. These questions can help:

• What kind of person is your supervisor?

• On what issues do you disagree with him or her?

• What are your supervisor's greatest strengths?

• Where do you feel he or she could do a better job?

• How were you and others treated by your supervisor?

• Has your supervisor ever helped you?

• What did he or she do that you particularly disliked?

• What did you do that your supervisor liked?

• What kind of people do you like to work with?

Job Objectives. It is necessary to know the applicant's objectives—that is, what he or she is looking for or wishing to avoid in a career or job. These questions can help:

• What is important to you in your job?

• What do you wish to avoid in a job?

• What do you want from your next job that you are not getting now?

• What is your overall career objective?

• What kind of a position would you expect five or ten years from now?

• What are your salary expectations?

Reference Checks. Once the applicant is deemed acceptable, a reference check is important. To conduct a meaningful check, you need to know what aspects of the applicant's background need verification. Any doubts or gray areas should be clarified in a reference check.

NOTE: The interview may provide leads that may not be on the application but which were discussed by the applicant. These should be checked.

Reference checks act as a quality control device because they may reveal information that could disqualify the applicant.

TIP: A time span of five years should be included in the references, and questioning should be thorough.

Reference checks are useful only if they come from credible sources, such as previous managers, college professors, and other comparable sources.

The Selection Decision. Poor employee selection is costly. Employees represent a valuable asset; therefore, a final decision should be carefully weighed. Evaluate the accumulated information.

IMPORTANT POINT: Your final hire/no hire decision should be guided by one further consideration: the applicant's potential for future growth and development.

The applicant may rate as only average for the job opening at hand, but he or she may one day become a most productive employee. To ensure that this occurs:

• Consider each step conscientiously
• Minimize your personal biases
• Follow-up on effective performance after the hire

DON'T OVERLOOK TEMPORARY HELP

Bank operation is one area particularly vulnerable to fluctuations in volumes of work. Rather than hiring full-time employees during peak productivity periods, and then trying to figure out what to do with them during slack times, temporary help may be a more viable solution.

FIVE PITFALLS YOU CAN AVOID BY USING TEMPORARY HELP

1. Paying costly overtime rates to regular employees during peak work time.

2. Establishing multiple shifts on a temporary basis which can involve premium pay rates for undesirable shifts.

3. Hiring people as regular employees when you suspect a heavy work load won't last, and then having to let them go.

4. Subcontracting some of the work to be done outside the bank which can cause communication problems.

5. Spending large amounts of money on more efficient and high-speed equipment.

Working with a Temporary Service. Although there may be an abundance of highly qualified people available for work on a temporary basis, it is wise to seek out a reliable temporary personnel service. One advantage is that the service will be able to save a bank from the time-consuming job of doing its own advertising and interviewing.

How to Make the Most of Temporary Help. Carefully analyze needs. Know what each task involves to ensure that people are matched to jobs. When evaluating a service, ask questions:

• Is the service well-known? Can it give you proof of its success in providing good help?

• Does the service normally do all the interviewing and screening of temporary employees it sends you? A good service will think of the personnel it sends out as permanent employees in its company.

• Do you need specialized service and does the service meet those particular needs?

Avoiding Temporary Help Problems. What do you do if the temporary is incompetent for your job needs? Complain to the service—it will be more likely to see that unqualified workers are not sent again.

> **TIP:** One way to ensure that you get good temporaries is to stick with one representative of the service. That way, the representative will consider you to be a regular and valuable customer. You'll be more likely to get the best people because the service knows you'll be back.

Another common problem is temporaries showing up for work who do not know what is expected of them. Assign a coach to explain what needs to be done. Also, don't forget to tell the temporary about wash rooms, cafeterias, and coffee machines. Make sure the regular bank employees know what work the temporary will be doing and to whom the temporary will report. This will avoid confusion caused by duplicating instructions.

> **NOTE:** A temporary may work out so well that you want to hire him or her on a regular basis. By using temporary help services, you have the opportunity to see how someone works before you hire him or her.

GUARDING AGAINST PERSONNEL PIRACY

Executive pirating in the banking business is increasing. There is such a need for good people, and apparently too few to go around.

> **ONE WAY TO COMBAT THIS:** Make management positions so profitable via benefits and incentives that new executives are attracted to the organization and current officers don't want to leave.

What One Bank Is Doing. Here is how one major banking institution in the midwest has been handling the problem of pirating*. Because the bank has so many young executives, it felt it was particularly vulnerable to raids on its staff. Top management felt more defenses were needed.

First the bank instituted a stock grant plan. An executive received clear title to 70 percent of his or her restricted stock grant if he or she stayed with the bank for five years. The executive would receive the remaining 30 percent if the bank achieved a compounded earnings growth rate of a set percentage during the five-year period.

ANOTHER VERSION OF THE STOCK INCENTIVE: A promising young officer receives stock in his bank, exercises voting rights, and receives dividends as long as he remains with the bank for the restricted period, usually five years. If he leaves within that time, his shares are forefeited.

KEY POINT: Because executive performance and bank productivity are as important as executive continuity, many banks have started programs that link their restricted stock grants to performance as well as retention.

One plan grants both performance shares and performance units. For example, some banks grant shares every two years, payable every four years if the goals are met.

THE FEATURE THAT KEEPS THE EXECUTIVE ON THE JOB: When one four-year plan pays off, the executive is half way through a second four-year plan that won't pay off unless he or she stays on the job for another two years.

* The bank in our example wishes to remain anonymous.

Life Insurance.   There is, among all sorts of plans, split-dollar life insurance. In a typical plan, the part of an executive's life insurance policy equal to an annual increase in the cash value is paid by the bank. The executive pays the remainder. The retention device in this plan is that the executive knows that the part paid by the bank (the cash value) rises each year. He or she also knows that the annual increase will eventually equal or exceed the annual premium. If the executive stays with the bank long enough, he or she will have free insurance. When the executive dies, the bank receives the accumulated cash value of the policy, and the executive's estate receives the remainder of the death benefit.

Cash Incentives.   Cash bonus plans are being reviewed at many banks and revised with tie-ins to performance. One large bank readjusted its annual cash bonus plan so that 25 percent of the potential revenue is based on a three-year cumulative performance and is paid at the end of the three-year period.

> **KEY POINTS:**   With a new three-year program beginning each year, the officer will think twice before leaving the institution and forfeiting his or her bonus.

Of course, one device often used to hold on to a good officer is to pay him or her more than the competition will. It may seem old-fashioned and not particularly sophisticated these days, but money still talks volumes.

> **CAUTION:**   There can be drawbacks with some of these bigger and better retention plans which could have a negative effect on a bank. An executive might be very unhappy in his or her job but not wish to leave because of the potential loss of benefits.

THE BANK MANAGER'S EXIT INTERVIEW GUIDE

The advantages of the exit interview are becoming more and more apparent, particularly in those banks where there is an abnormally large turnover in experienced employees.

There are, of course, many standard reasons given by employees who are leaving for a new position with another bank: "I've been here ten years and it's time I moved on," "I've been offered more money," "I don't seem to be getting anywhere here."

All these reasons seem feasible, but they may also reveal a flaw in the way a particular department is being run or the way a particular manager is treating his or her subordinates. However, it is not easy to ascertain the real reason a person leaves a job. After all, if a person complains about the boss on the way out, his or her new employer may find out about it and might make the employee look like a troublemaker. Nobody wants to leave under a cloud that will follow him or her to the next position.

The standard exit interview has been around for many years, but it has generally been a structured 5- or 10-minute meeting covering all the basic reasons for termination and is designed to elicit mostly yes or no answers. For instance, "Tell me why you are leaving. Is it for more money?"

In addition, many banks have formalized "clearance checklists," which are very structured forms concerning bank property, credit cards, and so on. More concern is given for the minute details of security and bank proprietary information than is given to the loss of a very valuable employee.

How to Conduct a Patterned Exit Interview. The obvious objective of the exit interview should be to discover the true reasons why the employee is severing relations with the bank and to develop a foundation for taking corrective action. Current approaches are not highly successful and should be replaced by the "patterned" interview, which allows the employee an opportunity to give a truthful account in a free and open manner. The patterned interview contains all the necessary questions but remains loose enough for the interviewer to follow up on leads and probe deeper in the right areas to gain full and complete information.

The interview must be planned and carefully scheduled and must be handled by the same department as all other termination interviews. The personnel department has the potential for being more objective than the department the employee is leaving. Another good reason to use the personnel department is that it already has the information needed (for example, job descriptions) and can be relied upon to develop the proper interviewing climate. The interviewer should assume a pleasant, nonjudgmental posture. He or she should be capable of decreasing any interviewee's stress and anxiety.

Each bank should have its own specific questions, but there are general areas that require coverage. These include:

- The establishment of a workable rapport
- Statement of the purpose of the interview
- Employee's attitude toward old job
- Determining reasons for leaving
- Comparison of old job with new job
- Suggested modifications of old job
- Interview conclusion

Questions concerning reasons for leaving the job should be avoided during the beginning of the interview to allow for the establishment of a feeling of rapport and trust. The interviewer should take notes during the meeting to permit further analysis at a later date.

Some typical questions on job attitudes are:

- Briefly outline the main duties of you job.
- Which duties were crucial to the performance of your job?
- Which duties did you like the most?
- What were some of the duties that you liked the least?
- Describe the amount of work and variety in your job.
- Give examples of satisfying and less satisfying incidents.
- To what extent were you given opportunities to use your educational background, skills, and abilities?
- Describe the promotional opportunities open to you.

Some sample questions relating to personal attitude are:

- Tell me something about the recognition you received on the job.

- Assess the general level of morale in your department.
- Assess the fairness of your salary.
- What is your assessment of the benefits provided by the company?

The interview should be concluded in as pleasant a manner as possible, leaving the employee with the feeling that he or she had an excellent opportunity to make his or her true feelings known.

> **NOTE:** When exit interviews are conducted in this manner, a great deal of information will be obtained that should permit the determination of trends and patterns concerning supervision, organization, and bankwide policies.

9

COMPENSATION
AND BENEFITS

At one time, and not all that long ago, banking was known as a secure place to work, which offered steady, long-term employment; however, the pay and benefits were generally less than in other types of business.

Not only is a job in banking no longer assured for life, but compensation and benefits have become much more competitive. This has evolved primarily because of the competition and the resultant need to compensate on a par with other businesses in order to get and hold on to capable employees. In fact, some banks are known for the benefits offered while at the same time demanding top performance from those hired.

TYING PAY TO PERFORMANCE

No bank can afford to pay premium salaries for the potential contributions of its employees. Today, more banks are using compensation to encourage improved performance.

What Your Bank Can Do. The following eight steps will assist you in gearing compensation programs to performance. To help your bank establish a compensation program that can be used as a lever to improve performance, you can:

1. Make sure part of an employee's salary is genuinely at risk—that is, the employee will not receive it if performance does not meet or exceed goals.

2. Make direct compensation a greater portion of total compensation. This will mean giving greater weight to salary, bonuses, and long-range incentive plans as opposed to non-monetary perks and benefits.

3. Set standards that are reliable measures of performance and use them to determine pay increases. This will take courage on the part of management because it will mean different pay for the same work if results differ and it can also lead to court challenges by protected classes.

4. Establish standards to measure team performance if necessary. Often, when a team rather than an individual is responsible for a task, managers stop appraising results rather than searching for innovative ways to do so.

5. Integrate the total compensation package (salary, bonuses, stock options, incentives, benefits, and perquisites).

6. Involve experts from many disciplines (economics, tax, law, etc.) in the design and administration of your compensation program.

7. Provide flexibility to allow selectivity in rewarding performance.

8. Always operate under the principle of higher pay for better work.

DEFERRED COMPENSATION AGREEMENTS

As competition grows for quality people, an increasing number of financial organizations are finding it advisable to arrange deferred compensation agreements for key officers. The following checklist of items may be of help in developing such an agreement.

• *Funding.* A funded arrangement is covered by the reporting and disclosure provisions of the Employment Retirement Income Security Act of 1974 (ERISA), an unfunded arrangement is not. If funded, vesting must depend on fulfillment of specific conditions, and there must be "substantial risk of forfeiture.

• *Election of Payments.* Where the officer can decide whether or not a specific amount of compensation should be deferred or paid currently, the plan should provide that the election is to be made in a year prior to the year in which the compensation is earned; otherwise the executive might be in "constructive receipt" of the compensation and taxed on those payments even though he or she actually does not receive the money until a later date.

• *Effective Date.* The effective date should relate to a period for which compensation has not been earned. Income that has already been earned cannot be deferred.

• *Amount of Deferral.* Adjustments are sometimes made to reflect the loss of a current tax deduction to the bank. The amount of deferral can be limited to the after-tax sum. This is the amount left after deducting an amount equal to the bank's deduction had it paid the executive immediately rather than deferring the compensation.

• *Fixed-Benefit Formula.* When the plan uses the fixed-benefit approach, the benefits may be integrated with Social Security benefits, or payments from a qualified pension, or profit-sharing and similar plans. The risk of inflation might be eliminated in part by relating the benefits to a cost-of-living index, or benefits might be geared to a final salary formula.

• *Phantom Stock and Inflation.* Another way to deal with possible inflation and provide larger benefits for executives is to use the so-called dividend plan. Here, the individual executive's account is credited with shares of the corporation's stock during his or her employment. The bank's earnings and the appreciation in its stock should largely offset the effect of inflation.

• *Valuation of Phantom Stock.* In phantom-stock plan, the calculation date of the officer's account should be clearly stated. If the officer's retirement date is used, the plan should choose the market value of the bank's stock on that date to determine the amount of benefits. It should also state the type of investment in which the funds will be placed during the pay-out period, such as two years after retirement. In this case the only difference would be that the date would be used as a valuation date.

• *Acceleration of Benefits.* The plan should give the bank the absolute right to accelerate the pay benefits before the date specified in the contract. The bank should be under no obligation to first obtain the consent of the officer or his or her beneficiaries. This provision gives the bank some tax protection in the event that it liquidates before the payments become due. By accelerating the due date of the benefits, the bank could then deduct the payments. If payments were made when the bank no longer was in existence, the tax deduction would be lost.

• *Assignment of Rights.* The bank may prevent the officer from assigning his or her rights under the plan. This is necessary if taxation is to be delayed until payment is made.

• *Double Benefits.* The plan should indicate whether or not benefits accruing to an executive under this plan affect his or her benefits under another plan provided by the bank.

• *Forfeitability.* When the plan provides that the executive is to remain in the employ of the bank for a specified time during which the benefits would be forfeitable, a clause stating exceptions in the event of disability or death should be added. When the officer is to remain as a consultant after retirement, the contract should state the area of consultation, the duration, and any compensation to be paid.

• *Restrictions on Compensation.* The plan may require that the officer refrain from competing with the bank. This condition, however, must be reasonable to be legally enforceable. For example, it should be limited to a specific field, geographical area, and reasonable period of time.

• *Trade Secrets.* The plan may forbid the executive's disclosure of secret procedures, know-how,, or similar information. Providing for the forfeiture of benefits in the event one of these conditions is breached may give the bank a better form of redress than a lawsuit.

• *Premature Death.* When life insurance is used to fund the plan, the pay-out formula should provide for an appropriate distribution of the benefits that would accrue in the event of the premature death of the officer. These benefits would normally be larger than the normal benefits and might require a different method of distribution.

• *Arbiration.* A provision might be included to refer all disputes to arbitration.

• *Saving Clause.* It is useful to include a "saving clause" to the effect that any provisions of the plan, if given effect, would serve to invalidate or disqualify the plan shall be deemed null and void.

CREATIVE EXECUTIVE COMPENSATION

Paying the average salary, or even a little above average, may not be enough for a bank to attract and hold onto its best executives these day. One reason for this is the new types of skills bankers must have. Just look at some of the functional areas found in banks that were not common or did not exist only a few years ago: sales management, strategic planning, human resources, financial relations, financial planning, systems and data processing, budgeting, risk management, cash management. The list goes on.

THE COMPENSATION PACKAGE

One area new to most banks is the need to consider executive compensation as a total package. This includes base salary, short-term incentives, long-term incentives, benefits, and perquisites.

A major problem for the majority of financial institutions is that base-level salaries are below those of many other kinds of businesses. This problem must be addressed; it might require a bank to pay above its general level in order to attract people with skills new to banking—that is, discount brokerage, cash management, and others.

Interestingly, compensation levels compared with other industries may depend on what the organization calls itself. For example, one study showed that financial holding companies ranked third in compensation, while commercial banks ranked twentieth, and thrifts ranked almost at the bottom in twenty-sixth place.

Where Are Compensation Packages Headed? Just as important as the current compensation situation is where the packages themselves are heading. To determine this, let's look at some of the components of the compensation package:

• *Cash compensation.* According to Arthur Young & Co., cash compensation is moving toward greater salary stability, greater opportunities for incentive pay, and the use of targets by which to gauge performance. These targets, by the way, are on both an individual and division basis. There also is a move toward compensation–deferral opportunities. These include such items as salary reduction (401 K plans), incentive elections, and insured programs.

• *Long-term incentive trends.* According to Arthur Young & Co., long-term incentives are getting increased attention. There seems to be an emphasis on offering multiple compensation plans, eligibility differentiation based on seniority and position, stock plans, stock appreciation rights (SARs), performance units, restricted stock, and performance shares.

• *Executive benefit programs.* There is a definite move toward flexible or "cafeteria menus" of benefits. The executive then can use the benefit(s) that suit his or her needs. It is a good idea for banks to be pragmatic and provide benefits that executives want. Any banking organization of size, Arthur Young & Co. believes, should have benefits such as physical fitness programs and facilities, as well as supplemental retirement, life insurance, and medical insurance plans. In addition, there should be some kind of income continuation plan as part of the compensation package in case of illness or disability.

Other Areas to Consider. Other attractive parts of an executive compensation package a bank should consider, and which are found in other organizations include:

• *Financial planning (tax related).* A bank would do well to stay away from anything bordering on investment counseling. If the advice doesn't work out, the bank suffers.

• *Automobiles.* This once attractive perk seems to be regaining popularity, probably because of the cost of autos and the ability to lease through the bank's leasing facility if it has one.

• *Employment contracts.* Although long popular in other industries, these contracts have made little headway until recently. A contract should include a specific term (five years is common); a provision to bar competing in the market area; a merger/acquisition contingency arrangement to protect employment in some way; and a consulting arrangement upon retirement.

> **NOTE:** The mix of components in an executive compensation package is dictated by a variety of factors: the region of the country, the shortage of particular skills, the level of competition in the area, and the benefits practices in the region. However, compensation must be managed as effectively as all other aspects of the banking business are. Only then will the compensation program be money well spent.

GETTING MORE FROM FRINGE BENEFITS

The competition for good people is tough in banking, and it isn't only better banks you must compete with. New electronics firms, supermarket chains, and other employers in town, regardless of size, add to this competition.

Fringe benefits by themselves probably won't help you hire top people.

> **KEEP IN MIND:** The absence of fringes could hurt.

At the same time the cost of fringes is skyrocketing. If you must spend considerable sums on fringe benefits, you ought to make sure the money is well spent.

You should consider the specific provisions of fringes that are so common you are almost forced to provide them. Also, you should look at the choice of other fringes. Ask these questions:

• Are the fringes what employees of your bank need and can use?

• Do they help the bank achieve the objectives they are supposed to meet?

Consider Insurance. Over 80 percent of all employees in the country are covered by some form of insurance. In most cases employers contribute the major share of the cost.

• *Life insurance.* Your program may be geared to the needs of married people with families. However, most banks employ a high percentage of men and women, who are single. Smaller benefits on bank-financial policies combined with voluntary, contributory plans for those who want more could save money and still protect employees.

• *Medical insurance.* A package program (from Blue Cross/Blue Shield or a private carrier) may include benefits not normally used by employees in your specific location. However, a program designed specifically to fill your employees' needs might not cost more (or perhaps less).

The Entire Package. Look at all the components of your present benefit program. Perhaps improvements could be made by shifting emphasis or adding one benefit and dropping others. A more liberal vacation policy could be offset by a decrease in retirement provisions. Costs could be similar but the money more efficiently spent.

Employers often make a big deal about benefits when they hire employee's, but then forget to tell the employees what is being done for them each year. One easy way to make employees aware of the benefits—and their cost—is to issue a statement each year detailing the benefits they are receiving and how much the bank is paying for them. It is part of the total compensation package; such communications could remind employees that the bank is an employer concerned with their welfare.

10

MANAGEMENT TECHNIQUES

Explaining and teaching how to be a good manager or how to be a more effective manager has become an industry unto itself. This is a good idea, but, unfortunately, there are so many books and seminars on the subject that it is often difficult (if not impossible) to determine what advice is good or even useful. At the same time, management techniques can be of considerable help and not a waste of valuable time.

The techniques and suggestions in this chapter are based on those used in banks which have been adapted from other businesses for use in the banking business—and they have been proven effective. Although they are not all-inclusive, the techniques described here should give a bank manager a head start over his or her associates.

HOW TO MANAGE TIME BETTER

Every aspect of banking is short on time, which makes the need to improve time management vital for most management. Here are some guidelines that can help:

• Handle important matters—the central concerns of your job—first.

• Give yourself daily "think time" for planning and evaluation.

• Always clarify your objectives before deciding what to do and how to do it. You can frequently find yourself wasting time because you don't know what you are really trying to accomplish.

• Divide big projects into smaller, workable units, setting several interim deadlines rather than one final one.

• Establish priorities, using a written list if necessary.

• Estimate how much time tasks are really worth and stick to your estimates.

• Avoid perfectionism on secondary or marginal matters.

• Practice how to say no in advance so that you don't take on more than you can or need to handle.

• Use devices like recorders, calculators, and so on to multiply your time.

• Always search for easier ways to accomplish tasks.

• Avoid procrastination by confronting the feelings that cause it.

• Delegate work. Don't try to do it all yourself.

• Make sure the deadlines you set are realistic and achievable.

• Allow time for an occasional break from productive work. This will refresh and recharge you, making you more productive in the long run.

• Confront your hang-ups about time. People generally fall into five categories in terms of their behavior regarding time utilitization: (1) the person who constantly rushes, (2) the person who strives for perfection, (3) the person who tries to please everyone, (4) the person who tries harder but usually accomplishes less, and (5) the strong, silent type who endeavors to do everything single-handedly. By recognizing your type of behavior, you can employ the appropriate techniques to counteract it. Example: If you're a perfectionist who squanders time by making the most trivial thing perfect, discipline yourself to do one thing imperfectly every day. If you rush through your tasks, slow down and see how much more you get done.

NOTE: Although there are certain factors that dictate your schedule as a manager, practicing sound time management techniques will allow you to control time rather then letting it control you.

HOW TO IMPROVE MANAGERIAL PRODUCTIVITY IN YOUR BANK

It is not only the clerical staff of a bank that should be the focus of productivity improvement, say the experts at the consulting firm of Arthur D. Little, Inc. The managerial and professional levels should also receive attention because that is where it can do a lot of good. After all, higher-level positions, too long immune from scrutiny, represent more than half the white-collar payroll and offer greater leverage and higher returns.

According to A.D. Little, Inc., those employees with the greatest number (managerial and professional), representing the greatest labor cost component, and having by far the greatest impact on the operations of an organization, have ironically received the least amount of attention.

However, maximum white-collar productivity gains will not come simply from across-the-board increases in new technologies and approaches.

> **KEY POINT:** The real gains, the experts say, will come from deploying capital to support professional and managerial workers, who up to now have received roughly one-half to one-third the investment in automation tools as their secretarial and clerical counterparts.

Business's demonstrated reluctance to invest money and effort on managerial and professional productivity is attributed to several underlying factors. Not the least of these, the consultants observed, is what is perceived as difficulty in establishing a definitive set of tasks for a manager.

Moreover, it is generally acknowledged that there is no uniform relevant timeframe for measuring a manager's output and productivity. Such things as creativity, flexibility, quality of output, employee satisfaction, and customer satisfaction must be considered along with the more traditional kinds of productivity measurements. Yet, this doesn't fully explain why managers have been slow to embrace efforts aimed at improving productivity within their own ranks. One must also consider what is at stake from a personal point of view. Redefining jobs could very well result in realization that some management functions are in fact redundant.

The ADL experts believe the key to productivity improvement for managers and professionals is in finding the means to improve their decision-making capabilities. This can be accomplished by improving the quality of information available and the effectiveness with which that information is communicated to the decision-maker. A manager's decisions must also relate to the correct issues.

Corporate strategy, the consultants pointed out, should dictate a management system which leads to better resource allocation and the proper tools to support decision making.

Today's office equipment is becoming much more attractive to the manager/professional because it is relatively easy to use, portable, and multifunctional. Tools such as an executive work station complete with display terminal, audio-visual teleconferencing, boardroom graphics tied to a minicomputer, and computer-aided design and retrieval systems are likely to become commonplace fixtures in tomorrow's executive offices, the Arthur D. Little, Inc. consultants predicted. For example: An executive work station is designed to handle a manager's routine desk activities, which can consume up to 25 percent of his or her time; in addition, it can serve as a support in internal communications, problem-solving, and analysis. With teleconferencing, a manager can reduce the high cost of time lost in traveling and can deal more effectively with problems that previously would have been too minor to merit personal visits.

The availability of better tools to do the job and a clearer definition and structure of management tasks—both of which are linked to a corporate strategic plan—will provide the impetus for managers and professionals in their quest for improved productivity.

NOTE: Can such productivity improvement be measured? Yes, say the Arthur D. Little, Inc. consultants, provided that measurements are not merely the traditionally bottom-line kind, but also take into account the organization's strategic objectives.

WHAT TO DO ABOUT MANAGEMENT SUCCESSION

Management succession is of prime importance to the ongoing progress of a bank. It is also one of the major areas that bank examiners consider paramount to the survival of the bank. Yet, the only way examiners can determine if a bank is prepared for succession is to review the time, effort, and methods devoted to proper training. This requires a total commitment by present management.

To have an employee with a title sitting and waiting for a job to be turned over to him or her is no substitute for not taking that person into the confidence of present management. Just sitting there does not help the employee understand the reasons for loan and investment policies, nor understand the bank's attitude toward each of the major customers of the bank.

Frequently, bankers get so involved in day-to-day operations that they fail to pay any attention to this critical issue. How many times have we seen or heard about the bank with an 80-year-old president, a 73-year-old executive vice-president, and the third person in line, whatever his or her title may be, only 28 years old? In many instances, this may be an exaggeration, but, far too often, it really is not. In fact, there are too many banks in which there is no preplanning as to who will take over the reins after present management leaves.

Here are some of the more pertinent reasons for this malaise:

• Present staff may feel there is no suitable choice for succession. If this is the case, it should be corrected immediately. Certainly, it is usually possible to bring in top talent from some other bank at the last minute to take charge, if the present manager gets sick or dies and no successor has been trained.

> **CAUTION:** This approach, however, has a dramatic effect on all the other officers and employees because it makes them feel there was no one on the staff that was worthy or competent enough to run the bank.

• Present staff may well recognize that the bank is not prepared for the future; therefore, staff members may question what will happen to their career paths if the bank they have chosen to work for collapses suddenly.

• Failure to develop new talent frequent demoralizes much of the talent that is already in the bank.

• Present management may feel no one else can do the job as well as it can. Although it is frequently true that the top people in a bank may be so efficient that no successors could possibly replace them, somewhere along the line, management must bite the bullet even at the risk of operating at a poorer level of proficiency.

• Present management may not plan for successor management because it feels this plan might reflect badly on it and the way it has run the bank during its years of tenure. It is sad to note, but nevertheless true, that some people would rather see an institution fail after they leave so that their stewardship looks strong in retrospect rather than prepare for future management so that the bank can continue to grow.

Management succession affects all levels of the bank, not only senior management. It applies to the comptrollers and auditors as well.

> **TIP:** Make sure there is a replacement for *your* job. Teach, train, guide, and direct that person.

Be sure he or she understands why and how decisions are made. Accept the fact that the person may not do the job in the same manner as you. Allow for growth into the job.

SELLING IDEAS TO SUPERIORS

Many top bankers insist that most of their job entails salesmanship—not only with customers but with their bosses and the board of directors as well. As one senior official of a New Jersey bank said, "If you can't sell, you won't cut the mustard."

Three Key Ingredients.

What are the best techniques for selling the boss and for keeping him or her sold? In all cases there are three key ingredients in a successful campaign to convince the boss or the board to do what you urge:

- Clear written and/or verbal communications
- Anticipation and refutation of possible objection
- Enhanced involvement of those you seek to sell

Communication. It is frequently a good idea to put your cconcepts across in both verbal and written communication.

> **RECOMMENDATION:** First test out your plan in verbal discussion with those you wish to convince. Later, follow up with a brief written statement of your suggestions for action.

Before the verbal discussion, you may want to rehearse by role playing with your spouse or with a trusted subordinate. In any case, keep the verbal discussion and the written communication concise and relevant.

Refuting Objections. Regardless of the soundness of your proposals, there will probably be objections to at least parts of what you propose.

> **RECOMMENDATION:** Be sure to anticipate as many of the possible objections that you can. Be prepared to explain why the objections are more than offset by the advantages of your suggestions.

This is an essential step that is often overlooked or underrated by executives.

Enhancing Involvement. It is important to secure some involvement from those you expect to convince.

> **RECOMMENDATION:** Arrange a face-to-face discussion before you submit final written proposals.

In this way, points or questions raised by your seniors can be covered in the written proposal, helping to make it as much their proposal as yours. In addition you will get a better idea of any objections to your proposal and have additional chances to overcome them (or to recognize that the objectives are valid and to adjust your thinking accordingly).

Furthermore, you should consider all feasible alternatives in formul. ing your recommendations. You might touch on these alternatives with your seniors in the course of verbal discussion, but don't dwell on any rejected alternatives unless you are asked to do so. Your boss or your board should indeed be concerned that you have evaluated all reasonable possibilities but they don't really need a full recitation of what all the possibilities are.

> **NOTE:** One banker informed us that he sometimes presents three alternatives to the chairman of his bank. These alternatives consist of the plan the banker wants to sell and two other plans which will appear far less attractive to his chairman. Supposedly, the chairman will select the preferred plan because it appears more attractive than the

others, even though he might have rejected the plan if it had been submitted singly, without the alternatives.

11

PLANNING
FOR YOUR BANK'S SUCCESS

Planning for a bank's success is another area that previously was not of great concern to many, if not most, bankers. Yet, today, at a growing number of banks, the planning function is an important part of the management process. Not only that, the head of planning is often, rightly, at the vice presidential (or higher) level.

Banking has become too complex to be left to chance. Plans are essential if a bank is to move forward with any real chance of reaching its goals.

The topics in this chapter will assist you in planning to reach those goals.

A BANKER'S GUIDE TO STRATEGIC PLANNING

In the new banking environment, strategic planning is the key to survival

Stategic Rules to Follow. The basic rules of strategy can be compared to those of warfare. These include:

• Define the business. By precisely defining the business you are in, you will avoid the two pitfalls of imitating the competition and scattering your resources.

• Concentrate on specific markets and products. This will enable you to marshall your resources to build your basic or core businesses and differentiate yourself from the competition.

• Surprise the competition as often as possible.

• Reinvest in key capabilities. Build on your strengths as well as exploiting competitors' weakneses.

• Once you have achieved victory, don't let the competition recover. Guard your market share.

Formulating Strategy. To formulate sound strategy, your bank must identify the important strategic issues facing it. Although the banking industry faces many common problems, each bank will have to contend with some issues unique to it. How well and how thoroughly you examine these issues could spell the difference between success and failure in the coming years.

There are three levels of analysis inherent in the strategic planning process:

• Economic analysis
• Market analysis
• Competitive analysis

The economic analysis, which is really the bedrock of the development process, looks at overall industry attractiveness and the general economic environment.

Market analysis weighs the opportunities and cost of production systems; the general requirements for success, customer use, and demographics.

Competitive analysis examines relative positions, strengths and weaknesses, competitive actions and reactions, and product and customer strongholds.

> **NOTE:** Competitive analysis will become an increasingly vital ingredient in strategic planning in the years ahead as banks face competition from new sources such as brokers, retailers, and high-technology companies.

> **KEEP IN MIND:** Sound strategic planning will also help to improve bank performance in all cases.

BALANCE SHEET PLANNING

Many bank's balance sheets are compiled by major departments from individual and uncoordinated activities and often without any thought being given to objectives started by senior management as to the desired structure of the balance sheet. In short, the balance sheet is not planned.

Today, a number of banks are conducting research to evaluate balance sheet issues that reflect senior management's policies, philosophies, and objectives. This kind of goal-setting affects both sides of the balance sheet; hence, management requires an in-depth analysis of the major departments (that is, loans and deposits) that will provide the bank with the ability to state a set of objectives for each major balance-sheet classification. Once the objectives have been agreed upon, a base is established for creating parameters within which the bank can operate.

A Recommended Approach. Senior management is concerned with identifying areas that will increase earnings through in-depth analyses of balance sheet structures. The recommended approach is to conduct evaluations that include operational as well as policy-oriented considerations; the objective is to provide the bank with the facility to act in a responsive manner with respect to constantly changing economic conditions.

To accomplish this, a clear definition of bank policy and philosophy is needed. For example: Capital allocations should be identified; portfolio targets should be structured for the bank; cash costs for credit lines should be quantified; and domestic and international capital reciprocity policies should be established.

Similarly, the commercial loan portfolio, in addition to providing management with the facility to track overall bank commitments by class, industry concentration, delinquency, yield, and account profitability, should be monitored to track the effects of all commercial borrowing, changes in rating mix, and maturity analyses. Peripheral areas that should be analyzed in terms of balance sheet impact and desired structure include:

• Liquidity (that is, true liquidity versus assumed liquidity)

• Dividend payouts as a percent of earnings

• Cost of capital (which is flexible) as it relates to return on capital and leasing objectives in relation to funding

There is concern for capital adequacy, liquidity, control of credit expansion, and a clear need for a conservative and integrated approach to your bank's balance sheet issues.

General Guidelines. Although countless techniques have been developed to deal with the issues above, there is no single theory or structure that can be applied universally. It is necessary for you to clearly identify your bank's customer mix and its economic environment. The following guidelines can be used to analyze these conditions:

• Design a rate–mix matrix that will provide the basis for an evaluation of potential profitability and liquidity impact during various phases of an economic cycle. This structure, coupled with a full understanding of the cyclical interaction between rates and changes in balance sheet relationships will provide the basis for forming a strategy.

• Evaluate balance sheet effects of transactions involving federal funds, Eurodollars, certificates of deposits, repurchase agreements, and commercial paper.

The guidelines below will help you analyze when to raise offering rates on federal funds loans, certificates of deposit (CDs) or other liabilities in order to purchase reserves during a period of deposit outflow or increased loan demand. Conversely, a reduction in loan demand or inflow of deposits might cause the bank to reduce its offering rates on liabilities.

• Assess the adequacy of bank capital in relation to major types of risk that may have to be charged against the capital cushion.

• Review the bank's commercial loan portfolio analysis techniques in terms of management reporting. The scope of this effort might focus on:

- *Commitment analysis*—including a review of the effects of zero–actual and partial–accrual loans on the portfolio
- *Commercial borrowing analysis*—to stratify the portfolio distribution by ratings and loan size
- *Rating mix analysis*—to track changes between time periods
- *Margin overprime analysis*—to analyze period-to-period changes
- *Maturity analysis*—to review the effect of maturing loans on interest income

> **NOTE:** Bank policies should be evaluated as they relate to domestic and international lending opportunities in order to determine funding on a matched basis, trading opportunities, average rollovers, and rate/yield curves for each portion of a loan.

FOUR BALANCE SHEET PLANNING CHECKLISTS

These four checklists will help you to plan a bank's balance sheet.

Rate–Mix Matrix.

A rate–mix matrix establishes the basis for an evaluation of potential profitability and liquidity positions during the various phases of an economic cycle. This tool, coupled with an understanding of the cyclical interaction between rates and changes in balance sheet relationships, provides the basis for forming a strategy.

At a minimum, it is necessary to:

• Assess the bank's customer mix and economic environment.

• Highlight inherent relationships.

• Identify factors to be developed as a step toward planning a management strategy.

• Classify assets and liabilities according to interest rate characteristics.

• Identify "matched" assets and liabilities.

• Identify "variable" assets and liabilities.

• Identify "fixed" assets and liabilities.

• Identify the potential profitability and liquidity position during anticipated phases of the economic cycle.

• Analyze rate–mix factors.

• Rate–mix imbalance due to money-market rate levels

• Management strategy

• Develop action guidelines (establish balance sheet classifications structure and related financial structure in accordance with stated bank policy, philosophy, and goals).

Transactions Affecting Liabilities.

This analysis provides the bank with guidelines for raising offering rates on federal fund loans, certificates of deposit, or other liabilities, in order to purchase reserves during a period of either deposit outflow or increased loan demand. A reduction in loan demand or inflow of deposits would, on the other hand, cause the bank to reduce its offering rates on liabilities.

• Federal funds
- Determine the bank's net position
- Review major correspondent bank users and suppliers
- Evaluate reserve accesses in relation to reserves to meet contingencies
- Evaluate the impact of regulations (1) reserve requirements, and (2) interest-rate ceilings on borrowed funds

• Eurodollars
- Review balance sheet effects when excess reserves are generated because funds are transferred from a demand–deposit classification to a foreign branch liability
- Review excess reseves as a base for an expansion of loans

• Certificates of deposit
- Identify dollar transfers from demand–deposit to time-deposit liability

- Compute excess reserves generated as a result of lower deposit reserve requirements
- Review excess reserves as a basis for an expansion of bank credit

• Repurchase agreements

- Stratify repurchase agreements by maturity
- Evaluate reduction in reserve requirements because of debit to the purchaser's account at the bank
- Identify dollars retrieved from CD redemptions

• Commercial paper

- Identify dollars retrieved from CD operations
- Consider the reserve effects through the sale of commercial paper
- Consider the reserve effects through purchases

Assessing Capital Structure.

To determine desirable balance sheet structures, it is necessary to assess the adequacy of bank capital in relation to major types of risk that may have to be charged against the capital cushion:

• Review bank capital influence on lending operations.

• Determine liquidity in relation to capital.

• Evaluate ratios and formulas used to assess the bank's capital.

• Identify the types of risk that bank capital protects:
- Loan losses
- Investment losses
- Operating losses
- Bank-owned real estate losses
- Other (catastrophic)

• Determine the degree of risk the bank can take in its assets (loan portfolio) in relation to earnings availability to absorb losses.

Commercial Loan Portfolio Review.

The scope of this review should focus on:

• Commitment analysis

- Commitment rating for the current period

- Comparison of source of commitment usage with previous period(s)

- Comparison of source of commitment availability with previous period(s)

• Commercial borrowing analysis

- Review loans that move automatically with the prime rate

- Review loans that do not move automatically with the prime rate but rather at the next renewal date, end of month, end of the quarter, and so on

- Stratify loans by individual ratings and dollar ranges and compare with previous period(s)

• Rating-mix analysis

- Identify the source of change in the rating mix and identify loans with a change in status

• Margin Over Prime Analysis

- Analyze period-to-period changes in the margin over the prime rate and the effects of loan payoffs and advances on cash flow

HOW TO DEVELOP A CONTINGENCY PLAN FOR DATA PROCESSING DISASTERS

As banks move further into computerization, potential disasters have also arisen. Banks are prone to every conceivable kind of disaster, ranging from fires and blackouts to terrorist attacks. Yet, surveys reveal that business often fails to make adequate, or even any, contingency plans. One survey by the American Bankers Association, for example, indicated that 42 percent of banks with assets under $100 million had a disaster plan, 67 percent of banks with assets between $100 and $500 million had such a plan, and 82 percent of banks with assets over $500 million were prepared for a disaster.

The most frequently given reasons for the absence of a disaster plan are: "It can't happen here," "Cost is prohibitive," or "There are higher priority projects and staff resources are not available." However, protecting your bank's data center from failure or disruption is vitally important.

A contingency plan seeks to minimize and contain any disaster, provide rapid and smooth transition to a backup mode of operation, and quickly recover normal operations. Where other aspects of security may fail for any number of reasons and the organization is faced with a major interruption in computer processing, the contingency plan comes into play to provide the necessary measure of continuity until normal operations can be restored.

Here are some tips on how to develop your contingency plan:

• Determine the defensive threshold for the data center as a whole.

• Conduct a security analysis, taking into account various possible threats and the degree to which your particular data center is vulnerable. This will allow you to calculate your exposure.

• Identify what measures are available to reduce or eliminate those exposures and at what cost.

• Recommend additional measures which will effectively improve the overall defensive threshold in the data center.

Subjectivity occurs in the security analysis when you attempt to quantify the exposure in the data. Approaches vary from the use of subjective qualification such as high, normal, and low exposure to the use of discrete probabilities of occurrence. The security analysis model makes no attempt to differentiate between types of risks; that is part of the risk analysis.

Conducting the Risk Analysis. Risk analysis takes into account the difference in the value or the importance of data. The risk analysis quantifies the data processing security posture within the data center relative to the types and quantity of information it processes and the potential threats to that information.

The data processing department should identify the data assets. The users should determine the importance and estimate the loss for different periods of time. Data processing then completes the risk analysis by determining the backup computing resources that will be required and the alternatives to providing those resources.

The next step is to sell top management on the recommended approach. In seeking senior management's approval to commit corporate resources to develop a contingency plan, several factors serve as selling points including the cost of replacing the computing capability itself, the cost of reconstructing the data center, the cost of providing the appropriate level of backup, the cost of developing and maintaining the contingency plan, the income that could be lost because of the disaster, and the approximate cost of losing operational control.

When a major failure or disruption occurs in the data center, the conflicts among and the similarities between applications can quickly result in an unexpected collapse of operations. Also, a loss of customers may occur.

> **TIP:** Normally, it is far easier to preserve customers and the deposit base than it is to recapture them.

The protection of data and software assets is another important concern. If the bank loses data or software, a major interruption occurs which can incur a significant cost for repair. The total cost to the organization includes not only the cost of the business interruption but also the reconstruction of essential software and data that was destroyed. The cost to reconstruct the software could easily approach the actual value of the software, depending on the extent of the disaster. The value of the data can be assumed to be equal to either the value of the equipment or the software, whichever is greater.

Generally, the reconstruction cost following a disaster is very high due to the tremendous time pressure associated with the effort.

> **KEY POINTS:** In the final analysis, bank management is responsible for safeguarding

corporate assets and providing internal control systems. Sound business judgment dictates the safeguarding of computer facilities, information systems, and information that is vital to the bank. Moreover, regulatory requirements call for banks to develop well-documented, comprehensive data processing contingency plans.

ELEMENTS OF LONG-RANGE PLANNING

Although most bankers these days agree that long-range planning is useful, if not necessary, it isn't always easy to know where to begin—or end—the planning process.

To begin the long-range planning process, a bank should consider these guidelines:

1. The leadership for long-range planning should come from top management. Many banks have found that active participation by either the chairperson or the president is an excellent idea. However, regardless of the level of managerial sponsorship, the organization must adhere to a strict timetable for plan development.

2. Forecasts should first be made of each facet of the environment within which the bank functions. Banking as a business is inseparable from the community it serves. To this end, the reality of any long-range plan is related to the perception with which the development of community markets is viewed.

> **NOTE:** You can obtain considerable information from both the federal and the state governments. The local town hall or the chamber of commerce have some additional ideas. Also, don't forget to check with any major local employers to see if they have formulated any plans for expansion or relocation. Chances are they have.

3. You should endeavor to develop an accurate picture of where the community will be in five years or so. By working with the known relationships between your bank and the community over the past several years, it is possible to infer what the relationship may be in the future. *Remember:* One of the primary purposes of long-range planning is to allow the management of the bank to shape the organization's relationship with its enviroment to the greatest degree possible. This shaping should include a complete analysis of existing and contemplated banking services.

> **NOTE:** In this way, some basic and specific estimates can be formed: probable resources, demand for principal services, capital needs, staff needs, and so forth. Based on these estimates, management can formulate broad corporate objectives, including a written goal of profitability.

4. At this point all departments of the bank should be brought into the planning process. Whenever possible, committees organized at these levels should include a solid representation of junior but experienced officers. Each committee is provided with a written summary of the environmental estimates and the corporate objectives of the bank.

The officers are then free to improve and complete the plan. Their recommendations will logically fall within three areas:

- Suggested changes to the corporate objectives
- Departmental long-range goals
- Specific spots by which these goals can be achieved

> **IMPORTANT:** Grass roots participation by junior officers with imagaination is both important and prudent. It is important for the feelings of enthusiasm, contribution, and commitment, it encourages. It is prudent because creativity is not necessarily a byproduct of seniority.

5. After the individual departmental committees have outlined their suggestions, goals, and specific projects, their reports are reviewed by either top management or its staff group. Then the task of reassessing priorities, assigning resources, and integrating departmental development begins. When this is accomplished, the initial long-range plan has been formulated and projected financial statements are revised in accordance with the reworked goals.

6. Initial implementation occurs at this point. There must be no confusion about the seriousness of the endeavor. Long-range plans should not become folders filed away in a cabinet. They should be working documents, with every step complimentary to each other in a series of steps reaching toward goals of the bank.

7. Finally, there must be reviews at two levels. The first review checks if proper implementation has occurred. The second review determines if changes and updates to the plan must be be made as forecasts change and the planning horizon is pushed ahead.

> **NOTE:**   Do not overlook the need for
> common sense in the formulation of the plans
> as they apply to your bank.

Here is a review of the important ingredients in the long-range planning process:

• Formalize the planning process, but keep it flexible.

• Keep discussion open and encourage the broadest and most creative thinking.

• Ensure broad participation in the process, particularly by the junior officers.

• Make the plans practical by requiring specific steps in order to accomplish planned goals.

• Follow up all plans with reviews.

• Repeat the entire process at logical intervals.

12

MERGERS
AND ACQUISITIONS

Today, a great many banking institutions are either on the lookout for banks to acquire or they are acquisition targets themselves. Without question, this is the age of bank mergers and acquisitions.

Most mergers, at least until now, have been less than 100 percent successful. Some have been expensive and drawn out failures. Although it isn't possible to guarantee success, there really is no excuse for so many mergers and acquisitions to have turned out so poorly.

Planning and attention to easily overlooked details are necessary for success. This chapter provides guidelines for successful mergers and acquisitions.

Although hostile takeovers are rare in banking, they do occur, and they may be on the rise. Steps can be taken to guard against possible takeovers.

POOLING RESOURCES OR PURCHASING THEM

A bank interested in growth can heavily promote its business by building upon its asset base. It can also achieve growth by joining forces with another bank (merger) and pooling the resources of both institutions, or, it can purchase another bank (acquisition).

At a conference on mergers and acquisitions presented by Becker Paribas, investment bankers, a consultant from a major

accounting firm provided the following chart which graph-
ically shows the differences between these two approaches:

	Pooling	*Purchase*
A. Effect on income (Immediate)	Income (or loss) of acquired for the entire year of acquisition added to acquiring income; prior years restated.	Income (or loss) applicable to period subsequent to acquisition added to acquiring income; no restatement.
B. Diluation of ownership control and earnings per share	Usually dilutive since consideration must be voting common stock.	Permissible to give cash or nonvoting securities.
C. Net worth	May be higher level of net worth. Equity securities always issued. Net worth (or deficit) of acquired carries over.	May be lower level of net worth. Equity securities only sometimes issued. Net worth (or deficit) of acquired vanishes.
D. Effect of income (continuing)	Usually favorable when market rates below acquired portfolio rate—higher rate will be reflected in future income.	May be favorable when market rates above portfolio rate—"cash" goodwill—no lockstep amortization "noncash" goodwill—lockstep amortization.
E. Ability to restructure assets	None—historical book values carry over.	Substantial—assets and liabilities of acquired market to market.
F. Effect on return on assets	Whole equal sum of parts (sometimes neutral).	Unfavorable—nonearning asset created (goodwill).
G. Costs incident to combination	Current expense	Capitalized and amortized.
H. Contingent compensation	Not allowed	Allowed.

NOTE: The obvious lesson to be learned
from the comparisons above is that both
approaches are worth looking into, and neither
approach is necessarily best. That depends on
each specific situation.

THE IMPORTANCE OF DETAILS

You have just engineered a merger between your bank and
another institution. All the major details have been covered,
the announcements made, the stockholders have voted their

approval, the applications have been filed and passed by the regulatory agencies. It's time to relax, right? Wrong! Just look at what happened in these cases:

• A bank merged with another bank several hundred miles away. When the first bank took over the second bank's operations, it sent late notices to almost all the second bank's mortgagors, including the former chairman and his mother! Apparently, no one at the first bank had considered the possibility of delay in receiving payment coupons mailed from so many miles away.

• Another merged institution sent savings account statements to customers with different interest amounts for the same deposit amounts. It seems that prior to the merger, one bank had accrued interest on an actual 365-day basis, while the other used a 30/360-day basis. Naturally, the customers were confused, particularly those with accounts in both banks before the merger.

• A holding company used the media to advertise a new product in, among other locations, the territory of a newly acquired subsidiary. Unfortunately, the new product was also news to the tellers, managers, and the executive vice president of the subsidiary. They all received inquiries on a product about which they knew nothing.

Although these problems were hardly critical, they are common examples of the kinds of things that can occur in a merger situation. Senior officers must also deal with complaints from customers and explain foul-ups to board members. Beyond this, such problems can lower morale, which is often in a depressed state anyway because of the merger. In addition, the acquiring bank can have its reputation damaged when the public gets caught up in the loose ends of a merger.

SOME COMMONLY OVERLOOKED DETAILS

In the merger process there are three areas that require attention:

Personnel. One of the more common misconceptions about any industry is that different organizations within that industry are in the same business. Because a corporate organization and structure focus so much on corporate actions, each organization in an industry is considerably different. To ignore this corporate law in a bank-merger situation simply invites administrative anarchy.

Complying with this law underscores the need to train newly merged managements. They need to be familiar with and understand the new procedures if they are to sell the merged organization to customers and to handle customer and stockholder problems that are bound to arise during the period of adjustment following a merger.

Customer and Stockholder Relations. After a merger, when things go wrong, customers (who may also be stock-holders can be affected. Consider the merger in which savings account interest was accrued by two different methods. Most customers affected by the situation approached bank staff personnel for an explanation or adjustment, but, they could get neither from uniformed tellers.

A less tangible but just as touchy problem is the corporate cultural differences between two financial organizations. They can often be substantial. Some banks, to emphasize their own efficiency and the value they place on their customers' time, employ devices such as blinking lights to indicate that a teller is available.

Customer complaints, if they arise, are often resolved quickly but through channels. Other banks offer a more personal or "folksy" environment, one in which the teller always has time for a chat and can usually handle most customer problems that come up. Imposing either technique on the other without adequate preparation can result in the loss of customers—all too often the customers the bank would rather keep.

Operations. There are three significant points to remember about operations in a merger.

1. Without the back office people doing their sometimes tedious tasks, little or nothing would be accomplished.

2. An operation's details can make the critical difference. In banking, where many of the products offered are available from competitors as well, operational strength (or its lack) is often noted as the reason why a specificc organization is more or less effective, profitable, or admired by both analysts and the public. An organization's operation may well be what sets it apart from the others.

3. Recognition of differences in detail is most important in the successful joining of the two organizations. Many mergers are handled with the completely arbitrary adoption of one organization's operation. A more rational and effective method would be to select the best from each of the organizations.

> **TIP:** It probably is a good idea to bring in professional assistance in the early stages of a merger; that will preclude the likelihood that such experts won't have to be rushed in to help solve a problem later on.

Also, because in every merger situation there seems to be an unlimited number of jobs to be done in a limited amount of time, an action plan should be developed with guidelines that will ensure completion of the most critical tasks. The following guidelines are ones suggested by the merger experts at KMPG Peat Marwick Main:

• *Identify a team*—even prior to identification of a potential merger candidate—headed by an officer with sufficient authority to ensure that plans are carried out. Team representatives should be selected from the controllers, operations, audit, and all the other major business activity departments.

• *Clearly define responsibilities* for each team member. This is necessary since some of the tasks assigned may overlap. Tasks should be assigned in priority order.

• *Use outside professional help* to play a part—but not the starring role. Too much outside participation results in both increased costs and decreased management familiarity with the details of the merger. Management will have to live with those details long after the professionals have left.

• *Develop a schedule* of periodic progress meetings to monitor the timetable prepared for the completion of the various tasks. Because the tasks of many team members will be interrelated, the teams should be aware of one another's progress. This step allows for reporting and solving problems that might arise, which could delay completion of the merger.

STEPS TO STOP HOSTILE TAKEOVERS

Although hostile takeovers are rare in banking, they can occur. If an unwanted suitor comes to call, what can you do? Let's say the offer isn't good enough, or you don't want to marry into a particular family, or you simply want to stay independent. Here are some steps you and your bank can take:

Staggered Terms for Directors. One solution a number of banks and other firms are using is to stagger the terms of members of the board of directors. With terms ending at various times, another bank will find it more difficult to gain management control.

This is what shareholders of Security New York Corporation in Rochester did to stop a hostile takeover. The $1.6 billion asset bank holding company received an unsolicited offer from Albany's Norstar Bancorp. Because of rumors of takeover attempts, Security New York issued a proxy proposal three weeks before the Norstar offer was received. Three classes of directors would be established with only one-third of the total expiring at any one time. The proxy read, in part:

> The effect of the proposal may tend to protect management and members of the board from immediate removal and may also make the company a less attractive target for acquisition of control by an outsider who does not have the support of management.

> **NOTE:** In this instance the ploy was superfluous. Norstar made an offer the management and shareholders of Security New York found too good to refuse. Security New

York became a subsidiary corporation of
Norstar.

Another Example: Shareholders of Butler International
overwhelmingly approved a management-sponsored plan to
make it harder for bidders to gain control in two-step acquisitions.

In a two-step takeover, a buyer makes a tender offer for a
company which is usually less than 100 percent of the value of
the stock. The potential buyer may then use various tactics to
acquire the rest of the stock.

Under the amendment to Butler's charter that was
adopted, the owner of more than 20 percent of the company's
stock cannot force a merger without the approval of at least 80
percent of all shares, or two-thirds of the board of directors.
Previously, a majority vote of shares was enough. The charter
ensured that shareholders didn't feel pressured to accept a pro
rata offer for fear they may get a lower price if they held out for
more.

Director Liability. Defensive tactics can be risky. "Financial managers," according to Reinier Kraakman, business law
professor at Yale Law School, "enter a burgeoning legal controversy regarding the limits that fiduciary obligations to shareholders place on defensive gamesmanship."

In several decisions, the courts' rulings on recent shareholder suits have been to protect management's business judgment against allegations of improper self-interest. This has
insulated directors and senior management from personal
liability. However, these court decisions have met with dis-
agreement from other courts and may be contrary to some
state laws. Therefore, financial institutions must work to protect themselves from the possibility of a lawsuit.

Writing in *Counsel,* published by MGIC Indemnity Corporation, Professor Kraakman suggests four preventive courses
of action:

• Directors should do nothing that might interfere with a
thorough consideration of an offer since it may be in the
shareholders' best interests.

• Any offers should receive the entire board's full attention.

• Outside directors should take an active role in takeover discussions to guard against allegations of suspect interest.

• A record of thorough outsider inquiry into the terms of unsolicited offers is "perhaps the most effective safeguard against retrospective suspicion and potential liability."

Sometimes Things Work Out Right. Here's an example: Peoples Banking Corporation in Detroit, Michigan, wanted to buy Pontiac State Bank and Pontiac tentatively agreed to the offer Peoples Banking made. Then, other potential buyers came around, most importantly Comerica, Inc. with a better offer.

After a year Peoples Banking released Pontiac so it could accept the Comerica offer. Peoples Banking chairman and president Franklin Rittmueller put it this way: "Our long established policy has been to grow by merging into Peoples, banks that wanted to join us as partners with stock ownership in our company. In line with that policy, using a legal agreement to force a relationship is no way to form a productive partnership. PSB has agreed to a fair settlement of the legal and other expenses we accrued, and our parting has been amicable."

A TWO-PHASE PLAN FOR MERGING EDP OPERATIONS

Bank mergers and acquisitions have become a way of banking life these days. One of the most difficult parts of these marriages is the consolidation of data processing operations.

When the two entities are some distance apart (that is, not in the same city), which is likely to be the case when the interstate banking dam bursts, the first question is usually whether such a consolidation is at all feasible. Here's how to go about making that determination.

The *objectives of an investigation* should be to:

• Determine the operational and economic feasibility of centralizing computer operations in whole or part; and if feasible.

• Define what such centralization should be, how and when it should be implemented, and what benefits will result.

The primary focus of the investigation should be computer operations, but other areas of related operations or functions for which centralization might prove advantageous should also be included. A *work-program approach* includes two phases.

Phase I

This is an overview of the economic and operational feasibility of consolidation and centralization of computer operations. You should attempt to limit your inquiry to high-level and gross cost factors. With respect to certain factors bearing on the feasibility, it may be necessary to go to a lower level of detail and/or make reasonable assumptions to ensure the relative validity of the findings.

Significant Factors.   You should consider the management philosophies of each bank, the nature of their business and structure and the resultant data processing requirements, the probable structure of the data processing facility on a centralized basis, the impact on staff and compensation, probable future requirements, communications and/or transportation requirements and costs, equipment and systems software compatability requirements, and costs. All these factors should be approached on a level compatible with the objectives of this feasibility phase. You should:

• Obtain statistical data from each bank regarding volume and processing levels for all current applications.

• Obtain cost data from each bank regarding current equipment, personnel, and operating costs.

• Project current application volumes based on past history data and future growth projection.

• Evaluate the feasibility and potential processing problems involved in operating the varied applications on one central facility.

• Evaluate the impact of check processing and other operations on a central facility.

• Estimate the probable communications network requirements of a central facility.

• Determine the general hardware requirements of a central facility.

• Determine the general hardware requirements of at least one satellite center.

• Estimate a probable site location for a central facility.

• Determine the general staffing requirements under a consolidated setup.

• Estimate the total costs for a consolidated operation and compare them with the current costs.

• Analyze the alternatives and develop a recommendation.

The results of Phase I should be documented in a brief report with associated schedules containing findings, recommendations, and supporting data. After submission of the report and an informal presentation, management should be in a position to decide whether it wishes to proceed.

> **NOTE:** If a centralized computer operation is decided upon, an operations team should be assembled. This team would be responsible for Phase II of the move, which is concerned with the nuts and bolts of the consolidation and centralization of the two data processing operations.

Phase II

Contingent upon the results of the first phase and an affirmative decision by management, the second phase is concerned with the details of the who, what, when, where, and how of the consolidation and centralization. Any analysis and recommendations should zero in on the management, organization structures, staff and salary levels, skills mix, staff locations, responsibilities, and the like.

You should also deal with the equipment requirements; locations; data center layout and distribution of processing; retained, displaced, and additional costs; other operations areas to be centralized or consolidated in whole or in part; the location of the center or centers; and communications and/or transportation requirements in terms of what, when, how, and costs.

Finally, deal with implementation in terms of when each change must take place, the sequence of events, the methodologies for completing the operational and technical segments, the human factors and needs that must be dealt with, the elimination or minimization of impact on customers, interim processing arrangements, if any, phased functional transfer, and the like.

Use the following seven checklists to consolidate the consolidation program.

EQUIPMENT

• Determine equipment requirements of a central facility to fit the processing needs allowing for growth and expandability.

• Determine the requirements and needs for satellite processing centers, if any.

• Determine equipment that may be needed in satellite centers to support such areas as check processing, data capture, and report printing.

• Determine the requirements for input and output terminal equipment.

• Determine the most advantageous complement of leased, owned, and rental equipment for the centralized operation.

COMMUNICATIONS

• Conduct a communications audit to determine the communications requirements for equipment, lines, and volume.

• Analyze the information flow by region in order to determine the ability of the network and processing system to handle volumes of information, yet remain flexible enough to respond to growth.

• Determine alternative communications networks giving consideration to level of service, FCC interconnect rulings, line sharing, and tariff charges.

APPLICATIONS

• Determine suitability of current application software to run under a central facility concept.

• Analyze implications of software upon a multiprogramming, multibank environment.

• Determine, to the extent possible, any major application modifications needed to support a central and satellite operation.

• Determine all system software requirements and/or changes.

• Examine and redefine scheduling priorities where appropriate.

• Determine other appropriate system changes (for example, input), which would enhance consolidation.

ORGANIZATION

• Develop a probable organization structure giving consideration to its placement within the consolidated bank and its interface with each associated bank.

• Define duties and responsibilities of each organizational unit.

• Determine staffing levels at all locations.

SPACE REQUIREMENTS

• In conjunction with the communications effort, determine alternate site locations.

• Give consideration to possible future mergers and new services.

• Define and lay out details of site to optimize workflow and cost savings.

ESTIMATE TOTAL COSTS

• Develop estimated cost schedules for a consolidated operation, which includes equipment, personnel, and operating costs.

• Compare consolidated costs to current costs of the two-center operation.

IMPLEMENTATION PLAN

• Establish an implementation schedule for consolidation showing specific tasks and estimated target completion times.

• Recommend an implementation task force to oversee the consolidation effort.

• Recommend qualifications needed from people to take charge of specific tasks.

The results of this phase along with schedules addressing each subject area should be documented in a report.

DIRECTOR CONCERNS IN MERGER SITUATIONS

The Conference Board, a business research organization, reports that the continuing wave of mergers and acquisitions puts growing pressure on outside corporate directors. This conclusion was reached in a study made by the conference board based on the views of thirty outside corporate directors and chief executives who have had recent experiences with mergers and acquisitions. Although only some of the directors are with financial institutions, the results seem to apply quite specifically to banks.

The directors express these major concerns:

• Objectivity is often lost in the heat of takeover battles, which often become emotional tests of wills and egos.

• Defensive measures designed to block or defeat takeovers can be extreme, costly, and wasteful.

• Vital decisions must be made in a hurried, high-pressure situation, which is not conducive to rational decision-making.

• Productive, well-managed companies can be damaged, even when they successfully ward off challengers. Cited as examples are firms that have made unwise purchases or divestitures or have seriously weakened themselves financially in their fight for independence. "When the wolf is at the door, in whichever guise or form, outside directors are placed in a difficult position," notes Jeremy Bacon, The Conference Board's specialist in directorship practices. "They must make many painful decisions, such as weighing the short-term gains of a sale against potential future gains if their firms remain independent. They must also balance the interests of very different shareholders against what might be preferred by management or others who have a stake in the company."

Virtually all the directors emphasized that the board's ability to cope with major merger decisions depends largely on how effectively the board has been involved in the company's long-range planning process.

There is a strong consensus that directors should be informed early on when major acquisitions are being considered. Most say they are. Although merger and acquisition decisions are initiated and carried out by management, the director's role is the same as in other major corporate decisions: to advise, challenge, approve, or disapprove.

NOTE: In balancing shareholders' interests, directors say their bottom line is often price.

Both friendly or unfriendly offers are frequently weighed not on the merits of the companies involved but on whether shareholders will get a fair deal.

PART THREE

OPERATING
THE BANK

Running a bank is a complex, ever-changing proposition. It requires hard-working employees with considerable talents if the bank has any chance of performing adequately in this highly competitive environment. Moreover, a major objective should be to perform at a level higher than merely adequate.

These days, the pressures impacting on performance are growing as modern banking moves rapidly into difficult and challenging times. The chapters in Part III will contribute to the effective operation of any bank.

Areas of concern such as cost control (Chapter 13), security (Chapters 14 and 15), and insurance (Chapter 19) also have significant application today. They should, of course, be adapted for the needs of a particular bank.

The advent of electronic technology has dramatically changed bank operations during the past quarter of a century, and promises to continue to change things as technological advances accelerate. Chapters 17 and 18 address this topic.

13

HOW TO HANDLE COST CONTROL MATTERS

With profit margins shrinking and with the costs of goods and services consumed by a banking company ever on the increase, the importance of controlling costs increases greatly. The topics in this chapter are designed to do just this—simply control costs.

KEEPING OVERTIME UNDER CONTROL

Unless a bank installs adequate controls over the overtime worked by its employees, its costs could easily get out of hand. Here are a number of ideas designed to keep overtime under control that were suggested at a conference on human resource management sponsored by The Conference Board, an industry-sponsored research organization:

• Develop a policy statement on overtime and then make sure all employees understand it. The statement should clearly indicate that the bank considers frequent overtime to be a result of poor planning.

• Conduct inquiries to determine if overtime is necessary, particularly in those departments with excessive overtime.

• Examine the causes of the overtime annd determine if steps can be taken to eliminate or lessen overtime.

• Require prior approval of overtime except in emergency situations.

• Define the hours that constitute overtime. Many banks still operate on a 40-hour week, even though the normal scheduled work week may be less. In such cases, an employee should be paid straight time until the 40 hours have been worked.

• Eliminate casual, voluntary overtime.

• Cap the number of hours of overtime an employee may work, or the amount of overtime pay a person may receive.

• Let your overtime plan evolve slowly so that you can address any special problems that may arise.

> **NOTE:** Overtime is often necessary and even desirable in order to accomplish the bank's objectives in an efficient and timely manner. At the same time, abuses may occur when people need additional money for whatever reason. By putting the proper controls in place, you will ensure the constructive use of overtime.

HOW TO CUT LEGAL COSTS

In this era of lender liability suits, banks are learning to be more active in protecting legal rights and financial assets, seeking claims to which they are entitled as, for example, in the reparations that came about during and after the return of the hostages at the Iranian Embassy. Consequently, legal costs at banks have soared in recent years.

What to Do. Because the future holds the prospect of an ever-increasing tide of litigation, banks have begun to study ways to contain the mounting costs. Here are some helpful recommendations:

• Hire legal staff to take over most tasks from outside counsel. If you hire attorneys at a salary of $35,000 to $80,000 a year instead of paying the equivalent of $200,000 to $500,000 for the services of attorneys at law firms who charge hourly rates of $300 or more, you can save at least 50 percent.

> **NOTE:** The use of in-house counsel has other benefits besides cost savings. Attorneys with a primary allegiance to the bank and with a background in the bank's business can more easily practice preventive law—that is, warn in advance of potential legal pitfalls.

• Delegate as much work as possible to paralegals and nonlawyers. Paralegals today conduct legal research and draft preliminary leases and contracts. They also keep up with the steady flow of paperwork such as completing the numerous forms required by regulatory agencies.

• Automate as many of the legal functions as possible.

> **EXAMPLE:** One major bank recently installed a microcomputer, legal litigation system which stores and automatically produces, via a remote printer, required documents such as summonses, complaints, subpoenas, judgments, and income executions and computes all fees, interest, and payments involved. Such data are automatically updated. The system provides a daily reminder of specific actions required for pending cases, ensuring a timely response to all necessary legal requirements. It also generates reports for management thus requiring less clerical support while furnishing added security and better control.

• Tightly manage in-house staff by using time allocation methods and goal setting.

• Have your professional legal staff specialize where necessary or desirable.

• Shop for the most reasonable fees and best services when you do have to resort to outside firms.

• Keep your primary outside counsel on a retainer.

> **NOTE:** Perhaps the greatest cost saving measure is an early warning system to avoid major legal battles, damage claims, or painful publicity. Banks today can no longer afford to wait for lawsuits or government complaints to be filed against them.

CUTTING BANK FACILITIES COSTS

Even with inflation under control, the expenses for maintaining bank facilities and premises seems to be going in only one direction: up.

Steps can be taken, fortunately, to cope with these rising costs. Here are ten steps you can consider for your bank:

1. Stagger your leases and review them periodically. By not having all your leases expire at the same time, you'll have more flexibility. If you find you need less space, you can plan to consolidate operations at the next possible expiration date.

2. Divide and sublet any space you don't need. Be sure to negotiate sublet clauses in your leases.

3. Use modular, open-space office layouts wherever possible. This will save you time and money when you need to refigure space.

4. Install computer-controlled energy systems that automatically adjust temperatures and lighting to conserve energy and shave your energy bill.

5. Centralize your premises functions to establish control and economies. Centralization also allows you to hire the expertise you need in this area.

6. Get bids on all contractor and renovation jobs as well as on the purchase of all furniture and equipment.

7. Design a space inventory system to monitor all your space needs and match these with available space.

8. Watch for any irregularities because premises and associated activities are areas prone to problems. At times, overruns have been known to result from inefficient management and/or kickbacks.

9. Recycle space and furniture whenever possible. Establish good maintenance procedures. It is often less expensive to keep equipment and furniture in good repair than to purchase new furniture.

10. Plan ahead. Realistically assess space requirements and select sites carefully. Much money has been wasted because branches or operations have all too quickly outgrown allotted space. Accurate projections and sound decisions can save you dollars. Do it right the first time.

> **NOTE:** Constantly reconstructing and refiguring space is disruptive to both staff and customers. Moves and relocations have been known to cause snafus with customer accounts and employee-relations problems. These can be avoided by proper space planning and utilization.

REDUCING PURCHASING COSTS

The following checklist is used by one of the "big eight" accounting firms to review the purchasing practices of its clients. Use the checklist to review the purchasing practices at your bank. It will help to determine if any techniques have been overlooked in reducing your bank's purchasing costs.

• Reduction of purchase authorizations on repetitively used articles via a systematic program.

• Purchase authorizations for repetitively used articles under a stocking program based on lead time plus safety-stock considerations or period planning.

• Purchase authorizations designating data material will be required.

• Purchase authorizations containing technical and performance specifications so that agent knows exactly what to buy.

• Statement of purchasing policies covering corporate relationships, particularly buying responsibilities; competitive buying, source selection, and bidding; maintenance of multiple buying sources to protect continuity of supply; rules on commitments and contracts; reciprocity; and conflict of interest.

• Decentralized purchasing function coordinated so that locations do not compete with each other, thus maximizing purchasing power.

• Increased purchasing power through nationwide buying contracts and blanket purchase commitments.

• Supplying purchasing personnel with summaries of commodity buying and supplier buying volumes to facilitate negotiations with supplies.

• Purchasing agent participation in standardization, value analysis, lease-versus-buy analysis, and negotiations of options to purchase in lease agreements.

• Orderly plan to ensure materials delivery within time specified on purchase commitments.

• Procedures to foster accurate weights (for example, periodic testing of scales) and weighing routines that are not unduly expensive) (for example, use of statistical sampling).

• Policy on acceptance or nonacceptance of over- or undershipments.

• Purchasing agent informed quickly of promptness, quantities, and quality of shipments received.

• Costs accumulated and decisions made to charge suppliers for rework costs caused by defective goods and accompanying significant return freight costs.

• Payments deferred until due dates.

NOTE: Purchasing costs are reduced each time you aggressively seek out the best deal.

Yet, in the long run, sound organization and purchasing procedures will save your bank as much money as aggressive bargain hunting.

CUTTING COSTS WITH VALUE ENGINEERING

Bank profits are being squeezed from all sides these days. Regardless of what the inflationary rate happens to be, costs for most banks are going nowhere but up. That is why many banks have instituted ongoing cost-cutting programs. Unfortunately, cost cutting becomes more difficult over time. It is management's difficult responsibility to ensure that the long-term health of the bank is not hurt simply for the sake of short-term savings.

Value Engineering. Consider the possibility of using value engineering concepts (usually associated with industrial firms) at your bank. Basically, value engineering is a technique that rates the worth of a product or service to its cost. An attempt is then made to improve the relationship by increasing quality, broadening the utility, and, not incidentally, decreasing costs.

When applied to banking, value engineering requires all staff activities to be examined in order to identify functions where cost cuts can be made without harming operations. Part of the process is the careful balancing of quality, cost, estimated savings, and potential adverse effeccts. The result is a list of opportunities for cost savings, ranked in order of their desirability, and providing an explanation of the implications of their implementation.

A commitment by management to the program is essential. Implementation of value engineering programs require the strong but fair CEO who is committed to more cost-effective operations. Senior management must then support the CEO with the willingness and ability to follow his or her lead. Value engineering also requires a determination not to accept less than the target cost reductions, along with the willingness to draw sharp lines despite the often frequent lack of hard data.

The Dynamics of Value Engineering. Value engineering works because it is an interactive process: Users and suppliers of services join together and determine what is important and what can be cut. Some of the concept's dynamics that contribute to the success of value engineering are:

• Senior management with its bankwide perspective, has an opportunity to review the entire spectrum of cost-saving alternatives, which are customarily known to only lower-level management.

• The CEO, senior officers, and suppliers and users of services all share the responsibility for any cutbacks decided upon.

• Managers and supplier departments must identify suitable alternatives or else risk the possibility of appearing unimaginative.

• Managers of receiver departments must act prudently when confronted with a less costly alternative or else take the risk of appearing unreasonable.

The Workings of Value Engineering. Value engineering is a team concept, which includes the chief executive, a task force composed of top associates, the managers of all organizational units receiving or supplying overhead services, and someone experienced in value engineering. Here are the eleven organization and data-gathering steps:

• The CEO establishes a small, high-level task force to guide the process.

• The CEO and task force members set the cost-savings target.

• The task force identifies the organizational units to be reviewed for potential cost reductions.

• The manager of each unit identifies all services and end products that his or her unit supplies or receives from other units.

• The manager estimates the cost of each service and end product according to guidelines set by the task force.

• The task force organizes evaluation groups composed of the receivers and suppliers of related services.

• The evaluation groups identify alternatives for each of the services (such as elimination, substitution, or streamlining).

• Evaluation groups rank the alternatives in descending order of attractiveness.

• The alternatives list is passed up the management hierarchy for review and reassessment where appropriate.

• All rankings of alternatives are turned over to the task force for decisions.

• The CEO, with the assistance of the task force, makes all final decisions.

> **NOTE:** The key to value engineering is the team concept. Without this interaction, cost cutting may accomplish its goals, but it can also cause other potentially more serious problems.

CONTROLLING TELEPHONE SYSTEM EXPENSES

Even before the breakup of AT&T, independent telephone companies have been offering electronic tools for telephone management, analysis, and control. Most of these systems are based on a minicomputer, or a series of microprocessors that manage phone usage for cost effectiveness and also collect, store, and analyze data from the company switchboard. When connected to a printer or a video display screen, the systems can produce reports of telephone usage in a form programmed by the user. For example, a daily, weekly, or monthly printout of calls by caller, client or product number, and trunk line could be provided.

The availability of this information makes it much easier to verify the monthly telephone bill, check the use of WATS or tie-lines, and charge calls to the proper accounts including employees for personal calls. It is also much easier to determine if WATS or tie-lines are paying for themselves or should be canceled.

Passive or Active Systems. Phone management systems can either be passive or active. A passive system only monitors the switchboard and produces periodic reports. An active system does the same and more. Its minicomputer takes charge of out-going calls and automatically routes them through the cheapest means. Employees are no longer able to make expensive mistakes such as dialing direct when a WATS line, tie-line, or microwave transmitting service is available.

Both passive and active systems can be purchased, leased, or leased with a purchase option that gives credit for part of the lease payments. Some systems are a package that includes telephones, a switchboard, a computer, and a subsystem that routes calls in an active system. Some manufacturers will add a hardware–software package to an existing phone system. Most of the lower-priced systems are designed for use with the newer computerized switchboards. However, many systems can be adapted to any type of switchboard.

What to Look for in a System. Whether you are buying or leasing a system, you should obtain at least three competitive proposals. Here are nine features and options you should look for:

• Flexibility and easy expansion of the system

• Guarantee of reliable performance for three to six months

• Clear provisions for maintenance and service costs

• Reporting on all outgoing calls from all stations on all trunks

• Concise, accurate, and timely reports tailored to management needs

• Complete network control, including sensing of individual trunk as well as station use

• Modular design to allow for expansion

• Compatibility with push-button and rotary dialing

• Code entry to identify usage by personnel and charges to client or account

> **NOTE:** With phone costs increasing at least 15 percent each year, the payback period for a computerized phone management system averages two years or less. That's a quick payoff.

14

MANAGING YOUR BANK'S PHYSICAL SECURITY FACILITIES

A bank must keep its resources and both its employees and customers safe and secure. This is no easy task as crime rises in many parts of the country. Drug-related crimes in particular are on the rise because of the need for quick cash.

Physical security measures are covered in this chapter. Another aspect of physical security, dealing with automated teller machine (ATM) security, is covered later in Chapter 18.

PROCEDURAL SECURITY MEASURES

Physical protective measures, such as lock-up devices, alarms, surveillance cameras, anti-intrusion devices, and guards are all essential ingredients of a bank's total security program. However, some of the most far-reaching security problems are procedural in nature.

Shift Schedules. Many banks operate beyond their regular shift to a one-and-one-half, two-, or even three-shift schedule. The reasons: A better utilization of resources, lower costs, a need to process volume, and a host of related causes. This notwithstanding, a shift operation causes problems to the security officer.

> **THE BEST REMEDY:** Lock up those areas
> that are not in use other than during the

162 / Managing Your Bank's Physical Security Facilities

prime shift. For example: A bank's tape library is frequently not in use during the second and third shifts. As such, it should be secured. In some banks the tape library may be used during the second and third shifts, but the librarian goes home at 5:00 p.m. leaving the entrance area wide open. In some instances this is overcome by putting necessary tapes and disks on a cart where the computer operator can still have the necessary tapes for processing purposes.

This procedure can backfire, however, if the tapes are inadvertently destroyed and backups, which may be stored in the locked vault, are needed. The cost of a tape librarian for all three shifts is difficult, at best, to cost justify. Therefore, alternatives must be evaluated in terms of their effectiveness.

Regulations. In-house regulations governing keys, master keys, combinations, and the like should be clearly spelled out. This is a procedural task that is frequently glossed over and yet represents a basic security precaution.

TIP: Pay particular attention when combinations are changed or transferred to others: Account for all keys from retiring employees or employees who are leaving the bank, change locks when and where appropriate, etc.

Receiving, Loading Stations

• If a new site is being established, pay special attention to the receiving and loading stations where many security measures fall short.

NOTE: Ideally, receiving should be separated from loading to prevent switching.

• Keep pedestrians out.

• Employee exists should be on the opposite side of the building to lessen traffic.

• Place time clocks on the same side as the employees' exit to force them to leave by that side.

• Locker rooms should be located away from the receiving and loading stations.

• Employee parking lots should be away from the receiving and loading stations.

• Be sure that the trash area is away from the receiving and loading platform. Trash vehicles are notorious for hiding stolen material.

> **NOTE:** Management must put some kind of a lid on security cost because funding for this important aspect is limited. To this end, the cost of any security element must be weighed in light of its anticipated benefits.

HOW TO KEEP SAFE-DEPOSIT BOXES SAFE

The increased usage of safe-deposit boxes and the growing incidence of robbery attempts on safe-deposit vaults make security and operational procedures important considerations for most banks.

Here are thirteen steps you can take to ensure a smooth safe-deposit box operation:

1. Give each safe-deposit box holder a contract that states the rental rate, box number, length of the lease, and all names of parties who have access to the box. File copies of the contracts according to box numbers.

2. Make sure boxes are paid for in advance and rent renewal bills (including any tax) are made out in duplicate: one for the box holder as an invoice and one for the accounts receivable department.

3. Ensure that customers pay the appropriate fee for their size deposit box. If special concessions are made such as allowing a customer to use a $20 size box because no $15 ones are available, have the authorized officer initial the contract indicating the concession in order to avoid confusion when the customer comes to use the box.

4. Deposit amounts received from box rentals daily and maintain rental cards so that periodic checks can be made to ensure all rentals are accounted for fully.

5. Make sure all entrance tickets are signed by a person granted access to a box as stated on the contract, along with the date and time of entry, and have this initialed by the officer permitting entry.

6. Mark keyholes to boxes under multiple control to assist in observing access requirements.

7. Enforce access rules stringently if your bank keeps any of its own assets in the department.

8. Do not let employees maintain custody of keys to rented boxes.

9. Never let box holders use the master key.

10. Have attendants present when box holders return deposit boxes to the lock-up area.

10. Make sure box holders are present whenever attendants open locks to boxes.

12. Make sure locksmiths who change locks on boxes surrender their keys directly to an officer, not to the vault attendant.

13. Inspect booths where box holders open their safe-deposit boxes immediately after they are used by the customer.

> **NOTE:** Taking these simple precautions can pay off for your bank with a thriving safe-deposit box business, earning handsome fees, greater security against losses, and enhanced customer goodwill.

NIGHT-DEPOSIT SECURITY CHECKLIST

A bank's night-deposit facilities are a convenience for many important business customers. However, it is a system that does not always run smoothly. How can you be sure you don't run into snags? Following is a guide for internal control.

The Cardinal Rule in Night-Depository Security. Establish a system of double checks and then stick with that system.

Have procedures typed out and give a copy to each employee involved with night-deposit bags. Seven points to consider are:

• Keep all night-depository vaults and safes under dual control.

• Be sure all customers who use night-deposit services enter into a contractual agreement with your bank. This eliminates the possible problem of the occasional customer who, after making a night deposit, finds that it has been lost in the shuffle.

> **TIP:** You should also post a sign over the chute stating that your bank will not assume responsibility for noncontracted night deposits.

• Supply each customer with a set of lockable canvas bags to be used in making night deposits. Each bag should be stenciled with your bank's name and a serial number.

• Make sure the keys to the bags are issued only to the depositor. All other keys, including those belonging to un-issued bags, should be kept under dual control.

• When the night-deposit vault is opened in the morning, be sure an employee prepares a detailed list, noting both the customers who have made deposits and their bag numbers. This process should be conducted under supervision. The list should be signed or initialed by each person.

• The opening of the bags should also be conducted under dual control. At least one person should be a teller. Also, be sure to compare the amount in each bag with the amount on the deposit ticket.

• When a customer picks up the bag, have him or her sign a card, and then compare it with a card kept in a signature file. Also be sure the customer signs a separate receipt for each bag. The receipt should note the date and time of the issuing of the bag as well as its serial number.

Customer's Responsibilities. When a customer asks about using night-deposit facilities, be sure he or she understands the proper procedures. Especially cover the following:

• Suggest that he or she uses care in coming to the depository late at night. Robbers could be lurking nearby just waiting for an unwary merchant.

• Explain your internal security procedures and how the customer can help by making accurate deposit counts and by following the bank's policies.

• Suggest the customer take extra care in safeguarding the depository key as well as the keys to deposit bags.

> **NOTE:** Insist on dual control, no matter how long any employee has been with the bank. Also rotate different employees to handle this job.

DATA SECURITY CHECKLISTS

Data protection involves making sure the security systems extend to personnel, access, and communications and that these systems function during emergencies, such as bombings or riots. The checklists following provide reminders for the security-conscious systems manager.

PERSONNEL SECURITY

• Is a background investigation performed on all employees?

• Are all new employees given a security briefing?

• Does bank policy provide for patent and noncompetition agreements and/or employee pledges?

• Is periodic refresher orientation provided?

• Has a system of accountability records been developed?

• Is there a termination checkout and debriefing session?

• Are nonemployees trained in security procedures?

• Are, at the least, limited background checks required for and performed on nonemployees working at the facility?

• Is there an orientation session for nonemployees?

ACCESS SECURITY

• Are personal identity documents required?

• Are bank badges and passes worn at all times?

• Are visitors required to register and be escorted by a bank employee?

• Are guards and receptionists situated at strategic locations?

• Are alarms provided for detection of unauthorized entry?

• Is area surveillance by film record or remote observation provided?

BOMB AND RIOT SECURITY

• Have organization and communication links been established for assigning evacuation decision responsibility?

• Are procedures estabished for contacting local police and fire departments when the bank is under actual threat?

COMMUNICATIONS SECURITY

• Are terminal control techniques reviewed, including:
- remote job entry
- assemble availability
- programs and users
- terminal usage statistics?

• Are code control techniques evaluated, including:
- passwords
- security codes
- authorization codes
- lockwords
- security tables
- personal identification methods?

• Is the system terminal network analyzed for cost effectiveness?

DEALING WITH KIDNAP/HOSTAGE SITUATIONS

Although your bank probably won't be faced with such a frightening situation, the kidnapping or holding hostage of bankers has increased alarmingly in recent years. It is advisable to be prepared if this situation happens.

Below is a memo one bank president sent to all officers and employees. Some changes were necessarily made so that it would apply to any bank.

MEMO

Following is the procedure to be followed by the officers and employees of the bank in the event a member of this staff or his or her relative is held hostage or kidnapped for extortion purposes:

1. Each officer or employee is to complete an employee family information form which will be kept on file in the bank vault. This information will be held in the strictest confidence and contains vitally impo'rtant data needed to safely return anyone on our staff or their family that is taken hostage.

2. Each officer will maintain a supply of the caller questionnaire forms to be used in the event that a threat is made via the telephone concerning a kidnapping of a relative.

3. If you should receive a phone call informing you that a member of your family is being held hostage and a ransom is demanded from the bank for their safe return, do the following:

(a) Remain as calm as possible.

(b) Do not upset the caller.

(c) Remember, the caller is counting on you to panic and act without thinking.

(d) Request proof that the caller is really holding the person hostage.

(e) Ask to speak with the person to determine his or her well being.

(f) Make notes of the entire conversation paying special attention to:
   (i) sex of the caller
   (ii) voice characteristics
   (iii) exact time of the call
   (iv) exact words of the caller
   (v) any background noises

(g) If possible, notify an officer and try to have the call traced.

(g) Be sure to indicate your willingness to cooperate.

(i) If a hostage is being held, try to arrange a simultaneous exchange.

(j) If a ransom is going to be paid, try to arrange a person-to-person payoff rather than a drop.

(k) While packaging the ransom money, be sure to include bait money (in this case, use teller's bail money in the package).

4. The longer the caller remains on the phone, the more valuable information can be obtained. While talking to the caller, interrogate him or her using the caller questionnaire at your disposal.

5. Be sure to detail any instructions received.

6. Try to verify the threat by calling the would-be hostage, e.g., your wife at home or your child at school.

7. Immediately after the call, notify an officer and the Federal Bureau of Investigation.

8. No information should be given to the press by the individual involved; this is to be handled by a member of senior management.

(a) Do not release names, addresses, or photographs of bank employees or their families, the exact amount of money paid, or the fact that bait money was included.

9. Bank officers should not answer telephone calls personally. Calls taken by other staff members should be screened, asking the caller's name, business association, and purpose of the call. If the caller does not satisfactorily identify him- or herself, take a message so that the bank officer can call back. (A kidnapper will not be anxious to give a phone number thereby revealing his or her whereabouts.)

10. Because of the increase in kidnap/hostage cases, it has been suggested that bank officers follow certain procedures at home in order to protect themselves and their families. Each individual will have to decide for him- or herself which protective device works best.

(a) Installation of protective devices in the home from inexpensive plug-in sonar or radar units, which detect room movements, to highly sophisticated burglar and fire alarms, in each room and on each floor and window.

(b) The installation of a second keylock on each door and window.

(c) Outside glass doors with deadlocks on them. In the event the glass is broken and the knob is turned, the deadlock still prevents opening.

(d) Any solid door that has a doorbell should have a viewer so that the person outside can be observed before he or she is admitted. It is recommended that a good solid chain lock be installed.

(e) Glass doors that open onto a patio should have chain locks attached to them and a bar placed strategically at the bottom so that the door cannot be opened without shattering the glass.

11. Taking security precautions in the bank and at home can reduce the chances of your bank being hit by a kidnap-ransom attempt. However, in the event such a threat does occur, the main point is to remember to remain calm and think clearly. This is much easier to do if you already have anticipated the emergency and have outlined a procedure to follow.

15

HANDLING BANK SECURITY: FRAUD

Fraud, both internal and external, is plaguing the banking industry. Although measures to detect and limit fraud have become more sophisticated, so have the attempts to perpetrate embezzlement and other fraudulent acts. As a result, a bank cannot take too many precautions in curbing fraud.

This chapter provides several checklists which offer relatively easily discernable means to determine where danger spots—or potentially dangerous areas—exist. Identifying these dangers then enables a bank to take steps to guard against criminal activities.

SEVEN STEPS TO FRAUD CONTROL

The incidence of fraud at banks is on the rise. The following measures will make it more difficult for perpetrators and may discourage others from trying their hand at fraudulent schemes.

1. Never allow one person to have complete responsibility for a transaction from beginning to end without some outside intervention or control.

2. Thoroughly investigate all newly hired employees. Be alert to recommendations of an evasive or cautious nature. If prior employers hedge on answers to direct questions concerning an applicant, investigate further.

3. Keep computer programmers out of the computer operating room. Do not, under any circumstances, permit them to run their own programs. Be sure all programs have

173

been approved by outside authority before running; keep a log of all programs run.

4. Enforce the rule that all employees take two consecutive weeks of vacation to provide an opportunity for others to perform the vacationing employee's work and learn what is going on.

5. Rotate jobs wherever possible. Changing jobs does not allow employees to become so entrenched that they discover ways to defraud or identify outsiders who might aid in deceitful practices.

6. Bond all key employees. Bonding company investigations may provide an additional safeguard concerning employees' past performance.

7. Maintain a continuous program of employee security and auditing training.

HOW TO CATCH COUNTERFEIT SECURITIES

A trick that keeps coming back like an old song is the pledging of fraudulent securities as loan collateral. This is usually accomplished by printing stock certificates with a name that can easily be altered to another name, most often a major corporation. To guard against this, lending officers should be aware of the characteristics of real securities.

The stock exchanges have gotten together to establish specifications for the printing of stock certificates. The bank note companies used for printing the certificates use a strict printing process, including the engraving of major portions of them. *For example:* The New York Stock Exchange requires the engraving of human figures on the certificates. Other safeguards include paper features and special inks built into the process.

How to Find the Phonies.   Here are some quick checks to help detect counterfeit certificates:

• Look for randomly placed planchettes (discs of paper) imbedded in the paper stock. (Not all certificates use planchettes, however.)

• Run your finger across the paper; it should be etched because of the engraving.

• Use an ultraviolet light. Red and yellow planchettes used in American bank note certificates will glow under the light.

• Vignettes, sometimes of human figures, should be clear. If they are muddy and the lines are indistinct, the certificate is probably a counterfeit.

• The color should be clean and identical to all other certificates of the same company and the same denomination.

What to Do if You Find a Phony. The Securities and Exchange Commission has set up an information center to assist in tracking missing, lost, counterfeit, and stolen securities. Such securities should be reported to the center.

The center should also be contacted any time securities are pledged or assigned in order to determine the status of the securities.

COPING WITH CHECK KITING

Consider the following example: Widget, Inc., one of your accounts, has a payroll to meet. Unfortunately, it doesn't have sufficient funds to cover it. The company expects a $10,000 payment from a client in a few days. However, in the meantime, the owner of Widget attempts a shady expediency. He cashes a check for $2,500 at your bank drawn on his out-of-state bank and uses the $2,500 to pay his employees. He then deposits in his out-of-state bank a check for $3,000 drawn on his account at your bank. Before this can clear, he deposits a check in your bank for $3,000 drawn on the out-of-state bank. Then his $10,000 payment arrives and he rushes it to his out-of-state bank for deposit. As far as Widget is concerned no one is the wiser.

This is considered an unauthorized loan. The owner of Widget is not a "typical" con man and has no intention of permanently robbing the bank. However, he is kiting. In this case, he took a chance because he was certain the money from his customer was on its way. Yet, the fact is, he passed checks between banks that had no collected funds behind them. He made one worthless check seem to be good by writing a second worthless check and then a third.

> **KEY POINT:** The operation is flatly illegal and your bank's employees, especially tellers and bookkeepers, should know what signs indicate that a kite may be taking place.

What to look for. Kites can be very difficult to spot when cash and legitimate checks are mixed with kited items. There is a pattern to kiting, however, which bank personnel can spot.
Tellers should:

• Be alert for checks that are deposited regularly and signed by the depositors.

• Take notice of customers who made frequent inquiries about their balances or other account activities.

• Watch for checks drawn on other banks and signed by the depositor.

Bookkeepers should:

• Watch for unusual activity, even if it seems harmless. Frequent large deposits and off-setting withdrawals should be investigated.

• Note checks payable to the maker deposited in another bank.

• Watch for a pattern in clearing checks and for a rapid growth of uncollected funds.

> **NOTE:** If you are suspicious that kiting is taking place, instruct your tellers not to cash checks on any uncollected funds for the involved accounts and put the accounts on hold. Then begin investigating the suspicious patterns and make some discreet inquiries.

CAUTION: Don't act precipitously. You risk embarrassing your bank or provoking a lawsuit if you scream "kite" where there is none.

HOW MONEY IS LAUNDERED

The government is taking a closer look these days at the "laundering" of criminally obtained money through financial institutions. You and your staff should be aware of how laundering schemes work.

In the FBI "Law Enforcement Bulletin," agents Vincent Doherty and Monte Smith describe the laundering of money by organized crime. They point out that organized crime has invested $20 billion or more into 15,000 to 50,000 business establishments in the United States. Organized crime businesses take in an estimated minimum of $48 billion in gross revenues annually, with about $25 billion in untaxed profits. The purpose of laundering funds is to commingle legitimate and illicit monies so that they cannot be separated, while simultaneously preventing the discovery of the introduction of illegal monies into business.

Although laundering money can be accomplished in a wide variety of legitimate firms, certain domestic businesses have characteristics that lend themselves to successful laundering operations. For example, the business selected as a "laundry" must be capable of absorbing a large volume of cash income because most illicit income is received in the form of cash.

Law enforcement officials have adapted new methods such as sampling, ratio analysis, and flowcharting to discover laundering operations and to successfully prosecute the people involved in the conversion process. Sampling is simply a statistical procedure wherein several customers of an organization are counted randomly, a conservative estimate is compiled of the amount of money spent by each customer, and a projection is made of how much money is actually received by an enterprise in the ordinary course of operation.

> **CAUTION:** Although law enforcement agencies have been relatively successful in detecting and exposing domestic laundering operations, it should be known that underworld organizations have developed and perfected several international money-laundering operations that traditionally have been immune to detection and exposure.

Although these international "laundries" vary greatly in form, organization, and complexity, the object is still to disguise the true nature and origin of funds derived from illegal activities.

International laundering schemes often involve the use of dummy corporations and numbered bank accounts, or they may use securities or financial instruments issued by banks located in countries with little regulating of banking.

Cash Flow Is the Key. The successful use of businesses to launder "dirty" money depends on keeping the cash flow "in house" and creating such complexity that investigation into the operation appears to be too complicated to undertake. Experience has shown, however, that these laundering operations are not complicated and can be investigated successfully.

Investigators have been assisted by the passage of the Bank Secrecy Act and the Treasury Department's regulations implementing its provisions, which establish reporting requirements for any person importing or exporting currency or other financial instruments totaling more than $5,000. Further, banks and financial institutions must report currency transactions in excess of $10,000 to the Internal Revenue Service.

The law also requires all U.S. citizens having a financial interest in, or signature authority over, bank securities or other financial accounts in foreign countries to report this relationship annually to the Treasury Department.

> **NOTE:** Procedures for opening new accounts should be reviewed to ensure that adequate checks are made on accounts with large cash deposits.

COUNTERING BANK CARD FRAUD

A customer inserts his or her card into an ATM and enters his or her personal identification number. If these procedures are followed properly, funds can be withdrawn from the checking account or a deposit can be made. Yet, banks are finding such security measures often inadequate and are experiencing Electric Funds Transfer (EFT) losses. These losses can be traced to the ease with which most bank cards can be altered.

Methods of Duplication. According to the Federal Deposit Insurance Corp (FDIC), the two most common methods of duplicating magnetically encoded data are skimming and buffer recording.

• *Skimming.* This technique involves placing a piece of recording tape over the magnetic strip of a valid card and applying heat. (The heat can be applied with a common household iron.) Next, the recording tape is placed over the blank strip of another card, and heat is applied again. Using this technique, it is possible to produce several duplicate cards without seriously degrading the recording quality of the information.

• *Buffer recording.* This technique produces a duplicated card of high quality. However, this method is electronically complex and expensive. Buffer recording requires an electromagnetic reader and buffer storage. The card is read and the data are stored in the buffer memory, later to be written out on a blank card. Building an electromagnetic reader would likely require some knowledge of both electronics and the data format of the good card.

The FDIC reports that in order to render cards less susceptible to duplication, some plastic vendors are advocating the incorporation of secure card properties. This requires the introduction of some random property that will vary from card to card.

One such technique, for example, utilizes two sets of magnetic bars, configured in an interleaved pattern and printed on the inner core of the plastic stock of the card. This forms a protective magnetic fingerprint, and no two cards are alike. The card could also contain additional safeguards by incorporating heat-sensitive and pressure-sensitive materials that would invalidate the card if any attempt was made to alter or duplicate it.

Other countermeasures are being tested by various vendors. These include the dilution of nonlethal radioactive isotopes into the plastic. Each card produced in this manner would have a unique set of identification properties that could be machine-read and computer-verified while still being extremely expensive and difficult to duplicate.

CHECKLIST FOR CONTROLLING FRAUD

There are three basic rules for controlling bank fraud. They have been around as long as banking has and are even more important today in this age of electronic banking:

1. Mandatory vacations
2. Separation of duties
3. Rotation of employees

Although these basic rules cannot cover all situations or possibilities, they do a good job when followed. Here are specific questions, based on suggestions by the American Bankers Association, that expand on these rules.

	Yes	No
Do you have one person responsible for protection procedures and controls?	☐	☐
Does he or she regularly report directly to the board of directors?	☐	☐
Do you periodically have an outside audit?	☐	☐
Do you require every officer and employee to take a vacation annually?	☐	☐
Do you require them occasionally to be gone at the end of the month?	☐	☐
Do you rotate employees in their work at unannounced intervals?	☐	☐
Do you periodically spot check the work for which senior officers are responsible?	☐	☐

	Yes	No
Do you allocate work so that no one employee handles an entire transaction to completion?	☐	☐
Do you have each note initialed by an officer as evidence of its genuineness?	☐	☐
Do you have disbursements made by someone other than the officer initialing the instrument?	☐	☐
Do you have all disbursements made by check?	☐	☐
Do you place reserve cash, securities, and collateral under the joint custody of two persons?	☐	☐
Do you require a joint action of two persons to place in or remove such assets and property from the vault?	☐	☐
Do you segregate and control separately inactive commercial and savings accounts?	☐	☐
Do you have cash items centralized and under continuous control and follow up?	☐	☐
Do you have corespondent bank accounts reconciled by persons other than those who issue drafts against or post entries to the accounts?	☐	☐
Do you rigidly enforce a rule against the holding of savings passbooks in the bank?	☐	☐
Do you hold securities for customers under the joint custody of two persons?	☐	☐
Do you occasionally have someone other than the person directly concerned count cash, list and balance savings accounts, individual checking accounts, notes, and so on?	☐	☐
Do you, after balancing, verify by correspondence with customers at least a sampling of the loans and account balances to determine the accuracy of the bank's records with respect to notes, collateral, checking and savings account balances, and so on?	☐	☐
Do you have someone verify the authenticity of items charged to expense?	☐	☐
Do you have all income, interest, rebate computation verified, re-added and checked to the general ledger by someone other than the person making the original computations and entries?	☐	☐

	Yes	No
Do you strictly adhere to a prescribed protective procedure in permitting access to safe deposit boxes?	☐	☐
Do you keep spare locks and keys to unrented safe deposit boxes under dual control?	☐	☐
Do you have someone review all returned mail to ascertain if any irregularities are involved?	☐	☐
Do you keep adequate bankers blanket bond coverage as recommended by the ABA?.	☐	☐
Do you annually check your entire insurance coverage and the expiration dates of all policies?	☐	☐
Do you maintain adequate internal records to trace and identify items which may become misplaced or lost in transit, or otherwise, to support your claim under your insurance coverage?	☐	☐
Do all tellers have control of their own cash?	☐	☐
Do you provide adequate equipment for the protection of teller's cash at night?	☐	☐
Do you instruct employees on what to do should a holdup occur?	☐	☐
Do you provide each teller with a package of "decoy money" on which the numbers have been recorded?	☐	☐

NOTE: If you answered no to five or more questions, your bank could have some serious problems. Remedial action is recommended in these instances.

16

EFFECTIVE
AND PROFITABLE
BRANCH BANKING

The reports of the death of bank branches have been greatly exaggerated. With the advent of ATMs, it was once believed that branch offices would be superfluous.

That certainly has not been the case to date. Although the number of branches has been reduced at some banks in some sections of the country, the branch remains an important feature of the banking business.

Streamlining and staff reductions, however, have occurred but this has been done to increase the importance of the branches that exist by putting greater emphasis on the effective management of those branch offices.

HOW TO GET MORE FROM A BRANCH OFFICE

What can be done to maximize the effectiveness of branch offices? One key to successful operations at the branch level is to have a branch coordinator who considers the branches as mini-institutions, with their own individual market problems. In essence, the coordinator is the buffer between the branches and the main office.

Here are some other tips to help a bank get the most from its branch offices:

• *Involve branch managers in profitability accounting.* In setting up a branch system, consider each office a full-fledged, cost-revenue center with its own budget. This involves the branch manager directly in all areas of administration from personnel cost control to supply purchases.

• *Use job descriptions.* Ask the branch manager to have each employee write his or her own job description. These should be reviewed by the manager who, in turn, should give the branch coordinator a written evaluation of his or her own efforts.

• *Hold regular on-site branch evaluations.* Do not rely on spot audits by bank examiners to turn up deficiencies. Branch evaluations (or mini-audits) can and should go much deeper than regular audits. Include such items as branch security, cash control, personnel evaluations, review of the physical plant, inventory, and logistics to markets.

HOW TO REORGANIZE A BRANCH FOR INCREASED EARNINGS

Sometimes a branch office may be unprofitable, and it might be advantageous to close it down. However, this decision should not be made too hastily even though it often seems to be the conventional wisdom to do so these days. It may be possible to improve profits through reorganization, or improved equipment and reduced transaction costs could possibly be a solution. The local market area could also be targeted with a special advertising campaign to sell loans and bring in deposits.

> **NOTE:** Although these alternatives might help, one of the surest ways of improving profitability is to increase the productivity of the branch staff.

At many banks, changes in staff and clerical assignments have produced better service with lower overhead. When these changes are handled well, morale also gets a boost—a factor that should not be discounted.

Restructuring. When a branch office is being restructured, the following areas should be considered:

• *Responsibility.* Customers should never have to jump from line to line or wait in line only to find they must first see an officer. *Someone must be responsible for each service performed at the branch.* Jobs should be assigned and then monitored to ensure they are handled effectively.

• *Staffing.* Traffic patterns must be studied to learn when traffic peaks and ebbs. Then staffing can be matched to the patterns. *Overstaffing must be avoided.* Part-timers, along with shift employees who can move from job to job are essential to most branch locations.

• *Staff allocation.* The best employees should be placed in the most important jobs—unfortunately this is not always the case. Money-making services or services that appeal to customers with high balances should always be handled adequately. Employees, particularly those dealing with more important customers should be trained to cross-sell. Of course, success in any cross-selling should be rewarded or recognized.

• *Leadership.* Officers should become involved whenever their help is needed. *They should not be permitted to use their status to withdraw from routine service demands when their help could be beneficial.* Officers can be put on the floor during peak hours to assist customers. They also should be kept out of the back office and away from long lunches at times when their help is needed most.

• *Specialization.* Most customers come to the branch office to perform only simple, quick transactions. However, they may find themselves waiting in long lines while other customers ask for money orders, make loan payments, or transfer monies to and from various accounts. *Specialized lines should be established for routine transactions to avoid needless waits.*

• *Morale.* One way to improve morale is to develop a system of bonuses which recognizes outstanding contributions by staff personnel to the success of the branch. Rewarding excellence encourages others to strive for success.

> **NOTE:** Some of the points made here depend on the effectiveness of the branch manager; however, they apply to virtually all branches. Those in charge of branch

administration should make sure each branch is organized and staffed to provide the best possible service at the least possible cost. Only then, if a branch remains unprofitable, should it be closed.

MEASURING A BRANCH'S PROFITABILITY

One way to increase a bank's overall profitability is to increase the profitability of each of its branches. To improve branch profitability, a bank needs the following basic information of profitability measurement:

- Deposits a branch generates
- Interest costs of the deposits
- Operating expenses
- Loan income

The bank must then evaluate this information.

Two common approaches for measuring profitability: the profit-center system and the contributory system. In the profit-center system, each branch is evaluated as a separate business unit. The branch's loan and deposit income is balanced against all costs that can be attributed to the branch. Each branch is also charged for its share of general overhead expenses for the bank as a whole. These expenses might include salaries for central administrators or marketing expenditures boosting a service the branch does not provide. Each branch bears these costs according to its relative size within the overall system.

Critics of this approach argue that it masks profitability by charging branches for general expenses they do not incur. These critics prefer to measure a branch's contribution to overall profitability. Their contribution approach limits deductions from branch profits to direct branch costs. Within this system, the actual and relative contribution of each branch to bank profitability can be evaluated.

Information the systems provide often results in operating efficiencies or an altered marketing emphasis. Yet, branch managers are also critical of both systems. They contend the systems mask or distort the effectiveness of their management. Three common complaints of profitability measurement systems are that they:

• Distort the rate of return on funds. The simplest method for measuring the rate of return on branch funds is to credit a branch for income and deposits based on the average yield of loans and investments for the entire bank. This rate is an average of the bank's loan and investment portfolio. This bankwide average, however, can hide a below-average return on deposits. It also prevents a branch from receiving credit for any highly profitable loans it books.

• Obscure market differences. Certain branches handle primarily consumer business. Other branches attract substantial real estate or corporate business. Consequently, some branches have greater expenses per dollars than others. Branch managers generally insist that the system of profitability measurement relate performance to each branch's service mix and portfolio. They contend that if the system does not, it will lead to erroneous conclusions about branch effectiveness.

• Fail to correlate noninterest expenses to activity level. A branch may maintain or reduce its noninterest expenses. However, this apparent control of expense does not indicate whether the quality of a service has been maintained or if the demand for the service has diminished. Output may have decreased or there may be expensive unused facilities at the branch. Noninterest expenses should be related to activity so that the rise and fall of these expenses has meaning.

> **NOTE:** Although measuring profitability is important, it is also important to understand the shortcomings of different systems of measurement and to adjust those systems to give the truest picture of your bank's

profitability. *To be most useful:* A profit measurement system must follow profits and expenses over several years to show the existence of trends.

HOW TO SELECT THE BEST BRANCH LOCATION

Although most talk these days is concerned with closing branches, that doesn't mean new branches are not sometimes necessary. However, because a high investment of resources is needed, it is important to take a disciplined approach when you decide where to locate the new branch.

Situation Analysis. This analysis includes coding deposit and other customer records by government census tract or other territorial classification of government demographic statistics, summarizing the bank's performance in each tract, and comparing the tract results with estimated potential per tract as derived from demographics and other data.

The analysis can supply information about the bank's current service areas, show areas where it is not making a dent in the marketplace despite the presence of nearby offices, and reveal the types of people served as well as those not served. This may suggest other actions besides branching, such as changing advertising or promotional emphasis or introducing new services.

The specific data to be developed in the analysis include:

• The bank's customer totals by demographic area

• The percentage of the bank's total customer base represented by a specific demographic area to identify which areas are supplying the most customers

• The number of households in each area

• Estimates of the number of savings accounts or other service units available in each area

• The number of accounts held by the bank expressed as the number held by the bank per 1,000 households in each area

• The bank's penetration or share of the estimated savings accounts available in each area

Each service or product can be analyzed in a similar manner.

Large-area Screening. The situation analysis leads to large-area screening to identify the best opportunities for branching. This is accomplished by ranking the demographic areas by selected criteria.

The screened data typically include the area's population, housing, income level, employment, retail trade, industrial base, and financial institution competition. The criteria used in screening set minimum levels for some or all of these factors. The result of large-area screening is a list of the top areas for consideration as potential branch service areas.

Site Selection. For each potential site identified, the proposed service area should be defined through the study of natural and man-made boundaries (for example, parks, railroad tracks, roads, and so on), traffic patterns, the draw of nearby shopping areas, and location of competitors' offices.

Each proposed site should be judged upon:

• Economic and demographic data

• Planned service penetration of the bank based on the potential, the bank's current penetration, and the number of competitors in the area

• Cost of the proposed site (building, equipment, operations, and funds)

• Income projection based on the projected funds provided

• A breakeven analysis of investment versus income in order to determine the payback

From such analyses the best sites should emerge.

> **TIP:** With costs being what they are, this kind of thorough research is the only way to go.

CONSOLIDATING BRANCH OFFICES

Just a few years ago, marketing studies invariably showed that customers chose a bank on the basis of convenience. Accordingly, banks opened as many branches as possible based on the market area and the local laws. Now, of course, banks are finding that full-range, brick and mortar branch networks are too costly to maintain, and in addition, electronic facilities make many branch offices unnecessary. *Result:* There has been a growing trend toward consolidation or closing of unprofitable or marginal branches.

When to Consolidate. If research shows that a particular branch does not meet your institution's overall marketing objectives, it might be time to consolidate that office with another or close it completely.

Profitability is the key to the business decision. Regularly scheduled performance reviews of each branch assist managers in determining profitability. However, whether or not a branch is currently profitable is not the only consideration. Long-range analysis takes into account factors such as the average account balance, the number of accounts opened versus the number closed, and a profitability history and projection. Such statistics paint a telling picture. What may seem at first glance to be a marginally prosperous branch may, in fact, be a potential candidate for consolidation.

> **TIP:** The expiration of a lease is a particularly opportune time to assess the worth of any branch. Some banks automatically schedule a performance review one year before the branch's lease is due to be renegotiated. Before pouring hundreds of thousands of dollars into a longterm commitment for branch office space, management wants assurance that the capital investment is wise.

Providing Alternative Service. In making the decision to close a branch, bank managers must act responsibly, assuring that customers will be able to obtain alternative services. Usually, that means a nearby branch. Less often, it may be possible to arrange for another institution to take over the business of the branch to be closed.

Today, new innovations such as ATMs and banking by telephone and/or home computer offer additional options.

> **TIP:** If only routine day-to-day transactions are required, an automated location with a pair of ATMs can be operated for a fraction of the cost of running a full-scale branch.

Drive-in facilities present another alternative.

Steps to Successful Consolidation. Closing or consolidating a branch may adversely affect a bank's relationship with an important corporate, institutional, or commercial client that transacts business through that particular office.

> **ESSENTIAL POINT:** Inform all bank departments before any public announcement is made so that if there are serious internal objections the decision can be reviewed quietly, and rescinded if necessary.

If a go-ahead decision is made, representatives from the appropriate banking departments must meet to determine the effective date of the action and to assign responsibilities. Only then is it time to go public with the news.

It is most important to tell the employees before the branch is closed that they will not lose their jobs. Because of the high turnover in branch staff members of most banks, it is usually not difficult to place these individuals elsewhere in the branch system.

The branch's equipment must be inventoried and marked for disposition such as resale, transfer to another branch, storage in a central equipment pool, or otherwise disposed of. The physical facility itself may have to be sold or sublet if the move doesn't coincide with the expiration of a lease.

A special team of experts conversant with branch closing procedures usually assists branch personnel with the remaining operational aspects of shutting down the facility.

> **TIP:** If such a team is not available within the bank, it might be a good idea to hire consultants with this capability.

Such a team can also provide guidance on record retention, account transfers, and system utilization.

> **NOTE:** Careful planning for a branch consolidation or closing ensures the efficient continuation of business. It also minimizes the risk of adverse employee and/or customer reaction.

HOW TO ANNOUNCE A BRANCH CLOSING

There's probably no tougher move for a bank, from a public relations point of view, than closing a branch. Once the decision to close a branch has been made, the announcement should be handled skillfully.

Here is a press release from a bank in New England that does the job the right way:

> Decreased customer activity and lack of anticipated growth has resulted in an announcement by Old Colonial Bank that it will close two of its offices.
>
> According to Robert A. Apple, senior vice president, banking offices at Old Colonial Bank, the bank's office in Barnwell, and its office in New Farmingham will be closed at the end of business on March 31. All employees presently assigned to these branches will be reassigned within Old Colonial's banking offices group.
>
> "Besides looking at these closings from a purely business point of view, we have examined both branch closings from a community service stand-

point," Apple said. "The closings of these branches will not interfere with Old Colonial's ability to service the banking needs of the customers and communities involved because of the close proximity of other offices. Old Colonial fully intends to continue serving these areas and its valued customers."

The Barnwell office, which is located in a former shopping center...was opened in 1964. "The shopping center has been vacated by most of its retail establishments, and limited customer activity does not warrant keeping it open," Apple said. "In addition, the Barnwell Community College needs and wants to occupy the space we have." Customers of this office are encouraged to use [nearby offices].

The New Farmingham office was opened five years ago in order to take advantage of the proposed rebuilding of Route 17. "The long delay slated for the highway's construction will not allow this branch to develop as we anticipated," Apple said.

17

EFFECTIVE SYSTEMS MANAGEMENT FOR YOUR BANK

Technology has permeated the banking industry with an ever-increasing array of electronically based systems.

It is all too easy for a bank to become innundated with and/or enmeshed in a jungle of systems, both good and bad. To avoid this, the following requirements are necessary: skill in the development of a systems project, proper selection of systems, awareness of what any given system can (and cannot) do, and placing effective control over the systems.

CHOOSING THE RIGHT SYSTEM

What is the best or most appropriate choice for your organization? For a large bank, this might call for only a partial change in equipment. For the medium-size bank, this could involve substituting one service for another, establishing or closing an EDP center, or perhaps joining a group. However, to get the best results and make the best possible decision, an organized approach is absolutely essential.

To institute changes in your bank, an outside consultant should first be contacted although it may be possible to do without one. Still, an outside consultant can bring an objectivity not otherwise obtainable.

TIP: This will mean added costs, but if the consultant is used only at key points where he or she is most valuable, as outlined below, the charges shouldn't amount to much over the long run.

Consulting arrangements achieve the best results when the consultant and the bank staff work as a team. Each has a different contribution to make in the success of the project. The bank staff knows the bank's situation and culture. The consultant, having faced similar problems numerous times, knows the range of workable solutions. Together they can choose the best solutions.

Task Force Study. A task force composed of four elements is recommended for an effective EDP evaluation:

1. *Management Committee.* This committee should consist of senior officers representing the major areas of the bank impacted by data processing (operations, controller office, and so on). They are the deliberative and recommendation formulation body. The project manager should be chairperson of the committee.

2. *Staff Group.* This group should consist of experienced staff from areas within the bank that will be impacted by data processing. They should be responsible for detailed data collection and analysis. They should be under the direction of the project coordinator, and, indirectly, the consultant.

3. *Consultant.* This person should be the best all-round consultant possible. One way to think of a consultant is as a surgeon into whose hands you would entrust the life of your offspring—in this case, the bank.

4. *Project Coordinator.* This bank officer acts as the primary contact for the consultant on a day-to-day basis, paying a leadership role coordinating the other elements of the task force (1 and 2 above).

Implementing the Program. The work program should consist of the following steps:

• *Establish the decision criteria.* To evaluate various alternatives, establish a set of criteria with differing priorities. These include such obvious items as cost, quality of service, system reliability, and less obvious factors such as capability for innovation. The consultant works with senior management, the decisionmakers, in identifying and setting an appropriate priority for the criteria, by proposing various factors for consideration based on prior experience.

> **THE RESULT:** A list of criteria by priority which would be used in the evaluation of the various alternatives.

• *Determine the bank's requirements.* Requirements for any new system should be collected and documented, if not already available, for comparison with each of the proposed alternatives. This comparison should be the responsibility of the staff group under the direction of the project coordinator and the consultant. The requirements should be organized along four levels for ease of comparison:

- Application: the key service being provided (for exammple, on-line, real time, name and address file change).
- Function: the particular subactivities within each application (for example, the daily accrual of interest).
- Procedure: the manner in which each function is carried out (for example, interest calculation formula, format of input).
- Report: the structure, form, and content of all system outputs. The result of this step is a list and explanation of all user requirements in an easily referenced format.

• *Gather data on proposed alternatives.* This process is usually begun by requesting proposals from the various computer services and consortiums.The bank, with the aid of the consultant, specifies the content and form of these proposals. The bank should look for specific data on the services offered, the service itself, and the terms, conditions, and cost of the service itself. Typically, other documentation of a proposed system must be studied to obtain a complete and thorough understanding of the system. Secondarily, the review of that documentation affords insight into the management of the computer center. This work should be done by the staff group under the direction of the project coordinator and consultant. The results should be documented in a form that would facilitate an analysis.

• *Visit proposed centers and interview management.* Obtain and/or clarify information in the proposal or systems documentation, and observe the center and the center management in operation. The actual visits should be made by the project coordinator, the consultant, and any interested members of the management committee.

• *Visit and/or survey other users.* To obtain insight into the quality and reliability of the service provided, and to confirm information provided by the servicer, direct contact with specific users is essential. Such contact can be made by mail, telephone, or personal visit, whichever is most appropriate. It should include, wherever possible, banks that had left the servicer for whatever reasons. The direct contacts in this step should be handled by the project coordinator and the consultant. Members of the management committee could participate if they so desired. The results of this step will be a brief fact sheet on each serviced bank contacted.

• *Evaluate the data processing alternatives.* The staff group should prepare a matrix and supporting documentation comparing the various characteristics of each alternative. The form and content of that analysis should be provided by the consultant. The matrix and documentation should then be submitted to the management committee for review, deliberation, and formulation of a recommendation to senior management. The consultant should participate in this analysis and offer recommendations to the committee where appropriate. The consultant should also clarify issues and the meaning and impact of the various alternatives for the committee.

THE RESULT OF THIS STEP: A recommendation as to the best data processing alternative under the circumstances, along with supporting documentation.

The consultant should outline the structure of that report.

NOTE: Recommendations of the management committee and the consultant should be presented to senior management in whatever manner they find appropriate. The consultant and the project coordinator and the members of the management committee should then be available to answer questions and provide additional information.

HOW TO ORGANIZE AND MANAGE A SYSTEMS PROJECT

Tangible benefits from the investment involved in developing workable systems calls for effective project organization and management. Key areas of consideration for successful project organization and management are: project recognition, definition, planning, control, and evaluation.

• *Project recognition* is the process of identifying a change that constitutes enough potential savings or benefits to justify the initiation of a project. A key issue to raise at this stage is: Where are we today and where do we want to be. These two stages can best be compared and evaluated when characteristics of both the current system and potential modification or new system are measured against the following standards:
- Corporate policy
- Production costs and production performance
- Product cost, quality, and timeliness
- Risk, security, and regulatory considerations

• *Project definition* states the reasons (problems and/or opportunities) that initiated the project, the analysis of design alternatives proposed, and the selection of the most attractive systems solution. The first step in project definition is to define the opportunities/problems faced and the reasons why the current system is unable to provide a satisfactory solution.

One way to clearly state this definition is to create a problem definition statement that can be used as a reference and for control during further stages of development. Such a document should include:

- Name of current system and description of products provided
- Brief description of system procedures and methods, including flowcharts
- Areas and departments affected
- Related systems
- Problem statements—problem identification and problem sources
- Optional requirements

The next step under project definition is process analysis and design alternatives. In this step possible system solutions to the problem should be evaluated. Considerations include:

- Automated versus manual processes
- Revisions of manual and or automated processes or procedures
- On-line versus batch processing
- Enhancements to existing equipment
- Risk, security, and regulatory considerations
- Development time and development costs
- Equipment and software costs
- Operational costs
- Resource requirements

The description of each design alternative should clearly show how solutions to problems and optional requirements will be achieved and how the overall objectives of the system will be met.

• *Project planning* covers the determination of the activities to be performed within a project, the scheduling for those activities, and the defining of the costs and resources required for them. Basically there are three levels of project plans. They are the preliminary project plan, the integrated project plan, and the phase or activity plan.

- *Preliminary project plan.* This plan is used during the early stages of a project, and as scheduling costs and resources are defined in more detail, it will evolve into an integrated project plan through an updating process. Preparation of the preliminary project plan requires determination of:

+ Project objectives.
+ Development phases such as functional analysis, design development, design implementation, installation, and acceptance.
+ Control deliverables including cost analysis, system evaluation reports, site installation plans, system approvals, and sign-offs.
+ System deliverables such as functional specification programs and supporting documentation and documentation for system and acceptance tests, user procedure and operations manuals, installation, maintenance, and modification.
+ Project activities associated with each phase of the project, which should be presented in a manner for easy tracking.
+ Project milestones—points at which the project's progress or the entire project is reviewed. Although project milestones are basically for tracking purposes, sometimes failure to meet a major milestone may be reason to cancel the project.
+ Time, cost, and resource requirements—all resources needed and their associated costs.

- *Integrated project plan.* This plan evolves from updating the preliminary project plan and adding more detail. For example, activities are broken down into tasks and possible subtasks.

- *Phase or activity plan.* This plan is developed for those areas of the project, which, because of their nature, complexity, or duration, require a more detailed breakdown than that provided by the integrated project plan.

• *Project control* is a continuing responsibility of the project manager throughout the project life cycle. To achieve adequate control, the project manager should:

- Monitor performance and achievement
- Review products and deliverables
- Update project plans
- Conduct project milestone reviews
- Motivate project personnel

• *Project evaluation* should serve two purposes: (1) to give senior management the opportunity to confirm that objectives have been met and (2) record organization, management development methods, and procedures used and their effect in terms of successful completion of the project.

HOW TO SELECT SOFTWARE

The selection of software for your bank is a most important decision; poor selections can be costly in terms of money, inefficient operations, and lost time.

Here are some ideas to help you make the right choice when software must be selected:

1. Make a checklist of the features that are critical to the operation for which the software will be used.

2. Make a list of your minimum specifications and send a copy to potential vendors. Request literature and a certification that the software they supply will meet your specs.

3. Review the product literature and eliminate vendors that are less desirable in relation to your specifications.

4. Make a checklist of desirable features.

5. Based on an analysis of the information received, rank the vendor's software.

6. Make an evaluation of the vendors, using such factors as experience, size, support facilities, stability, company references, and any other factors important to you and your bank.

7. Select the top 3–4 vendors and ask them to visit the bank and make a presentation.

8. Following each presentation, rate the product against the list of desirable features (no. 4).

9. Rank the products after all the presentations have been completed.

10. Contact existing users of the software for their experiences, which will help to confirm your rankings.

Select a minimum of two software products for final evaluation and to negotiate a contract. Remember, software vendors are competitive and pricing is more an art than a science. The following guidelines may help in the purchase process:

• If the product is affordable, buy it.

• If it is to be leased, you can expect to pay a minimum of 3 percent of the purchase price each month.

• Expect, and arrange for, a purchase credit against a substantial portion of the lease payments.

Evaluate the terms of the contract. The following points will help you with the final contract:

• Don't buy any software that is not warranted against program defects.

• Expect the vendor to accept some financial liability, at least the purchase price of the product, should the software fail to perform as specified.

• Don't sign a contract without a guarantee from the vendor that it has clear title to the software.

• Maintenance terms and costs should be spelled out in the contract before it is signed.

• Make sure the specifications of the product are delineated in the contract prior to signing.

• Expect a "right to use" arrangement or a long-term license, not a title, when you buy.

In addition, the software supplier will expect you to guarantee that your bank won't reproduce or distribute the software. The vendor will also indicate that any customer modifications will invalidate the warranty. These are generally standard requirements and should be agreeable to you.

ON-LINE SUPPORT FOR SOFTWARE

There are three basic types of electronic user support: on-line documentation, on-line help, and computer-based tutorials. This discussion will concentrate on the first two.

The first issue in providing electronic support is the system itself: If the software application is designed with attention to human factor issues, then the task of support becomes easier and simpler. If the screen design, flow of information, and logical architecture is designed from the user's perspective as well as the computer's perspective, there isn't too much support needed.

Providing effective on-line support can decrease the learning time required to become productive on a system and decrease the amount and severity of problems while running the application. Providing on-line information results in users who know what to do, are more satisfied, make fewer errors, and need less emergency hot line phone support.

> **TIP:**   One of the best ways to provide support
> is to have quick answers available to the users
> while they are running the application.

This is typically known as *on-line help*. On-line help might include the following types of information: a brief introduction or overview of the application; screen descriptions; field descriptions, including format of entry, an example, and possible choices; and a glossary of terms.

The most effective on-line help pays attention to the following issues:

1. Keep it short. The help message should be short, preferably one or two lines, a window of information, or one screen.

2. Quick answers only. The help message should act as a memory jogger. It should not try to convey complex material or teach concepts.

3. Provide examples. If the help message is a field description, give an example of how to enter data into the field.

4. Quick and easy access. Make access to the help message fast, simple, and easy to use, such as pressing a function key.

5. Experienced first, novice next. If you have a two-part or/two-page help message, put information for the more expe-

rienced user on the first page, followed by additional information for the novice. The more experienced the user becomes,
the quicker it should be to find information. The novice can go
the extra step of asking for more help if the first page does not
answer the question.

> **NOTE:** If more than quick help is needed,
> then on-line documentation might be a
> solution. Information available in an on-line
> manual may include the following: orientation/
> introduction to the application, concepts,
> procedures, and reference material.

On-line documentation is typically longer than the quick
help message, and additional issues become important:

1. Provide selective access. Users should be able to quickly
access the particular information needed. If users want information on the uses of a particular command, they should be
able to get to it without having to page through introductory
material or descriptions of every command.

2. Make navigation easy. It is important for the user to be
able to move back and forth between pages, then skip, and exit
quickly and easily.

3. Be selective. Not everything in the hardcopy manual
will need to go on-line. Choose carefully the information that
should be on-line. Some information, such as how to install
system software, how to log on, and what to do if the system
crashes should obviously not be on-line.

SOFTWARE INSTALLATION CHECKLIST

There is a standard approach to take when purchasing a
software package:

• Determine your requirements

• Gather information on the products of competing vendors

• Narrow the field to products most suited to your needs

• Make a comparative study of the flexibility, cost, and performance standards of competing packages

• Then make your informed choice

This approach is both logical and effective. Yet, one aspect of this purchasing process that is often overlooked is installation, which can lead to serious problems. Banks that choose software packages without fully investigating installation sometimes suffer installation costs that exceed the price of the package.

Some of the aspects of installation you should discuss with vendors are:

• Does the vendor have a prompt delivery record?

• Does the package contain everything necessary for installation?

• What preplanning decisions are necessary before installation?

• Are installation procedures clearly defined?

• What effect will installation have on existing systems? How will it affect your current procedures and forms?

• How many labor hours will be expended in installation?

• Does the supplied documentation contain the appropriate information for full use?

• What changes will have to be made in your data files? When and how will the changes be made?

• Will installation of the product affect labor power? How many people will be affected? What retraining will they need?

• What hardware is required for full use of the product?

• Will the product cause any reductions in your bank's hardware? If so, what are they? How will unnecessary hardware be phased out?

• What savings will the installation of this package produce?

• Do other users of the product verify it functions as stated in the user's guide?

• What problems have other purchasers encountered during installation?

• What additions or modifications in your operations practices will be necessary to support the package?

• How will the shift to the new software be managed? Will there be a period of parallel operation?

> **NOTE:** Look at price, compatibility, flexibility, and performance when considering a new software package. However, do not forget installation issues as well; otherwise, an installation job may take months longer than you planned or not operate at peak levels.

WHAT MANAGEMENT INFORMATION SYSTEMS CAN AND CANNOT DO

Management information systems (MIS) conjure up thoughts of huge computer systems with high-density storage capacity and sophisticated throughput. As new versions of MIS are announced, everyone rushes to implement the latest techniques, frequently without having fully implemented an original version.

> **EXAMPLE:** One bank purchased a financial management information system four years ago. The MIS is composed of several modules, including a general accounting module, responsibility reporting module, budgeting, cost accounting, and the like. During the past four years only the general accounting and responsibility reporting portions of the system

have been implemented; the bank has not had the use of the complete system during this period.

At last review it was estimated it would take an additional two elapsed years to fully implement the system at an in-house cost of the bank running in the low six figures.

This bank is not alone in its predicament.

Many banks have purchased large systems during the past few years only to realize that the implementation effort, to date, has been a nightmare.

No system is a panacea. Too frequently, a bank will buy an MIS with the idea that the system will meet all its information requirements and also provide a method of replacing outdated, autonomous systems.

This result is realized only rarely for at least two reasons: (1) The time frame frequently needed to implement the system is grossly underestimated, and the integration or elimination of existing systems is put off until the new system is operational; and (2) a bank's information needs change constantly so that even when a huge system has been finally implemented, its information capability is seriously outdated.

The financial management information system the bank in the previous example purchased four years ago did not include any capability for asset/liability management, mathematical modeling for budgeting purposes, or "what if" capability for balance-sheet structuring purposes. Of course, these are all capabilities a modern bank must have to survive. Yet, the bank purchased the system with the idea that all its information needs would be satisfied for a long time to come.

An MIS systematically gathers and reports data that relate to the activities of the bank and which are necessary to manage and operate the bank efficiently. The system should also assist in complying with the bank's external reporting requirements. Certain broad objectives should be developed which will:

• Perform all reasonable functions to help collect necessary data

• Be flexible enough to respond to constantly changing conditions and new operating procedures

• Provide information in the best form for each task or function to which it is directed

• Reduce duplication of effort and information

• Provide a high degree of control

Unless the system can be installed within a reasonable timeframe and at a reasonable cost, the bank may not have the use of the system during a long implementation cycle. It is important to evaluate the system in terms of its probable life. Normally, the system becomes obsolete within five years.

NOTE: The system should not be purchased with the thought of replacing all other systems.

PASSWORD CONTROL OF TERMINALS

As commercial banks move totally into the on-line, real-time processing world of general purpose terminals, password control over terminal use becomes essential. Although some banks make a science out of terminal control, and the industry as a whole does a sound job, it is still surprising how many banks do a poor job of terminal access control.

Here are some guidelines with which to compare your own bank's performance.

PASSWORD CONTROL CHECKLIST

• Is an adequate password control procedure in practice to protect usage of the system?

• Is the control over issuance and use of passwords effective?

• Are all passwords changed and reissued at least semiannually, and are passwords immediately deactivated upon termination or deauthorization of their holder?

• Do procedures exist whereby a user can have his or her password invalidated immediately and a new one issued when it is believed secrecy may have been compromised?

• Must special authorization be received before passwords can be circumvented?

• Are the special circumvention conditions defined in the procedures that describe the password control system?

• Are the procedures to circumvent the password control system restricted effectively?

• Is there a control procedure over the use of the same password at different remote locations within a specific time period?

• Is the password system structured to permit varying degrees of data confidentiality?

• Is the password system designed to prohibit specified users and/or locations from access to certain data?

• Does the password system provide a control over access rejections?

• Is the password long enough to have sufficient combinations so that it cannot be easily broken?

• Is a security code utilized in addition to the password?

• Is the control over issuance and usage of security codes effective?

• Does the security system prohibit override of security codes?

• Is control exercised over user authorization?

• Is the authorization code structured to permit the user to perform (that is, either reading or updating)?

• Is the user authorization system designed to secure and protect file information on a data element basis?

• Is the control over issuance and usage of authorization codes effective?

• Are adequate controls maintained over coding systems for passwords, authorization codes, security codes, and lockwords?

• Are nondata processing personnel responsible for the maintenance of the security tables?

• Are there effective controls over the accessing, updating, and reporting procedures applicable to maintenance of internal security tables?

• Are internally balanced security table totals required after each update and before the resumption of data processing?

REVIEWING YOUR INFORMATION SYSTEMS

Equipment systems reviews are usually predicated on the belief that present methods do not meet present management needs or will fail to meet them in the immediate future. Therefore, it is a logical extension that the primary need is to determine what management information the system needs to generate.

It is apparent that the larger the institution, the greater the demand will be for information, if only from the standpoint that more levels of management will need more kinds of information. Also, there must be a clear definition of the subroutines required to produce management information. For example, a savings deposit can be traced from the point of transaction through its ultimate reflection on the financial statement and its supporting schedules. In addition, information may be required in relation to the type of transaction, average balances, hold orders, and volume statistics.

Volume Factors. Transaction volume levels create a distinct factor in arriving at preliminary conclusions concerning the types of equipment the operation needs. The greater the volume, the greater the justification for more sophisticated equipment. Volume factors can be gathered from these sources:

• Self-logging sheets
• Present machine transaction volume
• Subsidiary ledger transaction counts
• Source document counts

Alternate Applications. Because of the proliferation of equipment systems being marketed by nearly as many manufacturers, it is important that adequate comparisons have been made before finalizing a recommendation to management. Although the ultimate decision is the bank's, pressure from excluded manufacturers (on multiple proposals) may result in the bank indicating that its decision was based on a consultant's recommendation. Therefore, adequate and proper justification should be in evidence as the basis for the consultant's recommendation. There are two general areas of consideration in arriving at a particular systems application:

1. Operational feasibility
2. Economic justification

Operational Feasibility. Operational feasibility refers to the capacity of the individual equipment system to perform the intended job application(s) in a satisfactory manner. Obviously, the best source of such justification is the performance of the same type of equipment in an existing installation. Consultants normally have access to such performance data among their many clients.

> **NOTE:** Where completely new systems are being proposed and are not yet operational, more weight must be given to the manufacturer's statements about the equipment's capability. The quality of these statements is generally as reliable as the firm's reputation. Consultants who are not expert in equipment systems application usually secure the advice and counsel of those in the industry who are qualified to pass such judgments.

Economic Justification. Economic justification is not only a comparison between the various equipment systems being considered, but also a comparison against existing systems. Generally speaking, if more than one system possesses the capabilities to perform the operation being reviewed, the ultimate choice will probably be made on economic comparisons.

Factors for consideration in arriving at economic justification are:

- Book value of existing equipment
- Depreciation methods used
- Trade-in allowance
- Adjusted basis for depreciation
- Service maintenance contracts
- Conversion and setup costs
- Supplies costs
- Personnel costs
- Rental versus purchase comparisons
- Lease-purchase arrangements
- Space requirements

> **NOTE:** The recommended system should provide the greatest justification from a standpoint of operational and economic feasibility. However, one further point needs emphasis: Future requirements must be analyzed in any evaluation of systems for current use. If a system is recommended to meet a bank's needs today and has to be replaced within a year or so, the process will be a waste of valuable management time and a considerable amount of money.

18

AUTOMATIC
TELLER MACHINES
AND POINT OF SALE

One of the most noticable signs of the electronic age in banking these days is the automatic teller machine (ATM). Following rapidly on the heels of ATMs is the proliferation of point of sale (POS) terminals in retail establishments.

These devices, however, also present as many problems as they do opportunities. The issue arises of whether to join a network, which greatly expands the worth of an ATM to a customer. There is also the need to select the right site, and then make the site secure.

For POS terminals, there is always the concern over failure(s) in the system. This chapter will help you to deal with many of the problems involved with ATMs and POS.

SELECTING AN ATM NETWORK

ATM networks have been growing dramatically in number and size. Increasingly, third-party vendors, companies whose main interests lie outside the traditional banking structure, are involved in the delivery of one of banking's key functions: the debiting and crediting of transaction accounts.

Even experts define third parties differently. Some experts include the subsidiaries of bank holding companies, in their definitions. Others restrict their definition of third-party vendors to companies which are not in any way involved in services that hallmark a bank, namely, the taking of deposits and the lending of monies to commercial entities. These companies' services for an ATM network can run the full gamut from merely sorting transactions through the switch to selecting terminal sites and being responsible for supplying the terminals' cash.

There are many advantages for a bank to join a network run by a third party, including:

• The immediate ability to offer customers more locations to conduct their banking transactions at little, if any, extra capital expense.

• The opportunity to use generic advertising for the network to market your institution's participation.

• The benefit of having data processing, card processing, servicing of the machines, and customer assistance functions performed by the vendor.

Four Points to Consider in Making a Decision to Join a Network.

• To what degree will you lose control of your proprietary program? Each individual bank must look at its own strengths. If terminal placement has been a major facet of strength in your bank's services, joining a network that predetermines sites could be a disadvantage. If the quality of your service team is high, participating in a network that operates these services may have an impact on the degree of customer service.

> **KEY POINT:** A third-party vendor may be operating aspects of your services that you would rather control yourself.

• What considerations has the third-party vendor given to security? Most individual banks struggle to make certain that personal identification number (PIN) security, fraud, loss exposure, and the integrity of the data base are given high priority in their ATM operations.

KEY POINT: In joining a third-party vendor, it is important to know what precautions and security measures it has established that will enhance—not detract—from your ATM program.

• What leverage will your bank have in the governance of the network policies and regulations? What type of organization will the decision-making body of the network have? What role will the third-party provider have in deciding the direction of the ATM network? Will bank participation in governance be determined by asset size, transaction volume, size of card base, or some other criteria?

• What effect will third-party vendors have on competition? It could be that by entering into an agreement with a third-party vendor your bank may be restricted to a certain set of service offerings limiting the types of products your institution has available to its customers.

NOTE: Under this type of arrangement, the incentive to independently offer different services to the public would be markedly decreased.

PITFALLS TO AVOID WHEN SHARING AN ATM NETWORK

A network of ATMs is an attractive proposition for most banks. After all, ATMs help a bank compete in the modern business environment.

An ATM network can be used to attract a desirable market segment that tends to use multiple banking services. It enhances a bank's image and forestalls deposit erosion. An ATM network, however, requires heavy capital expenditures and is beyond the resources of most banks. For this reason, those small banks, which believe they require an ATM network to protect their market position, often join together to form a shared ATM network. In this way a group of banks provide services that are beyond their individual means. However, watch out! Not every shared electronic network succeeds. Some of the most common causes of failure are:

1. *Authority is not delegated.* An ATM network is a major commitment, thus senior managers try to stay involved. The bank employees who are supposed to coordinate the planning of the system, however, are then inadvertently denied sufficient authority to shape the network. They report back to their superiors to discuss and resolve even minor problems. The network evolves without a central coordinating force and with costly slowness.

2. *An overextended consultant or vendor.* The successful installation of an ATM network is a major technical and administrative challenge. It also requires the competent attention of an ATM consultant or some organization that has experience with ATMs. Unfortunately, ambition sometimes exceeds ability and a consultant will become overcommitted. In this case, the consultant has neither the time nor supplies needed to make the network a success.

3. *Poor initial planning.* For an ATM systemn to be profitable, it must attain a certain level of card distribution and transactions. On occasion, bank syndicates have taken an overly optimistic look at their potential transaction level. The syndicates have not honestly determined whether a profitable level can be attained. If the necessary transaction level cannot be reached, the banks should not proceed or else seek additional members for their organization.

> **KEY POINT:** Participating banks must also understand that an ATM system usually takes about eighteen months to mature. Until that time the system will generate a deficit. Participating banks must be willing to support this deficit. They cannot leave the syndicate because of its initial unprofitability.

4. *Poor marketing effort.* Occasionally, a syndicate fails to designate a full-time marketing person to coordinate the efforts of its various banks. Direct mail, lobby displays, and media advertising are used effectively at some banks but sporadically at others. As a result, the syndicate's overall customer base is not properly cultivated. The syndicate has not sold its new facilities aggressively. Instead, its managers have acted as if the ATM facilities would sell themselves.

MODELING ATM SITE SELECTION

Computerized models are being used by a number of banks to determine the best sites for branch offices and ATMs. With costs rising for both, sound decision-making in choosing a location is essential.

What Should Go into a Model. Facility site selection models are usually full five-year balance sheet and income statement forecasts. Such models also rank deposit and loan gathering potential of possible sites, and forecast and rank their profitability using the calculated income statements.

Nine Attributes of a Properly Functioning Model. For a model to function well, it must have:

• The capacity to examine a multitude of sites and rank them by deposit and loan potential plus ultimate profitability.

• The ability to differentiate among trade areas in making forecasts, based on local data.

• A computer-based network to speed examination time, but not through the data processing area because of its ongoing support of the bank.

• Comprehensiveness, by incorporating the wide variety of deposit and loan patterns found in diverse branches as well as their implications to many noninterest costs.

• Standardized input, using only readily available data in order to minimize expense and ease difficulties of collection.

• The capacity to be updated as often as necessary, for interest rate changes, inflationary expense, and so on.

• Flexibility, which allows for whatever changes management feels would be beneficial.

• Reasonably swift delivery of forecasts, so opportunities to bid on sites could be reviewed with model results.

• Minimal ongoing costs which would not affect the decision to model or not.

> **NOTE:** One of the first decisions to make is whether to go with an in-house version or to tap models already in existence. Some banks and service firms offer models for sale. In evaluating whether or not to buy the outside service, it is wise to consider how current the data are on which the particular model is based and what the vendor charges for each site run.

TEN STEPS TO ATM SECURITY

Keeping ATMs secure concerns all banks these days. The following tips will help:

1. Get your security officer involved in ATM discussions early in the planning phase. Do not wait until the ATMs are operational or until some serious assault or fraud loss occurs.

2. Attach a high priority to crime prevention and risk avoidance in early ATM planning.

3. Confer with law enforcement officials and bank security equipment experts early in ATM planning. Often, they will be able to suggest crime prevention and risk-reduction techniques that have proven successful in other installations. Indeed, seeking the advice of law enforcement officials is one of the mandatory requirements of Title 12 of the U.S. Code for all federally regulated financial institutions. This Title relates to security measures.

4. Make sure ATMs are considered to be security devices as well as marketing systems and replacement tellers.

5. Adopt the standards for ATMs that have been approved by Underwriters Laboratories (UL). Compliance with these voluntary standards provides a higher degree of protection. In addition, proving that UL standards were observed can have a positive effect on insurance underwriters, judges, juries, and so on, and can significantly reduce liability in the event of litigation or claims against your bank.

6. Give careful consideration to the need for camera or closed-circuit television (CCTV) surveillance as part of each ATM installation.

7. Give serious consideration to the safety and protection of employees and customers when selecting the exact location of the ATM. Avoid deserted locations where the risk of crime is high.

8. Locate ATMs in well-lighted areas. Some security experts recommend a minimum standard of 100 foot candles at the machine and 40 foot candles in the vicinity of the ATM as guidelines.

9. Locate ATMs in areas of high-density pedestrian and vehicle traffic so that the ATMs can be readily observed by the public.

10. Provide employees that are servicing ATMs with a safe and covert duress signaling device in the vicinity of the ATM so they can let you know if any untoward situation develops.

> **NOTE:** Paying close attention to ATM security will pay off, not just in fewer difficulties for the bank but in increased customer acceptance and usage of your machines.

MOVING FROM ATMS TO POS*

At some point, the majority of retailers hopes to have POS registers at the check-out station that electronically debit the customer's bank account. In a study on POS developments, The Federal Reserve Bank of Atlanta reported on the comments of a number of supermarket officials. When asked if they viewed in-store ATMs as a stepping stone toward point-of-sale terminals, many of the respondents said yes.

An official of one large southeast chain of supermarkets even implied that AIMs were being installed soley as an intermediate step. Another supermarket official said, "ATMs are going to work in certain locations, but they won't have the impact that POS will. Ulimately, POS will do away with check cashing. ATMs are simply another service for our customers."

In actuality, ATMs in supermarkets represent a role reversal between banks and retailers. Instead of absorbing processing costs and paying deposit fees to a bank, the bank pays the store a rental fee for the ATM space. The store receives the rental fee, and the owner of the ATM and the operator of the switch split the transaction fee. The customer's bank pays that fee, although it may pass the charge along to the customer. However, the store pays nothing.

If the supermarket or convenience store owns the machines, it receives the transaction fees and (hopefully) generates profits. However, retailers are usually content to let the banks or third-party networks own the ATMs. Still, if the banks or networks do not provide the customer coverage desired by the stores, they might well purchase their own terminals. For example, in one state where the banks seem to have not cooperated with the stores, a retailer said, "Owning our own machines is a major possibility if the banks don't get with it themselves." Interestingly, while the majority of retailers appear to welcome a transition to POS, there have been few moves made in this direction.

---

*This material was prepared with the assistance of experts at Tandem Computers, Inc. Tandem is heavily into POS equipment and systems.

The advantages to retail establishments of POS systems are obvious, because they extend the benefits they now receive from in-store ATMs. However, it is important to remember that the retail industry is consumer-driven.

Benefits Needed. It can be expected that POS facilities will only be implemented if the customer finds them beneficial. One study by the retailing industry indicated that the greatest priority of customers is a quick checkout. The rapid check-out times of POS registers could be a decisive factor.

The potential for POS is enormous. A study by The Antietam Group in Summit, New Jersey indicates that at leasts 11.3 billion annual transactions are prospects for an automated POS system. This was about one-fifth of the total payments handled by retailers in the study.

For banks, the implications of POS are also staggering. There undoubtedly would be a move away from checks. Certainly the volume of check cashing would be reduced, if not obliterated—a development most banks would welcome.

> **NOTE:** The potential use of ATMs for banks is there for the taking. Agreements for in-store ATM networks should not be entered into lightly, however. They should be considered with an eye toward the prospect of electronic POS systems in a future that is approaching rapidly.

DEALING WITH THE POS REVOLUTION

For years, people have been predicting the advent of a cashless–checkless society. Now, the movement toward making the prediction a reality is picking up speed. It could be that implementation is just around the corner.

Installation and acceptance of ATMs is the first real step toward the concept of "paying with plastic."

> **KEY POINT:** More important, ATM networks will serve as a base for the next

significant evolutionary step: the widespread implementation of electronic funds transfer at POS systems by retailers.

Concepts and Technology. Electronic POS systems allow consumers to make purchases using credit or debit cards by eliminating the inconvenience of carrying cash or writing checks. It is expected that shortly, billions of POS purchases currently paid with cash and checks will be transacted via electronic systems.

> **RESULT:** Merchants will benefit from improved cash management and reduced collection risks because both credit and debit cards will be approved or declined by the systems' authorization processes.

POS systems consist of three features:

- Merchant interface
- Switching process
- Authorization process or customer data base

The merchant interface—electronic terminals at the retail location—can be provided by the acquiring bank. However, some merchants have developed their own systems.

After information has been entered into the merchant terminal, the second step is authorization of the transaction. With credit cards, the information is switched to the authorizing service or bank, checked, and then the response is switched back to the merchant terminal.

Bigger Role for Retailers. Overall, POS networks are being developed as a result of the work that went into building ATM systems, which are controlled mainly by banks. However, in the POS world ahead, retailers are expected to pay a significant role in the owning and delivery of services. Many retailers would rather establish proprietary input, authorization, and switching systems which are then connected to a bank, instead of the bank placing terminals in their locations. *Their objective:* To allow retailers to deliver convenient services to customers more inexpensively.

The number of regional networks will probably decline through mergers. One or two networks—each with switching capabilities—may emerge in each regional area. The survivors will be the ones that provide superior service at reasonable cost.

Keys to this service will include network availability and functionality, as well as flexibility to allow retailers to run their businesses in whatever way suits them best.

> **KEY POINT:** Retailers will require 100 percent system availability which provides access to data bases or some other payment system process that allows them to make decisions regarding customer transactions.

Currently, rules governing who assumes the risk of accepting bad checks or cards—the bank or the retailer—when a computerized authorization system fails are not well defined. If authorization is not available, a database capability at the switch could eliminate this problem.

In addition, POS switches need to handle up to hundreds of transactions in just a few seconds from the time when a transaction is entered on a terminal until the authorization is received.

Finally, the needs for system security and data-base integrity are also important issues. With debit card transactions, for example, money is transferred during the authorization process, which requires a high degree of integrity in the data base to maintain strict financial control.

> **NOTE:** In the future, retailers and banks will find it increasingly necessary to cooperate in forming POS networks. This trend should allow retailers to play a much larger role in the POS market than in the past.

HOW TO PREVENT POS SYSTEM FAILURE

Consider the following example:

Because of competitive pressures, you decide to establish a POS network with neighboring banks in major retail and supermarket chains in your community. The cost of the network will be spread among network participants. You are asked to join a broadbased committee to oversee the design and installation of the POS system.

Your first concerns are technical in nature:

- What hardware and software will you purchase?

- How will they be installed?

- Will you need switching equipment to accommodate the computer systems of the different banks?

- What changes will you make in your back office staff?

These questions must be answered successfully. However, POS system failure is seldom caused by the failure to resolve technical problems. Rather, POS system failure is usually attributed to the following factors:

- *Point of sale apathy.* Management of supermarket and retail chains supports the POS concept. They understand that the convenience of POS terminals may bring additional customers to their stores. Also, supermarket executives find the check guarantee aspect of the POS service attractive.

> **PROBLEM:** Management sometimes fails to convey its enthusiasm for the service to the clerks who operate the equipment.

Consequently, use of the equipment varies according to the whims of individual clerks. At some stores clerks are intrigued by the equipment and encourage the customers to use the service. At other stores the clerks can't be bothered. Such clerical apathy reduces both customer interest in the service and transaction volume on the whole.

• *Some banks have a prejudice against joint ventures.* These banks are uncomfortable joining a banking network supported by their usual competitors. Some banks have a preference for ATM and telephone bill payment EFT services. They maintain that these services will attract the greatest consumer support in their marketplace. Some banks consider the merchant-oriented POS service superior to the consumer system. To them the POS merchant service is less susceptible to marketplace vagaries.

Because of these biases, these banks make only a tentative commitment in time and resources to the POS service. They argue that by limiting their commitment they will limit potential losses.

> **PROBLEM:** By limiting commitment, these banks are practically ensuring loss will occur.

• *Market considerations.* Each POS market has different regulatory, competitive, and demographic characteristics. The POS network also must adjust and market the service so that it will appeal to the consumer in this marketplace.

For many POS systems, marketing is inadequate. Strong initial efforts fade and customer usage does not increase after the first year of the service.

> **PROBLEM:** Network members fail to make coordinated marketing efforts and satisfactory transaction volume is never attained, or, the system makes a poor start and the expense of remarketing the service is prohibitive.

The POS service can be successful. However, success comes when network members know their customers and explain the services in terms their customers will accept.

> **NOTE:** If your bank decides to offer the POS service, do it right. Otherwise, you will

have to withdraw the service. An expensive investment, which is unused, is unproductive. It also will become technically obsolete.

19

HOW TO HANDLE YOUR BANK'S INSURANCE

Adequate insurance is necessary for individuals and for business firms; this also certainly includes banks.

In addition, with costs soaring in recent years, it is necessary to keep the cost of insurance under control as much as possible. A number of ideas for controlling the important issue of insurance costs are provided in this chapter.

IS YOUR BANK ADEQUATELY INSURED?

Insurance protection is vital to the safety of a bank's assets and personnel, particularly in these days of increasing lawsuits. The first step a bank should take is to conduct an audit of current insurance coverage. There are several objectives of this audit.

• Examine the manner in which bank policies on insurance coverage are fulfilled through procedures established by the insurance department.

• Examine the compliance with procedures by employees of the insurance and other bank departments.

• Examine records and reports relating to insurance operations.

• Report on the manner in which the controls are operating in relation to bank policy.

The audit should not attempt to cover such matters as the technical provisions of insurance policies or the adequacy of limits of liability because the auditor may not be qualified to give an opinion in these matters. It is advisable to have the extent of coverage generally defined in bank policy and specifically applied by the insurance department in consultation with any necessary outside counsel. The following procedures can be used to audit your bank's insurance program.

1. Secure and examine statements of bank policy covering insurance, and discuss these with the insurance department.

2. Review written procedures, memoranda, and other material to determine that:

a. Instructions are in force covering the procurement and maintenance of coverage in accordance with bank policy.

b. Procedures are adequate for both the insurance department personnel and personnel of operating units reporting on insurance matters to the insurance department.

3. Review contract files, lease files, and pertinent correspondence files in the insurance and other departments (such as real estate, construction, and purchasing) to determine that the insurance department is informed of risks to which the bank may be exposed so that adequate coverage may be maintained in accordance with bank policy.

4. Prepare a schedule of policies in force with outside carriers showing:

Coverage
Exposure
Locations
Premium
Other pertinent data

5. Review policies to ensure that types and limits of coverage are maintained in general accordance with bank policy.

6. Examine policies and related correspondence to verify that:

a. Policies on file are listed in the schedule and policies listed on the schedule are on file.

b. Policies are safeguarded adequately.

c. All significant data are shown on the schedule.

d. The bank is shown as the insured.

e. Where applicable, subsidiary locations and companies are specified.

f. Endorsements are physically attached to policies.

g. Required premiums or deposits were reasonable and accurate.

7. Review and test the procedures followed by the insurance department to assure that:

a. When orders for insurance are placed, binders and policies are received.

b. Renewal of policies is adequately controlled.

c. Policies are considered for renewal in sufficient time to permit consideration of changes.

d. Invoices for premiums and deposits are reviewed and approved by the insurance department before payment.

e. Financial position of small local insurance carriers is periodically checked.

8. Secure a copy of any reports rendered to management on general insurance department operations.

a. Test-check any financial figures shown on reports, such as premium cost, insurable values, claims paid, and savings made, with appropriate original records.

9. Discuss uninsured losses with the insurance department manager to determine whether losses arose because of a risk assumed under bank policy or through failure to follow established procedures.

10. Fom your knowledge of bank operations and background, discuss with the insurance department any risks which may not seem to be covered by insurance to determine that these risks are considered in the determination of bank policy. *Discuss also any situation where there is any question in your mind regarding the necessity of insurance presently being carried.*

11. From observation and discussion, determine situations in which the insurance department control and operations appear to be handicapped because of poor coordination.

12. Test-check premium charges, as derived from the insurance department records, with entries on the bank's accounting records.

> **NOTE:** These procedures require certain assumptions as to general policy and assignment of responsibility that may vary considerably from the situation in any specific bank.

> **EXAMPLE:** The program assumes that there is an authoritative and comprehensive statement of bank policy in insurance matters and assignment of responsibility for the insurance program to a specific insurance department. A normal outcome of this particular situation may well be a recommendation in the audit report—showing from the audit findings that a statement of bank policy or more definite assignment of responsibility is necessary for effective administration of the insurance program.

REDUCING INSURANCE COSTS

When the public thinks of bank crime, it usually thinks about robbery. However, robbery is only one of the crimes that affects the cost of blanket bond insurance premiums. Insiders scheme to embezzle depositor money; conartists attempt to pass worthless checks. A bank suffers needless insurance costs when these and other crimes are abetted by inadequate security procedures.

The checklist following presents seven security measures your bank can undertake in areas most often criticized by insurance companies.

SECURITY CHECKLIST

• *Cash on hand.* Institute better control of teller and vault cash. This means working with your bank's accountants to determine peak business hours when more operating capital than usual will be needed. Even during peak business days, move cash out of teller stations and into the vault on a frequent basis. Schedule armored car pickups accordingly.

• *Alarms.* Consider installing sophisticated central alarm stations for the main vault safe-deposit area, night depository, teller cages, and branch locations.

• *Audits.* Consider using a full-time audit department or retaining outside certified public accountants to do annual unqualified audits that would include a high percentage of verification.

• *Loan practices.* Meet with your bank's senior loan officers and ask them about the lending practices of your bank. Insurance companies continually cite the failure of banks to adhere to proper lending practices, particularly where collateral is concerned. They often ask, "How much collateral is ever verified?"

• *Personnel.* Work with your personnel department to ensure new employees are screened properly. The entire staff should be fingerprinted, and careful checks should be made on their business and personal references. You should receive reports from personnel on current employees who may be in financial difficulty or have had a brush with the law. Many insurance companies make the additional suggestion of using a polygraph test for prospective employees in sensitive areas, such as tellers, computer programmers, and certain operations personnel.

• *Check processing.* Suggest all checks be recorded on microfilm before they are sent off to a processing center.

• *Prosecution policies.* Develop with senior management clear-cut policies on prosecuting employees or outsiders who defraud the institution.

> **NOTE:** Study your security procedures in these seven areas. Determine what changes you can make to enhance your security. Then inform your insurance agent after you have tightened procedures.

> **KEEP IN MIND:** A slight modification in your security arrangements may produce savings in insurance costs over the next several years.

FULL COVERAGE FIRE INSURANCE

Let's suppose your bank establishes a new branch. The lease contains options to purchase the building where the branch is located. If the branch is successful, you plan on making major improvements in the premises before purchasing. To protect your bank's interest, you should be sure the improvements are insured against fire loss.

> *EXAMPLE:* In one case in New York, unwary tenants of a motel–restaurant found themselves in an untenable position: A fire rendered their purchase option worthless, and the fine print in their policy limited them to less than a 7 percent recovery for their losses.

In the example above the tenants operated a motel–restaurant; however, the same thing could happen to any corporation that rents and improves commercial space. The one-year lease gave the tenants in the example an option to buy the property if they exercised the option at any time before the lease expired. Then tenants spent more than $15,000 in fixing up the premises and obtained what they thought was sufficient fire insurance coverage for "improvements and betterments."

Shortly before the lease was to expire and before the tenants exercised the purchase option, the fire totally destroyed their premises. The tenants then asked their insurance company to reimburse them for the value of the improvements.

The fire insurance carrier pointed to a provision in the policy limiting the tenants' recovery for improvements to only a portion of the loss prorated over the unexpired term of the lease. The tenants had only 23 days remaining on their lease at the time of the fire. Thus, the insurance company contended that the tenants could only recover 23/365 of their losses, or less than 7 percent.

The tenants maintained that the purchase option gave them a full insurable interest in the property, but this argument fell on deaf ears. A New York court ruled that the policy's language was very clear and that the tenants had no further right to any additional recovery. [(See *Vendriesco* v. *Aetna Casualty & Co.*, 414 N.Y.S.2d 64 (App. Div.)]

> **NOTE:** Do not let yourself be caught in a similar situation. If your bank has spent a considerable sum on improvements, obtain coverage in an absolute dollar amount that is not prorated over the unexpired term of the lease.

DATA PROCESSING INSURANCE COVERAGE

Insurance for data processing is one subject which seems mystifying at a distance but is really straightforward once one is able to obtain it. The guidelines that follow attempt to give you a head start in overcoming the initial anxiety of obtaining this insurance. They are designed to take you step by step through the items you should consider when deciding on coverage for your data processing installation.

DATA PROCESSING INSURANCE CHECKLIST

• Check individual lease contracts from vendors to determine liability for physical damage, equipment, disks, rental tape, and subleased equipment.

• Check insurance policy for exclusion due to electrical or magnetic erasure or damage.

• Determine replacement value of purchased equipment, subleased equipment, and all equipment located at remote sites.

• Consider transportation costs for replacement equipment.

• Define valuable papers and records versus media. This includes those records kept internally for billing purposes— that is, a check can be either a valuable paper or media depending on its status in the processing department. Is coverage provided for both?

• Is coverage provided for any installed cables for visual displays plus installation cost and connector fee?

• Consider transportation and installation costs of raised flooring.

• Consider vaults, card files, tape files, and disk cabinets which are normally listed under regular furniture and equipment.

• Determine maximum value, in both dollar amount and number of items, of papers, documents, and media that will be in the data processing center at any one time.

• Determine the amount of deductible, take into consideration the backup procedures, microfilm storage of original copies, and difficulty of restoration.

• Consider degree of security backup in relation to value of programs and documentation.

• Consider dollar value of forms on site at any one time: stock forms, preprinted forms card stock, ribbons, expendables.

• Consider value of business interruption. Study exclusions such as no coverage for the insured for services rendered to the parent company, subsidiaries, or affiliates.

• Consider dollar value of accounts receivable processed for other companies.

• Consider dollar value of bursting equipment, tape cleaners, and other auxiliary equipment.

• Consider errors and omissions coverage. Consider air conditioning units.

• Does policy include coverage on outside users of equipment?

• Is intentional and unintentional damage caused by the bank's own employee covered?

The following equipment and procedures should be considered because they tend to minimize damage, deductibles, or amount of coverage:

• Fire protection and smoke detection equipment to reduce rates

• Security installation to minimize or reduce damage from outsiders

• Fire drills using marked fire exits

• Emergency power OFF switch located by door

• Battle lanterns emergency lighting

• Loudspeaker system to alert personnel

• Fire-fighting equipment and extinguishers

• Personnel trained in use of fire-fighting equipment

• Extinguisher near trash can

20

OTHER OPERATIONAL CONCERNS TO CONSIDER FOR BETTER CONTROL

This chapter includes a roundup of operational items that do not fit specifically into any of the preceding chapters. They are all important, however, and the ideas presented can improve operations and exert better control.

ACCOUNT INFORMATION CONSOLIDATIONS: THE CIF SOLUTION

To develop a complete and current picture of an account at some banks, it is necessary to make inquiries at several different departments. Certain customers, for example, have checking accounts, savings accounts, and personal loans, and also are affiliated with one of a bank's major corporate accounts.

Tracking down information from all the involved departments can be tedious and time-consuming. This diffuse system of information storage also produces a considerable degree of record duplication and problems with determining account profitability. To surmount these problems, banks are turning to the central information file (CIF).

The CIF solution. A central information file brings together all the information on checking accounts, savings accounts, and loan information of a single customer. The advantages of purchasing this computer software and establishing CIF at your bank are:

• *Streamlined recordkeeping.* CIF reduces certain clerical operations such as bookkeeping and key punching and reduces a bank's paper needs. Because account information is stored in a single file, account maintenance is simplified. The bankwide file also makes it a simple matter to develop a current picture of an account relationship.

• *Improved account analysis.* CIF provides a bank with a means of identifying the scope of a relationship and a systematic standardized body of information that can be used to determine account profitability. CIF thus becomes a valuable tool when determining prices for your services.

• *Improved marketing.* CIF delineates a full account relationship and improves your capacity for intelligent cross-selling. In addition, because the full range of a customer's business is available to a teller whenever the customer enters your bank, the customer receives more convenient, rapid, and informed service.

> **CAUTION:** CIF is a valuable source of information when the information in the file is accurate. Often, however, tellers make errors (usually before a bank's system is refined), which require time and effort to correct. Furthermore, the system must be seen as more than additional software to your tellers if it is to be used properly.

Because CIF complements your marketing program and can be used to determine pricing, special training is necessary to reap its full benefits. Do more than train low-level personnel on CIF if you expect to get the most out of this investment.

> **NOTE:** When shopping for CIF, look for flexible software that does not require preconversion of files and which provides solid

documentation. Such features will make the software more effective both in the long- and short-term.

CHECK TRUNCATION CATCHES ON

A growing number of banks are truncating checks—that is, not returning checks to customers with their statements. It also seems that customers are not objecting or not objecting too strenuously.

Many of the banks that have been successful in selling check truncation to their customers promote free check storage instead of check truncation itself. They also promote the storage service in conjunction with ATMs, automatic transfers, and other innovative banking services. First-rate marketing is often necessary before storage service is accepted by consumers. However, bankers make the marketing effort because of the advantages and cost savings enjoyed by truncating banks.

The Paper Blizzard. The banking system processes an estimated 40 billion checks annually. To handle these checks, the banking industry has huge investments in laborpower and expensive check-processing technology. Truncation appeals to bankers because it reduces:

• *Staff size.* Bulk filing is the major back office precursor to check truncation. According to the Bank Administration Institute, bulk filing programs can reduce personnel needs in the check-filing area by as much as 60 percent.

• *Equipment costs.* There are currently two major check-truncation techniques. Banks using internal truncation store their own customers' checks. Banks using intercept truncation have other banks store the checks. These intercepting banks receive checks through the payment system, electronically capture magnetic ink character recognition (MICR) encoded data, and then send the information to the customer's bank.

• *Postage costs.* Monthly statements that include cancelled checks and promotional materials generally require extra postage. Monthly statements for truncated accounts generally require only standard postage. Over a year's time the extra costs for standard accounts can be significant.

A bank with an internal truncation system must have:

- A bulk filing system
- Adequate microfilming and check-sequencing capabilities
- Sophisticated data-processing equipment

Intercept truncation, however, requires little investment in technology from the payee's bank. Under the intercept procedure, the intercept bank microfilms, stores, and retrieves requested checks. In some areas, the fee for this service is less than the cost of supporting full standard check-processing services.

In the next decade check truncation may become commonplace at commercial banks. After all, the process is a sensible antidote to rising check volume and processing costs. There also are other factors besides the banker's desire to reduce expenses. For example:

- Competition from other financial institutions may force banks to promote the service. Credit union share drafts are comparable to checks. They are relatively cheap for credit union members to acquire because there is no return of the share draft. Commercial banks may soon have to offer "free storage" checking or they may begin to lose checking account customers and balances to the cheaper share draft service.
- Successful programs throughout the country have proven consumers will accept truncation. They accept the service when it is marketed as free check storage. They also accept the service if they have confidence that their cancelled checks can be located, microfilmed, and mailed to them quickly.

NOTE: If your operating procedures are effective and your bank's marketing is persuasive, your customers should accept truncation. Truncation, in conjunction with effective bulk filing, also will produce major savings for your bank.

HOW TO PREPARE FOR AN INTERNAL BANK AUDIT

Banks face audits from a variety of sources ranging from bank examiners and other supervisory authorities to internal auditors from the comptrollers of auditing departments. In addition, many operations managers may want to periodically conduct their own internal audits to ensure their operations are running smoothly.

Efficient auditing is developed in four stages: planning, verification, evaluation, and reporting. Of these, planning is by far the most important. It defines the scope and sets the limits for the examination. If an audit is started under one plan and the plan is subsequently revised, the entire audit may have to be started anew. Therefore, it is essential that audit plans developed carefully.

A Preliminary Survey. Once the major audit area has been defined, a preliminary survey should follow to determine the significant areas for concentration of audit effort. Its purpose is to get a quick impression of the operating problems and the kinds of controls needed to cover the risks. A preliminary survey should answer questions such as:

- What is the job?
- Who does it?
- Why is it done?
- How is it done?

The preliminary survey also gives the auditor a chance to understand the people doing the work and the type of managers who lead them.

The survey can be completed quickly if the auditor has a clear idea of what information is needed. Some of the records that should be requested by auditors include:

• Copies of management's policy statements, directives, and goals for the current period, plus statements of functions and responsibilities and delegations of authority.

• A copy of the department's organization chart showing the detailed organization and its position in the company's structure.

• The nature, size, and location of subsidiary organizations, if any.

• Financial information, such as operating statements, other regularly prepared reports, and information on assets, including their location and nature.

• Operations manuals.

• A documentation of operating methods, usually in the form of a flow chart.

An Exploratory Interview. An exploratory interview with the general manager is desirable.

> **SUGGESTION:** To avoid wasting expensive executive time, an advance appointment should be made, unless a surprise audit is required.

In setting the interview time, avoid the period right before lunch, the end of the day, or late on a Friday afternoon. If possible, set the interview shortly after the workday begins, while both the interviewee and auditor are still fresh.

Conducting the Interview. As a preliminary to the interview, learn something about the manager, such as his function, his language in that function, his experience on the job, and his results. Much of this kind of information should be obtainable from prior audit reports, financial statements, and other operating reports.

Here are some sample questions that are applicable to most operations:

SAMPLE QUESTIONNAIRE

• Has the department's role been documented and communicated to other departments?

• Has complete authority been extended to carry out the department's role?

• Is department performance measured by:

accomplishment of objectives
staying within budget
on-time performance
recovery of operating costs
customer complaints
number of people
cost savings
feedback from other departments
personal judgment

• Have acceptable performance standards been established in the areas chosen to measure the department's performance?

• Have the department's objectives been documented and ranked according to their importance?

• Is the accomplishment of objectives reported regularly?

• When objectives are not accomplished, what review or action is taken?

• Has senior management reviewed the department's annual operating plan?

• Are there any particular areas or concerns that you would like to have examined by the auditors?

The interview should be limited to one hour. After an hour the point of diminishing returns has been passed, and the worth of the extended interview diminishes as time expands.

Limiting the interview to one hour usually creates a more receptive atmosphere for additional conferences, should they be necessary. Even if all the points have not been covered in the initial hour, set up another appointment rather than prolong the interview. Conclude the interview as pleasantly as it began. Summarize your facts before leaving. Above all, thank the executive for his or her time.

> **NOTE:** During the interview, the auditor should take sufficient notes to stimulate recall but still avoid trying to record the entire conversation. Do not use a tape recorder.

THE UNRECONCILED DIFFERENCES TASK FORCE

Erratic behavior in an EDP system is often signaled by a mounting volume of differences—a volume too great for the regular staff of investigators to handle. When that happens, there is usually only one solution to clean up the situation: form a "difference task force."

Using a Tested Program. Following is a tested program for use by such a task force.

DETERMINE THE SITUATION

• Select a cut-off date and get copies of general ledger G/L and cash-proof system (CPS) reorts.

• Define accounts and cost centers to be included in the effort.

• Collect and/or locate all suspense tickets, transfers, documents, and items that have been posted to G/L or CPS.

• Sort items by date within cost center within account.

• Collect all free or extra items (checks), process (clear) items, and create suspense.

• Prove items to G/L and CPS as of the cut-off date by cost center:

- note items not on G/L or CPS
- note G/L or CPS entries with no items

TOUGH ITEMS GUIDELINES

• Set guidelines for tough items:

- lack of description
- number of days outstanding (based on cycle for each cost center)
- special cases

• Establish standards or work paper documentation for audit trail and develop an investigation worksheet.

• Identify all tough items for task force investigation.

• Order tough items in a priority list:

- dollar amount
- days outstanding
- type of items

CONDUCT INVESTIGATIONS

• Assign teams that include one person with specific knowledge of an area to be supported by those with general knowledge.

• Have each team select items for investigation from a priority list (taken in order) and follow the item to resolution to maintain continuity of the investigation.

• Document all investigations according to standards set up for work paper documentation.

• When each item is resolved notify the center that originated the item about its resolution.

• After an agreed upon number of days of unsuccessful investigation, list the item as a candidate for possible write-off.

ESTABLISH ONGOING MONITORING

• For each cost center, assign the responsibility for clearing differences and monitoring the center's suspense accounts.

• Arrange to send unmatched teller transfer and suspense account reconciliation reports to cost centers on a daily basis.

• Require each cost center to prove and reconcile these reports daily.

• Investigate outstanding items and clear them.

• After an established number of days of unsuccessful investigation, list the item as a candidate for possible write-off.

• Require the task force coordinator to monitor cost centers to ensure that daily proof is being done.

• Require the task force coordinator to ensure that no items remain outstandinng after a specified number of days, and, if they do, to justify these open items to senior management.

HOW TO SIMPLIFY FORMS LANGUAGE

Many states have passed legislation in recent years that requires banks and other companies to provide customers with understandable forms and contracts. Because courts may find agreements invalid due to a lack of understandability, it is helpful to have a set of guidelines to follow in creating these documents. Here are variations set forth in plain English by Carl Felsenfeld and Alan Siegel in their text, *Simplified Consumer Credit Forms.*

• Write well. Obtain a respected guide such as *The Elements of Style* by William Strunk, Jr. and E. B. White or Allen Bernstein's *Do's, Don'ts and Maybes of English Usage.* Then follow it.

• Design your document. Increasing emphasis is placed not only on the use of words but also on the format in which they are presented. Making each point visually important to the reader, once considered merely good communications, is fast becoming a part of contractual law.

If a well placed, clearly expressed provision of an agreement is contested, it most likely will be upheld in the courts even if a party to the contract failed to read it and was therefore unaware of it.

• Get help from communications experts, particularly if you are not a language specialist with a knowledge of readability testing and measurement procedures. Many lawyers, though willing to assist, are so accustomed to reading legal jargon that their review is often less objective than that of a good communications specialist.

• Test each provision for its business function. Your ultimate goal in preparing a form or agreement is to help the consumer understand exactly what he or she is getting into. Writing in a consumer-understandable style requires examination of each point in the context in which it is used. Some questions you might ask yourself in refining the writing and design are:

- Will the consumer take this seriously, as in the case of a loan agreement, or treat it as casually as a small appliance warranty?
- Will the reader have the assistance of legal counsel? In this case a more complex form may be acceptable.
- Under what circumstances will the consumer read the document? If the document will be read when ample time is available, you will acceptably be able to use less simple terms.
- What is the level of sophistication or maturity of the typical reader?
- Do statements made in the document lead the consumer to reasonable conclusions?
- Within the context of the transaction, how important is each particular provision? The document should be structured, whenever possible, to place the greatest emphasis on the most vital aspects of the agreement.
- Would further simplification of a statement make a significant difference in the meaning or understanding of a point in question? If not, it's probably worth making the change.
- What empirical evidence—that is, sources on language formula tests, results of comprehension tests, expert opinions, or changes from prior versions exists?

• Test the usefulness of the protections that the provisions of your contract provide, keeping in mind the specific needs of your bank. Some risks may be so minor you may not wish to cover them in the agreement. However, there may be perils that, however improbable, you do not wish to chance. Such decisions will be strongly influenced by the size of your institution and the type of transaction you are dealing with.

• Follow up your efforts with formal testing. Because the response of a person to any particular statement is affected by his or her background, for example, job, upbringing, education, prejudice, the document should be consumer tested prior to publication. Use any or all of the following methods:

- Although your document should not be designed specifically to pass a language formula test, such a yardstick, when applied well, can measure the true effectiveness after the writing is done.
- Use a test group of potential customers for a valuable question-and-answer session.
- A "plain English" test may be administered to sample customers, focusing on the understanding of terminology, facts, and principles and the ability to calculate what will happen under given circumstances.

> **NOTE:** Revising bank documents to conform to the "plain English" doctrine is more than a tedious exercise. Beneath it all lies the intrinsic public relations value of improving customer relations.

HOW TO ENSURE ADEQUATE DATA PROCESSING DOCUMENTATION

Documentation is one of the most talked abut issues in data processing. It is also the area most often criticized by bank examiners, external auditors, and internal auditors.

Here are some guidelines for adequate documentation developed for the regulatory authorities' own use.

DATA PROCESSING DOCUMENTATION PRINCIPLES

• Documentation principles:

- Documentation: collecting, organizing, and storing all recorded information about a given problem and its method of solution.
- Purposes of documentation:
  1. Simplify revision by providing full detail in support of each program.
  2. Aid in instructing new personnel by providing background on previous programs and serving as a guideline for new programs.
  3. Provide operators with current operating instruction.
  4. Serve as the basis for an evaluation of internal control.
- Basic forms of documentation:
  1. Run manual (complete program documentation): An organized collection of all documents pertaining to a data-processing problem and its solution.
  2. Console run book (operating instructions): An organized collection of all documents pertaining to the operation of the computer. The console run book is a section of the run manual. This section is duplicated, bound, and used to provide operating instructions for the machine room personnel.

• Typical run manual:

- General
  1. Title page
  2. Table of contents

As a permanent record, the manual should be organized as clearly and logically as possible. A title page and table of contents will improve the logical presentation and organization of the data.

• Problem definition

1. Original project request and approval programs are usually prepared in response to requests of user departments. The request should be approved by the data-processing manager and the systems analyst. The approved request becomes a part of the documentation in case there is a discrepancy between the resultant program and the desired result. In many instances, data processing may have finished a program in accordance with a user's request only to find the user had not defined the problem properly.

2. Problem statement: This is usually prepared by the systems analyst and is the basic source of information concerning the program.

3. Economic evaluation of new system: If the new program or system has an economic justification, it should be documented in the run manual.

4. Functions of control group: Because the control group is an integral part of the data-processing system, its function in relation to each program must be clearly defined. The control functions must be fully outlined and documented as part of the run manual.

• System description:

1. System flowchart: Indicates the source and nature of all input, machine, computer, and manual operations, and the nature and disposition of all outputs.

2. Record layouts are an essential part of program documentation and must be included for all inputs and outputs. For example, card layouts should include field names, field locations, field sizes, a description of control punches, a description of file identification, and the layout and content of all labels.

3. Other system information needed to explain and describe the system should be included as part of the run manual.

• Program description:

1. Decision tables are an aid in determining if all possible decision combinations have been provided for within the program. These tables, although they are not in common use, can be a very valuable aid to programming and should be considered for use in all installations.

2. Program flowchart: This is a pictorial representation of the logic of a computer program. These charts are an absolute requirement in any documentation effort.

3. Source desk or coding listing serves as back-up in case the source deck is lost or destroyed. Each listing should be dated and only the latest listing should be retained.

4. Assembly printout: A copy of the most recent program listing should be part of the documentation. Without such a listing, it would be almost impossible for anyone to follow the coding flow and logic.

• Operating instructions

1. Description of program: The machine operator should have a basic understanding of the purpose of the computer program. This allows him or her to operate the program with a more intelligent approach and helps to prevent him or her from committing gross errors. The description of the program should be brief and stated in as simple and straightforward a manner as possible.

2. Card layouts: The operator should have copies of layouts to guide in punching replacement cards in case cards are mangled during processing.

3. Keypunch instructions: A copy of the keypunch instructions for all input cards should be included to give the operator additional assistance in case it becomes necessary to punch replacements for damaged cards.

4. System setup diagram: The operator should be given detailed instructions on how to set up all the individual devices to be used during the computer run.

5. Operating instructions should define the operators duties in starting, running, and terminating the program. Nothing should be left to the operator's imagaination.

6. Console messages and halts: This is a list of all messages and halts contained in the program and instructions for the action to be taken in response to each message or halt.

• Acceptance record:

1. Test data (input): Copies of all test input should be preserved as part of the documentation. Every time a program is modified or changed, the test input should be processed and the output compared with the original test output.

2. Sample output: See test data (input).

3. Program change sheet should be a record of all changes made in a program since its original implementation. The record should show:

a. date of change

b. reason for change

c. approval of change

d. approval of change test results

4. Documentation review comments and approval: When a program is first prepared, the documentation should be reviewed and approved by a responsible authority such as the program manager or the data-processing manager. This review and approval should be recorded in the run manual. Every time a revision in the program is made, the manual should contain an approval of the revised documentation and an acknowledgment of the related correction or corrections to the console run book.

PART FOUR

THE BUSINESS
OF THE BANK

The facilities, personnel, and operational activities of a bank are all essential aspects of the banking business. However, they are all of little value without offering services to the public that result in income for the bank.

Banks were originally established as the safekeeper of funds, which of course, they still are. Then, the lending of those funds made banks more useful and profitable. Nowadays, banks are broadening their activities even further by providing new and/or more refined services and offering services that generate fee income. All of these new services increase the complexity of the banking business and increase the potential problems to bank management.

In this section, there is extensive coverage of banking services. Several chapters relate to commercial lending and retail lending. In addition, Chapter 28 specifically covers marketing and several other chapters cover the aspects of the overall marketing function or the selling of the bank and its services to customers and potential customers: advertising, business development, customer relations, and public relations. These areas are growing in importance as banks face stronger competition from within the industry itself and from other firms in the expanding financial marketplace.

21

EFFECTIVE MANAGEMENT
OF BANK SERVICES

If nothing else, banking is a service business. As such, it is vital for a bank to know what costs of its services are, which, in turn, allows the banks to price those services realistically in order to contribute positively to the bottom line.

This chapter includes some specific services that have been growing in importance for many banks: financing buyouts, cash management, and lock boxes.

HOW TO DETERMINE WHAT A NEW SERVICE COSTS

Consider this situation: Your marketing department recently surveyed the banking needs of the major corporations in your marketplace. The survey indicated very strong interest in the direct deposit payroll (DDP) service. According to the survey, about one-third of the largest corporations in your bank's marketplace already have the service. However, a majority of the remaining companies plan to introduce the DDP system in the near future.

Your marketing department is eager to develop and offer DDP. Soon after it received the survey, the department held meetings on the service. Preliminary decisions were made on product definition, strategy, and marketing costs. Then members of the department came to you and made a presentation. "Well," they said, "what about it?"

Determining the Cost of New Services. You cannot give the marketing people a quick answer to their question. However, you can set to work immediately and study the operational impact of the DDP service.

At a major regional bank, the initial aspects of new service investigations are conducted with the help of the following checklist. The list is used to guide the first stages of new product development. It also is used to ensure that no major operational facet of a new service is overlooked.

New Service Checklist. The checklist has three major sections as shown below.

TECHNICAL AND OPERATIONAL

• What is the new service? How is the service defined?

• What is the operations flow of the service?

• What equipment will be required? Is new equipment needed? Can existing equipment be used? Will existing equipment have to be replaced?

• What are the throughputs of the service? What are the input requirements? What are the output requirements?

• What will the equipment supporting the service cost? Should it be leased? What are the maintenance costs?

• What personnel will the service require? How many employees are needed? What is the midpoint salary range?

• Will the new service require additional personnel? Will you utilize current personnel? Are there retraining costs? Will the service reduce personnel needs?

• What forms and supplies will be required?

• Are there unique costs (for example, postage, special forms)?

• What are the occupancy requirements? Will the bank need new space? Can it utilize existing space?

DEVELOPMENT COSTS

• What are the development costs of personnel?

- What are the development costs of equipment?
- Are there other development costs? What are they? How much do they cost?

IMPLEMENTATION COSTS

- What are equipment installation costs?
- What are training costs?
- Are there other implementation costs? What are they? How much do they cost?

> **NOTE:** The checklist is meant to structure new service queries; however, it is only as good as the person who uses it.

IDEAS ON PRICING BANK SERVICES

Too often pricing of bank products and services is decided upon incomplete and/or inappropriate information. A simple solution frequently adopted is for a bank to simply follow what the local competitor is doing. The problem with this approach is that the competitor is probably doing exactly the same thing—a virtual case of the blind leading the blind.

Another solution entails the bank employing a very sophisticated pricing approach which systematically computes costs and adds a margin to arrive at a price that guarantees a profit. One problem here is that the costs to provide a regular savings account for an average customer during an average month may range up to $7 or $8 a month.

The main difficulty is that a typical financial institution offers dozens of products and services to hundreds or thousands of customers. Tracking costs to each of those combinations of products and customer segments is difficult at best. Also financial institutions have high fixed costs. When the controller decides where to allocate fixed costs, minor changes in allocation can result in huge differences in allocated costs. These factors are probably more important in explaining cost differences between institutions than any real differences in actual costs.

> **FACT:** The customer has a choice in the marketplace among the various banks offering financial services. Costs themselves are meaningless to the customer. The bank might be able to convince the customer that a certain service costs $3 or $4 a month to provide but if the customer can go up the street and get it for less, that's where he or she will go.

According to Dr. William D. Wilsted, former dean of the University of Colorado's Graduate School of Business, "Prices should not be based on what the competitor up the street is charging, or, for that matter, on the specific costs of providing financial services. Neither meets the criteria of complete and appropriate information." What does meet these criteria? Dr. Wilsted sees proximate value pricing as the answer.

> **KEY POINT:** The single most important factor relating to the price of products and services is the value of those services to the customer.

Proximate value pricing is a market-proven approach to pricing goods and services based on value to the customer. That value or worth is determined by four factors that constitute components of proximate value: product utility, customer alternatives, customer perceptions, and customer capacity.

Product Utility. By far the most important single factor to pricing, and the most important component of value to the customer, is product utility. Product utility is the usefulness of the bank's services to the customer. There are four generally recognized types of utility:

• *Form utility.* Form utility occurs when the bank designs a product based on economic or customer need. For example, a customer comes into a bank and asks for his or her single most valuable economic resource, a paycheck, to be accepted in order to create more valuable forms out of it; for instance, apply it to a checking and savings account and a mortgage. The bank can be confident of creating value because the customer came in voluntarily and surrendered the paycheck.

• *Place utility.* Place utility is the usefulness to the customer of the convenient locations at which banking services are available. Branching is one way to create place utility for customers; ATMs are another. The customer can go to a convenient location and take advantage of the majority of the bank's services without having to enter the bank's lobby.

• *Possession utility.* A customer is willing to pay a higher premium for possession than any other utility because it allows him or her to take possession at his or her discretion or take something in a different legal title form, which provides either tax or cash-flow benefits. The auto industry recognized long ago that customers are willing to pay hundreds more in options on automobiles for the opportunity to have the car right away instead of later. Each time bankers finance a lease or grant a loan they provide the customer with the opportunity to take something in a different title form to provide tax or cash-flow benefits. Possession utility is provided with every service sold.

• *Time utility.* Financial institutions know a lot about time utility. Bankers pay their own employees, or someone else's employees, to work through the night to account for transactions so that customers can walk into the lobby the next day and be given a complete update on their accounts. Now the normal work day is being extended through ATMs offering availability of many services twenty-four hours a day.

ANOTHER ITEM FOR CONSIDERATION:
Research shows that 60 to 85 percent of the bank's customers select an institution on the basis of convenience, and convenience is nothing more than time and place utility. Fewer than 15 to 40 percent make their selection on all other factors related to value as

product utility. However, there are other factors, too.

The Customer's Alternatives: the competition. In terms of competitive pressure, the classic pricing response is to reduce the price. Yet, analysis indicates that in 99 percent of all pricing situations, reducing the price is the wrong answer. Reduction in price reduces net profitability for the institution without solving any competitive problems.

To reduce a customer's alternatives to any extent, a pricing opportunity must be created. The most direct way to do this is through product differentiation. Customers must be persuaded that another institution's services are poor substitutes, and, thus, not real alternatives. A pricing opportunity is created by offering the customer better quality products and services.

Customer Perceptions. Frequently, there exist in the marketplace, perceptions about institutions and their products. Often, these perceptions are not based on fact. However, it is important to remember that when perceptions differ from fact, they often are more important than the fact in the marketplace.

To build a pricing program on information that meets the criteria of completeness and appropriateness, a bank must be able to measure and identify the existence of perceptions. It also must evaluate their impact on its ability to market its services in the competitive marketplace.

Customer Capacity. For a market to exist for a service, three things must be presented simultaneously: (1) market demand, (2) sufficient numbers of people who can afford to pay the price reflecting the value, and (3) sufficient numbers of people who can afford the price who also are willing to pay the price. These three factors constitute demand.

If the service cannot be sold at a price that returns the cost of its production plus some margin of profit, three alternatives are available.

• The cost must be reduced so that the price reflecting the value will cover cost plus the desired margin.

• The service might be redesigned to enhance its ability to meet customer needs, and, therefore, raise its value and price.

• The service can be withdrawn from the marketplace.

> **NOTE:** The correct price is set by the marketplace in a market where the customer has a number of alternatives for purchasing financial services. Products and services should be priced and promoted on the basis of proximate value rather than on the basis of "what the market will bear" or on what it costs to provide the product or services to the marketplace.

COMPONENTS OF A CASH MANAGEMENT SERVICE

A corporate treasurer sits at a CRT terminal in his or her office and calls up data on the company's financial position in order to make some investment and foreign exchange holding decisions.

The scene above is commonplace these days as sophisticated corporate cash-management systems have been introduced by many banks. Tight money, high rates, and the down cost of idle funds have all contributed to the realization of the value of sound cash management.

Fund Utilization. Today's cash-management techniques generally fall into three categories: cash gathering, including lockbox banking, wire transfer, depository transfer checks, freight payment plans, preauthorized payments; cash disbursing, including decelerated bill paying, playing the float, payable-through-drafts, and zero-balance accounts; and cash control, including information-only wire, account activity analysis, account profitability analysis, and computer models.

Cash-gathering activities are designed to accelerate the conversion of receivables to cash and to concentrate that cash in central points for maximum utilization. This is done by minimizing mail and check float and by rapid check collection and money transfer.

Lockbox banking attacks the problems of mail and check float and generates cash balances. Truncating checks at a central post office within a region in which they are drawn enables banks to reduce remittances in transit to one from as many as three days, depending on the location of the buyer in relation to the receivables office of the seller.

To minimize operating costs and to optimize customers' earnings potential, many banks are now stressing "bullet" lockbox systems—lockboxing checks only over a given dollar amount. The company instructs only selected customers with large dollar invoices to remit to a lockbox. All routine payments go directly to the company's own offices.

Retail payments for credit card purchases, installment loans, and insurance premiums are generally lockboxed because their processing costs can often run high, since the job is people-intensive and requires considerable sorting, listing, duplication of documents, and other handling.

Transferring funds by wire. There are as many formulas for determining the dollar amount and timing of transfers as there are companies using the technique. However, the formulas all center around transferring given minimum amounts over some predetermined compensating balance as the deposit funds become available.

Depository transfer checks (DTCs) offer the simplest and least expensive means of consolidating funds. Deposits are called into National Data Corporation (NDC) each day from all over the country where they are immediately entered into a computer file. At a given time each day they are transmitted by wire to their designated concentration banks, which prepare and deposit the DTCs.

Freight payment plans and preauthorized drafts are specialized cash-gathering techniques meeting the needs of particular industries. Under a freight payment plan, freight bills are sent to a bank, which immediately credits the checking account of the carrier and charges the checking account of the shipper. Preauthorized drafts are popular in the insurance industries, where the bank, on standing authority, periodically pays out an amount to a third party from a customer's checking account without the customer having to draw a check.

Slowing the Outflow. Cash disbursing methods are concerned with decelerating cash outflow and minimizing the time deposits that lie idle in checking accounts awaiting payment of outstanding checks.

Decelerated bill paying is perhaps the most common way of slowing down cash outlays. With this method, bills are paid due but in the slowest way possible, with the exception being invoices where discounts are offered. Most discounts are taken because it is almost always more profitable to give up the funds earlier and get the discount than to employ them elsewhere until the net due date.

Many companies also refuse to mail remittance checks to a post office box address, knowing it is probably a lockbox. They slow the payment by mailing the remittance directly to the company. Other large companies with disbursement accounts throughout the country conserve cash by paying west coast bills with checks drawn on east coast banks and vice versa.

Playing the Float. To the corporate treasurer, float is the sum of outstanding checks at any given moment. If understood and monitored closely, float can be employed for profit. By playing the float, the corporate treasurer is, in effect, using the funds twice.

The key to successfully playing the float lies in a company's accuracy in anticipating the timing of charges against its accounts and in its ability to forecast the amount of float available for investment. A constant charting of check flow is an absolute necessity.

Bank corporate cash management systems should be designed to allow the corporate treasurer to maximize the use of float provided there always are collected funds on deposit when checks are presented and that the base balance is maintained.

Zero Balance Accounts. These accounts are used to eliminate subsidiary account funding. The accounts are overdrawn daily and the bank is authorized to make daily transfers from a parent account to cover the overdrafts. The company deposits are made only to the parent account, effectively utilizing its balance.

The Importance of Cash Control. Cash control is primarily information management, the support function and the very heart of cash management. Among the components of cash control are:

- *Information-only wires.* Bank notifications of balances, deposit activities, lockbox remittance data, and any other such information a treasurer needs to monitor cash flow.

- *Account activity analysis.* The periodic comparison of the daily balance in the company's checkbook with the balance on its bank statement to determine the average float the company has to play with.

- *Account profitability analysis.* The placement of a dollar value on the services the bank is providing and the compensation the bank is receiving for those services. To the corporate treasurer, account profitability analysis is a measure of the effectiveness of cash utilization.

- *Computer models.* A system that integrates a company's total banking activities. Such models have built into them, in terms of mathematical equations, all the banking activities of a company, including company agreements with its banks, the price of bank services, agreed compensation terms, and all internal company policy constraints. By feeding into the computer data on the levels of account activity from monthly account analysis, cash-flow forecasts, and so on, corporate decisions on which banks should be used for disbursements or who should receive tax payments and other deposits can be optimized, conserving cash and minimizing opportunity costs. Computer models also provide programs for the maximization of investment and foreign exchange resources.

NOTE: Most banks' corporate cash-management systems offer increasingly sophisticated features for cash gathering, disbursement, and control. The banks whose systems provide the greatest accuracy, speed, and superior performance results in terms of its computer modeling will gain an edge in the marketplace.

LOCKBOX IDEAS

Lockbox, which is perhaps cash management's oldest product, will continue to remain an important product offering in a bank's relationship with corporate customers. Paper processing will be around for a long time to come.

Customer demand for lockbox services, albeit in a different form and using new technologies, will probably continue to be strong and these services will remain an important and integral portion of a total bank/corporation relationship.

Should a Bank Be in the Lockbox Business? A bank that intends to pursue the corporate market vigorously must offer lockbox capability. As the importance of traditional credit services diminishes, especially in the large corporate market, information and cash management services increase in importance. However, from a bank's perspective, lockbox services should be evaluated from a product, as well as a relationship, viewpoint. Ideally, a bank should be able to make a profit in a straightforward product profitability analysis. At the very least, a bank should attempt to have lockboxes break even on a product profitability basis. The capital and labor investment and the type of technologies and networks chosen by an individual bank will significantly affect its breakeven and profit levels.

Types of Lockbox Services: pros and cons. The least sophisticated lockbox operations involve conventional proof. These systems require low capital expenditures, are flexible, and can handle any kind of payment. However, they are also labor-intensive, have problems with peak volumes, and offer relatively few control mechanisms. This type of system has significantly declined in recent years.

The next level of sophisticated lockbox operations is a transactions-oriented system in which checks are scanned and micro-encoded and information is keyed into a terminal. The advantages of this type of system are that it involves relatively low labor costs and a modest capital investment. In addition, it offers increased controls, the ability to handle peak volumes, and a unique market positioning. However, it is relatively expensive to expand such a system.

Inventory-oriented systems offer yet more sophistication through image-lift technology. They provide lower labor costs, increased control, good peak volume capability, flexibility, and a unique market positioning. However, the initial capital investment is quite high.

One bank uses a system based on scanner-optics and image-lift technology. The process can be broken down into a number of steps:

1. Sort and reader sort incoming information.

2. Scan optically for terminal functions.

3. Operator 1 check, micro-encode, and enter terminal information.

4. Operator 2 verify.

5. Lift receivables information from the invoice to enter in the terminal and later merge with other records.

> **NOTE:**   What about the future? Here are some predictions about lockbox operations in the years ahead:
> - Companies will ask for and receive more customization and more information gathering capabilities.
> - Companies will be willing to pay the premium needed to get these services.
> - Banks' costs will decrease once initial automation investments are paid off.
> - Paper will remain the normal payment mechanism.

THE EQUIPMENT LEASING DECISION

At first, only the largest banks used lease financing. However, banks of all sizes are now finding that leasing is a profitable business which a growing number of customers desire. Moreover, because of the phase-out of interest deductibility for individuals, the 1986 Tax Reform Act makes leasing even more attractive to both banks and their customers.

There are several reasons why a lender may find it desirable to consider equipment leasing:

• Full service progressive image. Many lenders feel that by adding the leasing function to existing product lines, it places them closer to achieving complete financial service capability.

• Attract new customer base. Leasing may attract customers that previously obtained this type of financing from other sources, thus offering the bank an opportunity to cross sell other financial services.

• Maintain existing customer base. Leasing permits a lender to offer customers an alternative method of financing, eliminating their need to seek financing services elsewhere.

• Tax shelter. Leasing permits a lender to take advantage of the tax benefits of ownership, such as the investment tax credit and accelerated depreciation.

• Profits. Leasing may improve a lender's profitability by several hundred bsis points over the conventional lending rate.

Development and Implementation. To develop and implement a successful leasing program, three key ingredients must be included:

1. Commitment of senior management. Management of the parent organization must openly and aggressively support the leasing concept. This acceptance will filter down to other management levels of the bank.

2. Commitment of resources. From inception, the leasing operation must have the personnel, equipment, support services (legal and accounting), and a readily available and adequate supply of funds.

3. Constant force in the marketplace. The leasing company must develop an aggressive reputation of desiring new, good quality business on a consistent and regular basis.

> **NOTE:** A leasing operation must be managed with the same dedication and understanding as any other division or department within a well run and profitable organization. Knowledge is the single most important element to a successful operation.

It is important to understand the impact of decisions. If there is a doubt or lack of understanding regarding certain terms or conditions in a lease transaction, a bank should not be forced into closing until those doubts have been removed.

22

COMMERCIAL LOAN MANAGEMENT STRATEGIES AND TECHNIQUES

Commercial or business lending is in a state of flux at many banks. Banks are finding that a growing number of business customers are using other sources to obtain funds, often in the commercial paper market. Still, commercial lending remains— and always will remain—a mainstay of a bank's business.

This chapter, and the three that follow provide a variety of ideas, procedures, and recommendations to improve this segment of the market.

One problem some banks have faced recently is ineffective management control of the lending function. This cannot be tolerated, and Chapter 22 provides guidance in an area that will always be important in banking.

KEEPING LOAN POLICIES CURRENT

With credit regulations, market conditions, and sometimes interest rates changing almost daily, bank loan policies must constantly adapt to those changes. The problem is how to communicate these changes to all lending staff.

Put All Changes in Writing. After the bank's loan policy is adopted by the policy committee (and approved by the board, if required), the policy should be printed and distributed to all lending personnel.

Each time a revision is made, update the appropriate policy manual pages and send revised pages to all holders of the manual. Put a notice on the cover sheet to alert recipients that the materials must be read immediately before being added to the manual.

Updating Made Easy. With careful planning, loan policy changes can be successfully managed to reflect the ongoing business environment. Here are seven tips on how to manage these changes:

• Design for flexibility. Use a looseleaf notebook so that only changed sections have to be reprinted.

• Rate changes. Consider printing minimum rate schedules for all loan types on one sheet. Generally, loan rates change more than loan conditions so this will substantially reduce typing and printing costs.

• Telephone prime rate increases. Since many loans are keyed to the prime rate, telephoning remote locations in anticipation of the printed revision will give a day or two of extra income at the increased rate.

• Use form letter disclosures. Have a standard letter ready to advise customers of rate changes. This will speed the notification process while ensuring that required disclosures are properly made.

• Audit review. Have staff auditors check for adherence to loan policy, including the requirement that the loan policy manual be kept up to date.

• Loan review. Credit audits and normal loan review procedures should use the loan policy manual as their standard. Deviations should be reported to senior management.

• Management accountability. Management at all levels must understand their responsibility to make loans in conformance with loan policy. The directors must make it clear that this responsibility cannot be delegated.

HOW TO RATE COMMERCIAL LOAN RISKS

Many banks are trying to tighten their lending procedures and improve the quality of their loan portfolios. Does your bank have a system that compares the risk of a particular loan to other loans on its books? Pricing on each loan should be in accord with the risk of that loan. What system does your bank have for relating the price of a particular loan to the price of loans of comparable risk elsewhere in your bank?

One east coast bank, which specializes in loans to middle market companies (a growing market for many institutions), uses a risk-rating system to answer such questions as those posed above. At this bank a two-digit code is used to classify loans. The first digit indicates the risk of lending to a particular borrower. The second digit indicates the risk of making a particular kind of loan to that borrower. The code is reviewed each time a loan is reviewed or renewed.

Rating the borrower. The system used by the bank has four categories for evaluating the risk of lending to a particular borrower. These categories are:

- Cash flow

1. Very strong for five years
2. Definitely sound
3. Satisfactory, but possible problems
4. Acceptable, but historically erratic
5. Inconsistent, possible inadequate debt service coverage
6. Not dependable

- Financial condition

1. Very strong and liquid
2. Definitely sound
3. Satisfactory, possible future liquidity uncertainties
4. Acceptable, declining trend in liquidity and earnings
5. Definite problems: short-term borrowing supports long-term assets
6. Weak

- Repayment situation

1. Very strong, excellent debt service coverage
2. Definitely sound
3. Satisfactory, but possible problems

4. Sufficient, but threatened by economic, business uncertainties

5. Repayment from contingent financing

6. No clear repayment source

• Management

1. Excellent: strong and experienced financial team

2. Definitely sound: generally strong and experienced financial team

3. Satisfactory top management, but little depth

4. Acceptable know-how

5. Definite weakness, relies on outside advice

6. Inadequate

To determine an overall risk number for a borrower, loan officers add the appropriate number for each risk category and divide by 4; a rating 1 is great, a 6 is bad.

Transactions are also rated on a scale of one to six, with 1 being a well-secured loan to a highly rated borrower, and 6 being an unsecured loan to a low-rated borrower. There are three categories of secured loans, from 1 to 3, and three categories of unsecured loans from 4 to 6. The risk-rating system works as follows:

> **EXAMPLE:** Let's say a borrower has satisfactory cash flow (3), his or her financial condition is definitely sound (2), repayment situation is satisfactory (3), and management is excellent (1). Adding the numbers, the total is 9, resulting in a left digit of 2.2. Let's also say the loan will be secured by the company's receivables. Based on his or her knowledge of the customers, the loan officer assigns a right digit of 2. The final rating is 2.2/2.

The bank generally will make a loan if the two numbers are three or better. In this case, the loan probably would be made.

NOTE: No rating system is foolproof, and this one has the disadvantage of being partially subjective. However, it has the advantage of being easy to administer.

THE IMPORTANCE OF DOCUMENTATION

The use of bank deposits as loan collateral can be a great comfort. The collateral, for one thing, is accessible. Realizing the security, for another, requires only a few bookkeeping entries. There is no need here for a cumbrous foreclosure sale as with other types of collateral—for example, a car.

A pledge of deposits is the bank's right of setoff. A pledge of deposits, of course, is made by a written contract signed by a depositor, whereas the setoff is a right under common law or one specifically created by a state statute. Both enjoy much the same benefits, but they are not the same thing. This point becomes obvious when the two are in conflict with one another.

How Conflicts Occur.   For conflicts to occur, all that is needed is for a depositor in bank A to take out a loan at bank B and pledge his or her bank deposits in bank A collateral for the loan by bank B. When this happens, the bank with the deposits—(bank A)—will be relying on its right to setoff to cover any defaults of its depositor; bank B will be looking to those very same deposits as collateral for its loan. This sets the stage for potentially serious conflicts.

The bank most comfortable with this confrontation between a pledge and a setoff is the bank with the right of setoff. It, after all, has the bank account in its possession. However, this isn't always the case. *Example:* An Illinios Savings and Loan learned this hard lesson when it saw its admitted right of setoff thoroughly beaten down by a California bank's pledge. The case involved a depositor in the S & L who assigned two of his savings deposits in the S & L to secure a loan at a commercial bank.

The commercial bank had the S & L depositor sign a formal pledge agreement, and then followed through by taking all the steps necessary in California to nail down its security interest in the deposits. The depositor turned over his passbooks to the commercial bank while the commercial bank forwarded the assignment to the S & L for acknowlegment. The S & L signed and returned an acknowledgment, indicated the balance, and confirmed that there were no prior assignments. It also admitted there were no setoffs, claims, or defenses. Later, faced with a default by its own depositor, the S & L exercised its right of setoff against the two savings accounts. The commercial bank, however, felt the S & L's right of setoff was subordinate to the commercial bank's prior pledge. The bank won its case because of its prior pledge.

> **NOTE:** Securing a debt with a savings account is often a good way to boost the quality of a sagging credit. However, assignments must be properly executed and acknowledged before you have rights to the collateral.

> **CAUTION:** Particularly when dealing with other banks, make sure you have acknowledged assignments and signed sight drafts in hand before advancing funds.

REVIEW THOSE LOANS

Particularly since Penn Square, banks have been increasingly concerned about reviewing loans. A growing number of banks are setting up loan review departments to ensure that loan officers follow loan policy and that problem loans are identified.

Sometimes, however, a loan review staff is simply too expensive for a bank; for some smaller banks, the size of the loan portfolio doesn't justify the full-time loan reviewer.

Use Your Lending Officers. According to one senior loan officer who has worked at banks of varying sizes, any bank should, at a minimum, be able to rely on its loan officers to spot problem loans.

> **TIP:** In the senior loan officer's bank, for example, performance appraisals include the officer's loan loss ratio *and* whether the officer advises superiors of potential problems.

If troublesome loans show up only after a review has taken place, the loan officer must be able to supply a good explanation.

In the daily administration of a loan, there are numerous opportunities to review loans. When statements come in from a borrower's accountant, the bookkeeping department may be called upon for authorization to pay an overdraft or draw on uncollected funds. Information pertaining to the borrower may appear on the public record, or the credit department may receive an inquiry from other than a normal trade creditor.

These and similar items allow the leader to contact the borrower and can keep the bank on top of the loan situation. Any information gleaned from such instances should be put into the borrower's file for future reference.

> **NOTE:** Another step that can be taken is to have the auditing department check the loan documentation and other related paperwork that pertains to the less subjective areas of credit information.

> **TIP:** Spot reviews will also help to reinforce a bank's commitment to the loan review process.

EARLY WARNING SIGNS OF PROBLEM LOANS

A bank cannot simply react to troubles with its borrowers. It must anticipate and identify problems before they get beyond help. The following checklist, adapted from Citibank's "Credit

Doctrine for Lending Officers" provides some items to consider:

MANAGEMENT FACTORS

- Change in key executive or director or auditor
- Change in ownership
- Evasive answers to direct questions concerning recent or projected performance
- Any major acquisition
- Unavailability of internal information, such as projections, financial statements, and accountants' management letters
- Change in nature of the borrower's business or objectives
- Imaginative accounting
- Expressions of dissatisfaction with treatment by another bank or with present auditors
- Refusal of permission to talk with company's auditors
- Organizational transitions; for example, moving from an entrepreneurial management style to a more formal decentralized one
- Late submission of financial statements
- Poor financial controls
- Arrogance in place of borrower cooperation
- High-style personal and corporate living habits by the principals of young enterprises
- Diminishing margins of profitability regardless of how they are computed
- Decline in net income or unseemly growth in profits that may result from such changes as the purchase of another company or the opening of new sales outlets
- Decline in sales or too rapid rise in sales
- Adverse changes and trends in relation to key industry statistics; for example, sales per square foot of retail space
- Deviation from normal seasoned borrowing pattern

• Changes in the market value of equity in relation to book equity

LEVERAGE AND FINANCIAL FACTORS

• Major sale of assets

• Decline in inventory turnover

• Buildup in the ratio of receivables to sales

• Unfunded cash requirements, including large current or near-term debt maturities

• High leverage, not only financial but operational (for example, high fixed costs)

• Stretching payables

• Decline in net working capital

• Delays in seasonal cleanups

• Inability to finance outside the banking market

• For nonfinancial borrowers, the inability to clean up simultaneously at all banks

• Financing by other banks on terms less onerous than those your bank considers appropriate

• Slowness in trade

• Violation of covenants or agreements (yours or others)

• Credit refusals by other lenders

• Requests for refinancing or an extension of term loan payments or revolver maturities

• Delays in stock offerings or expected financing by long-term lenders

• Any public offerings at unusually high rates

• Unusual increase in overdrafts

• Downtrend in the ratio or retained earnings to total assets

• Any adverse industry information including regulatory

• Adverse stock market letter reports

• Change in ratings

- Adverse international developments
- Cresting markets, industries, or borrowers
- Unusual increase in trade inquiries
- Changes reflected in your own bank and trade checks

23

COMMERCIAL LOAN PROCEDURES

Chapter 23 contains several nuts-and-bolts ideas to assist lending officers in exerting control and more precise monitoring of outstanding loans.

LOAN APPLICATION CHECKLIST

One of the reasons for delays in the processing of loan applications is incomplete information. Delays also lead to complaints from would-be borrowers. The checklist below allows applications to be reviewed to ensure that the needed information is there.

- Introductory material
  - Nature of the business
  - Amount requested and for what purpose
  - Method and term of repayment
  - Security or collateral, if any
  - Estimated earning to be generated by loan proceeds

- Company history
  - Type of organization
  - Date established, ownership changes
  - Subsidiaries, where located
  - Industry background, company's position in it

- Names of principles, biographies, salaries, and so on
- Current financing

• Business activity

- Products and services
- Sales methods, market territories
- Kinds of customers, names of major customers
- Sales potential
- Competition, comparisons with
- Number of employees, morale (if morale can be determined)
- Internal operations, outside operations
- Principal suppliers
- Reserves maintained

• Physical plant

- Plant and equipment description
- Lease arrangements
- Expansion plans

• Management

- Organization chart
- Future needs
- Continuity plans
- Incentives, benefits
- Strategies, plans

• Financial Data

- Current interim balance sheet
- Current income statement
- Tax returns (past three years)
- Profit projections—short term
- Profit projections—long term
- Cash-flow projections
- Ratios—inventory turnover, receivables sales days, and so on.

SUGGESTION: You may want to add other more specific information, depending on the business involved, local economic conditions, and so on.

IMPLICATIONS OF THE TEMPORARY LENDING LIMIT RULE

The office of the Comptroller of the Currency has issued a temporary lending limit rule. This rule helps banks with declining capital by allowing them to treat their loan commitments as "loans" at the time the commitments are made.

Loans made by banks to one borrower are limited to a percentage of the bank's capital. Banks experiencing capital declines have a problem making loan commitments because they cannot be certain that the outstanding loans to the borrower will not exceed the lending limit to that borrower at the time the commitment is actually funded.

To alleviate this problem, the temporary lending rule provides that if the total of a binding, written loan commitment and all other loans and commitments to a borrower are within the bank's lending limit at the time the commitment is made, the commitment is deemed a "loan" and its legality under the lending limit is determined as of that time.

> **IMPORTANT POINT:** Because it is now considered a "loan," however, a binding, written loan commitment must be counted in calculating loans outstanding to a borrower in determining the legality of a subsequent loan, even if the commitment is not fully funded at the time of the subsequent loan application.

Banks are still permitted to make "overline" commitments—those that would exceed a bank's lending limit when issued—because such commitments are not treated as "loans" under the temporary rule until they are actually funded.

> **CAUTION:** A bank which has entered into an "overline" commitment will be in violation

of the loans-to-one-borrower limitations if it subsequently funds that commitment in excess of the lending limit.

INTERNAL LOAN DEPARTMENT CONTROLS: A CHECKLIST

How good are the procedures in your bank's loan department? The following checklist will help to evaluate the effectiveness of the controls now in place and point out the areas of weaknesses.

	Yes	No
1. Are proceeds on loans disbursed only after the notes have been properly approved?	☐	☐
2. Are approvals on notes reviewed to determine that such approvals are within the limits of the bank's lending authorities?	☐	☐
3. Are current lines of credit on file within the department?	☐	☐
4. Are new loans reviewed to determine that such loans are within the established lines of credit?	☐	☐
5. Are loans, which are in excess of established lines, referred to the loaning officer?	☐	☐
6. Are notes inspected for proper signatures and endorsements?	☐	☐
7. Are new loans reviewed to determine that such loans did not increase the borrowers' total indebtedness to an amount in excess of that authorized by the borrowers' corporate resolution?	☐	☐
8. Are all new notes assigned a control number?	☐	☐
9. Are such numbers assigned in numerical sequence?	☐	☐
10. Are new notes recorded daily?	☐	☐
11. Are maturity dates rechecked on all new loans by a second person?	☐	☐
12. Are all notes held in the vault overnight?	☐	☐
13. Are liability cards on which new loans have been posted reviewed to ensure accuracy of posting?	☐	☐
14. Is discount on time notes rechecked to ensure accuracy of original computation?	☐	☐
15. Is an old and new balance proof made of principal payments?	☐	☐
16. Are paid notes stamped paid after good funds have been obtained?	☐	☐
17. Is incoming collateral receipted for on a prenumbered collateral receipt form?	☐	☐
18. Is incoming collateral compared to collateral listing on note by a second person prior to deposit in vault?	☐	☐
19. Is collateral held under dual control?	☐	☐
20. Are securities inspected for negotiability and documentation upon receipt by the collateral clerk?	☐	☐
21. Are collateral record cards posted from the collateral receipt by other than the collateral clerk?	☐	☐
22. Is collateral valued upon receipt by collateral clerk to determine that the collateral value meets margin requirements?	☐	☐

23. Are vault copies of collateral receipts Recordaked after the securities have been placed in the vault? ☐ ☐

24. Are office copies of collateral receipts filed numerically? ☐ ☐

25. Are vaulat copies of collateral receipts initialed by a lending officer to indicate approval for withdrawal or substitution? ☐ ☐

26. Is the night box reviewed to determine that collateral is being placed promptly under dual control? ☐ ☐

27. Are receipts obtained covering collateral released? ☐ ☐

28. Are securities out for transfer, exchange, and so on, controlled by prenumbered temporary vault-out tickets? ☐ ☐

29. Are the department's copies of open temporary vault-out tickets reviewed to determine that the items are authorized and have not been outstanding an unreasonable length of time? ☐ ☐

30.Are coupon tickler cards set up covering all coupon bonds held as collateral? ☐ ☐

31. Are written instructions obtained and held on file covering the cutting of coupons? ☐ ☐

32. Are all coupons cut except those where specific instructions from the customer requesting noncutting are on file? ☐ ☐

33. Are coupon cards under the control of other than the personnel assigned to coupon cutting? ☐ ☐

34. Are credits to customers' accounts representing cut coupons agreed to the total of the coupon deposits? ☐ ☐

35. Are totals of loans made, paid, and renewed as shown on the daily loan report agreed to the applicable general ledger controls? ☐ ☐

HOW TO CONTROL LOANS SECURED BY WAREHOUSE RECEIPTS

Using a public or field warehouse is a good way to gain control and maintain possession of inventory collateral. The bank is assured of an accurate count of inventory pledged at the origination of the loan and that control will continue until the loan is repaid.

Even though the warehouse worker is required to exercise diligence to protect the interests of both borrower and lender, you should still monitor the arrangement closely. The following checklist identifies the most important controls you should have built into your collateral control system:

CHECKLIST

• Are the warehouse receipts signed by a representative of the warehouse?

• Are specimen signatures on file of all persons authorized by the warehouse company to sign the receipts?

• Do the warehouse receipts meet all the requirements of the Uniform Warehouse Receipts Act, including the date, location of the warehouse, and an adequate description of type, quality, size, and so on?

• Are receipts checked for any break in numerical sequence?

• Are the receipts in nonnegotiable form, except those covering such items as bulk whiskey, bales of cotton, or other readily marketable commodities?

• Are nonnegotiable receipts issued to show (_____) as pledgee for (name of borrower)"?

• Are negotiable receipts properly endorsed?

• Are negotiable receipts kept under bank control until payment for the goods is received?

• Is an accounting record-maintained of the merchandise deposited, including description, lot number, cases, and so on, and of the release price per item in those cases where the receipt does not provide for this information?

• Are all releases of goods from the warehouse posted on a register or on the warehouse receipts, including the date, number of units released, and the negative units remaining?

• Is a monthly summary provided by the warehouse worker showing the total of all goods on hand as well as the daily activity in dollars and quantities?

• Is a service charge collected and credited to the income account called "commercial loan charges" in those instances where the bank prepares the release form?

• Are loans limited to a percentage of the collateral valuation as determined at the time of making the loan, and do they not exceed the borrower's cost?

• Is adequate insurance obtained, including fire and extended coverage, to cover each loan?

• Does the insurance policy include a lender's loss payable endorsement in favor of the bank?

• Is an adequate tickler system maintained to provide for the renewal of existing insurance policies?

• Does the insurance policy recite the location of the goods covered?

• Whenever a provisional reporting policy is on file, does the bank receive a copy of the monthly report to make certain that the value of the merchandise in storage is reported accurately?

• Are quarterly inspections made to determine that the merchandise warehoused compares with the amount shown on the bank's records?

• Are the goods in the warehouse inspected periodically to verify that a loss of deterioration has not happened on occasion?

• Is the market value of the goods checked periodically to determine that an ample margin of security is provided?

• Whenever the value of the goods is found to be reduced, is the agreed-upon margin restored by requiring either a reduction in loan principal or a provision to pledge additional security?

• Is a monthly report issued by the warehouse worker advising the bank of any overdue warehouse charges?

HOW TO TELL WHEN A CONSTRUCTION LOAN NEEDS PROFESSIONAL ASSISTANCE

Loan officers rarely have the time or the expertise to monitor the progress of capital construction projects. Some banks often use design and construction professionals to handle this responsibility.

In the monitoring process, the hired professionals are asked to certify the percentage and cost of the completed construction, the amount of materials stored on the site, and the compliance of the construction with approved plans, specifications, and applicable government regulations. These reports are documented with photographs illustrating construction progress.

The professional loan officer can be expected to be generally attuned to the construction process on the project site and sensitive to signs that a project may be in trouble. An owner's or contractor's inability to pay for work and materials is one of the major problems. This can be caused by a low first estimate, unpredictable price increase, diversion of funds, or delays that increase time-dependent costs.

Another source of problems is the failure to pursue the work which is usually caused by indecision, changes, inadequate plans, site problems, conflict with the building authority, inability to crew the site, or inadequate flow of materials. As the inspection and certification process goes on, any problems, actual or potential, should be reported to the lender immediately.

Engineering Checklist.

A professional engineering firm has developed the following checklist for use by professionals engaged in this inspection and certification service.

PRECONSTRUCTION

• Review plans and specifications for completeness (are the plans sufficient for construction?) and compliance with any codes found in the specifications.

• Evaluate the cost estimate to ensure both proper costs by classification, including a contractor's fee, and that the breakdown is not unbalanced to front load.

• Evaluate the construction schedule for realistic durations of activities and of the total project.

• Verify that an investigation of the building site has been made to determine soil conditions by test borings, location of utilities, drainage, and public roads.

• Determine if the site and improvements comply with zoning and other codes and ordinances.

CONSTRUCTION

• Verify compliance of in-place construction with plans, specifications, and any building codes, including any code references found in the specifications.

• Verify quality control by reviewing materials test results and construction procedures.

• Verify that the reported completion is actually completed and that the backup for costs complies with the lender's requirements.

• Verify the cost of the stored materials and provisions to secure the materials.

• Review any changed orders and forward to the lender any change that affects aesthetics, function, construction cost, or duration of the project.

• Review administration of subcontracts for executed contracts, insurance, lien waivers, realistic progress payments, and receipt of payments.

• Determine if progress is adequate to maintain the construction schedule.

• Review continued availability of materials, equipment, specialty subcontractors, and the craft labor.

• Verify if other inspecting authorities are making required visits.

• Review the daily construction log.

COMPLETION

• Verify that final building inspections by building authorities are being scheduled and the subsequent certificate of occupancy is issued.

• Verify that the design professionals are listing punch items and the contractor is accomplishing these items.

• Verify that final lien waivers are being obtained and forwarded to the lender.

• Verify that the design professional has executed a certificate of substantial completion, and that the contractor has completed a certificate of payment and compliance.

> **NOTE:** If you use a professional engineer, be sure to give him or her as much information as possible about the requirements of the project.

HOW TO HANDLE PASS-THROUGH LOANS

There are all kinds of ways to make questionable loans worth putting on the books—co-makers, guarantors, and so on. One of the more esoteric techniques is the "pass-through" loan, where the loan is made to a more creditworthy party who agrees to immediately turn the proceeds over to the original applicant.

> **CAUTION:** This practice, although sound in some circumstances, is susceptible to abuses where there is a fine line between questionable bank loans and misapplication of bank funds.

The courts have defined three general categories where loans could be characterized as "sham" or "dummy" loans because there is little likelihood that the named debtor will repay. Bank officials that knowingly participate in such loans have a "natural tendency" to injure or defraud their banks and are guilty of willful misapplication of bank funds. The categories are:

• Cases in which the bank officer knows that the named debtor was fictitious or that the debtor was unaware of the use of his or her name for the debt

• Cases in which the bank officer knows the named debtor was financially unable to pay back the loan

• Cases in which the bank officer assures the named debtor that he or she is not obligated to repay the loan in the event of a default and that the bank looks solely to the intended beneficiary of the loan for repayment

What Is Acceptable. The situation is totally different, however, when the bank officer grants a loan to a nonfictitious debtor who is financially capable and fully understands his or her responsibility for repayment. There are really two loans: The bank looks to the named debtor for repayment of its loan while the debtor looks to the third party for repayment of his or her loan. If for some reason the third party fails to make repayment to the named debtor, the latter nonetheless recognizes that this failure does not end his or her own obligation to repay the bank.

The loan officer simply grants a loan to a financially capable party, which is precisely what a bank official should do. There is no natural tendency to injure or defraud the bank, and the official cannot be said to have willfully misapplied funds. This is true because, in any event, the loan was made on the basis of the named debtor's credit strength, not on the basis of that ultimate beneficiary.

What if the Banker Is the Third Party? It is quite a different matter when a bank officer procures the assistance of another person in obtaining the desired funds for his or her own use. Despite the fact that the intermediary may have been financially capable of repaying the debt and even undertook to do so, the banker is presumed to have followed this route to conceal his or her personal interest in the loan from the bank and to circumvent regulations restricting direct lending to bank officers.

> **EXAMPLE:** In one case, a Pennsylvania banker was able to get three friends to borrow $18,500 from the bank under the condition that they relend the proceeds to him. He was indicted and convicted for misapplication of bank funds. In addition, because the loans were fully and accurately entered into the bank's records but without any reference to the officer's self-interest, he was also convicted of

making false bank entries. The court reasoned
that the true nature of the transaction should
have been entered in the bank's records in
order to present examiners with a full picture
of the bank's actual condition. (*See United States*
v. *Krepps,* 605 F.2d 101.)

CAUTION: Pass-through techniques offer
legitimate ways to strengthen lending
opportunities. However, lenders must be aware
of the potential for abuses, including outright
fraud.

24

ASSET-BASED LENDING

Asset-based lending is a growing, yet often misunderstood, aspect of commercial bank lending. Some ideas in Chapter 24 will help to dispense with the mystery—and the risk.

AN EFFECTIVE ASSET/LIABILITY MANAGEMENT SYSTEM

Because many banks have had commercial loan operations automated for several years, and demand and time deposits for even longer, putting together an asset/liablity management system should be no problem. That often isn't the case.

Generally, the main problem is not in the categorization of loans or deposits as they currently appear in the computer systems and on the general books. It is accounting by "interest rate maturity."

For the most part, loan systems categorize loans according to principal maturity (that is, demand, time, term, and purpose, including commercial, consumer, and real estate). Loan records usually carry a principal repayment schedule and/or a final maturity. They also record the agreed-upon interest rate or the base rate designation, such as the prime or the London Interbank Offering Rate (LIBOR), and the add-on factor—for example, two points over the prime.

> **KEY POINT:** For asset/liability management, the fact is that information is not enough. By itself, without augmentation, it is essentially useless.

THE REASON: The primary tool of asset/ liability management is the "interest rate sensitivity gap report," and that report requires accounting by interest rate maturity.

To assess its current position in terms of interest-sensitive assets/liabilities, management needs to know certain information.

"Rate sensitive" assets/liabilities are loan or deposit interest rates likely to change because of fluctuation in some external rate, such as the prime rate. That is only one half of the definition. The second half is those rates likely to change within a given short time such as thirty days. All assets/ liabilities with those characteristics are generally classified as rate sensitive.

At one time, the short time period used for analysis purposes was one year. Today, because of the rapid changes in the interest rate market, that period is generally reduced to thirty days.

The remainder of the asset/liability portfolio must also be classified by the date upon which the associated interest rate may change. That may not be, and generally is not, as obvious as it sounds.

REASON: Principal maturities may or may not coincide with rate maturities.

EXAMPLE: A term loan that matures in five years for principal repayment may mature annually with respect to interest rate. That is, the interest rate on the five-year loan may change or be subject to change after one year and every year thereafter. Similarly, longer-term certificates of deposit or CDs that are presumed to be longer term, may be subject to interest change on specified interest rollover rates, and the rollover may cause the interest rate to have a much shorter maturity. All these must be reflected in their proper timeframes.

Other assets/liabilities may not have specific interest rate or principal maturities; nevertheless they must be classified. Usually, classifications are based on assumptions drawn from historic market behavior. These assumptions are then grouped according to interest rate maturity assumptions. Core deposits, by definition, have no maturity. Interest on mortgages may mature on the basis of the national average holding period, or some average peculiar to an individual bank or its local area.

> **NOTE:** Interest rate maturities are not necessarily obvious; they may require investigation to uncover them.

The "gap" analysis is generally portrayed on a report that lists all the bank's assets and liabilities in columns according to interest rate maturity. Using this method, there can be columns for the immediate rate-sensitive group (possible change within the next thirty days by definition), the 31-to-60 day change group, and other groups as the bank requires. This report tracks the level of interest rate maturities of assets and liabilities. The difference between the two is the gap, and it is based on what happens to interest rates.

In addition to the amounts of loan and deposit principal shown in the columns, an average interest rate associated with all these funds should be calculated.

The resultant report would show:

- Assets by interest rate maturity period
- Average interest rate for the assets in each period
- Liabilities by interest rate maturity period
- Average interest rate for those liabilities

> **NOTE:** From this report, management would be able to determine in dollars and percentage

rates each unmatched segment of its asset/ liability portfolio.

APPRAISALS MUST BE ACCURATE IN ASSET-BASED LENDING

When a bank does asset-based lending, it is important to know the value of the asset.

That's why appraisals by an outside, independent appraiser are necessary. But how can you be sure the appraisal is accurate? Has the right valuation technique been used?

Here are some guidelines suggested by Rosen Systems, Inc.* of Dallas, Texas, to help ensure that a machinery and equipment appraisal is on the right track:

• Review the Statement of Limiting Conditions for any restrictions that relate to value.

• Are assumptions as to the condition of the assets made? If so, are those assumptions reasonable?

• Does the value concept include a "distress" situation and "forced sale" connotation?

• Are nonstandard assets valued? If so, does the appraiser present support for the value, and are the values conservative?

• Exclude any value for fixtures, dies and molds. Note that an appraiser's estimating of such items should serve as a signal that he lacks expertise in the liquidation value concept.

• Are values other than scrap accorded to such items as process wiring, piping, etc.? If so, they are an indication of the appraiser's inexperience.

• If the report is typed and not computer-generated and recapped, check all mathematical computations, including total value.

• Review machinery and equipment descriptions for possible lease items which have been valued.

*Used with permission from "How to Get Your Money's Worth from an Appraisal," published by R.S.I. Appraisal Group.

• Review in detail all items above your established "threshold" dollar amount. Items considered material should be discussed with the appraiser to determine a confidence factor.

• Check for value consistency in quantities of similar items within an appraisal. If not consistent, appearance may be a factor, or problems may be indicated.

• Are the appraiser's qualifications, definition of value, method of valuation, and effective date of the appraisal included in the report?

• Identify and question any large dollar amounts which relate to summary listings. An example could be $100,000 allocated to office furnishings and equipment.

• Does the Statement of Limiting Conditions explain discrepancies, unique situations, or qualifiers which may invalidate a portion of the report or the entire value concept?

• If a dissenting opinion is filed when several appraisers are involved, determine the reasons.

• Does the appraiser note machinery and equipment appearance?

• If code structures are used, are these defined?

• Does the recapitulation page at the front of the report agree with the total value shown at the end of the listing? Generally, do the totals throughout the report support the overall valuation?

• Is the value concept defined? Does the definition coincide with generally accepted terminology?

• Is the method of appraisal based on a sales comparison approach, or on replacement cost less depreciation? For asset-based lending decisions, the latter is not appropriate except in rare instances.

WHAT AN ASSET/LIABILITY MODELING SYSTEM SHOULD DO

Banks and other financial service institutions have been evaluating asset/liability management to a high-priority function in recent years. This is due to the increased pressure on earnings and the increased need for capital adequacy. In fact, the Federal Home Loan Bank Board has proposed that thrift banks develop formal policies and procedures for review by the boards.

There are numerous software packages available to assist in gap analysis, balance sheet projections, and reporting on spreads and ratios. What should an institution look for in selecting a microcomputer or mainframe package? A major bank recently published results of a survey that sets forth the fundamental features an asset/liability modeling package should contain:

• A chart-of-accounts routine that allows the user to group and subgroup various line items

• Adequate storage capacity for at least one year's worth of monthly balance sheet information

• Balance sheet forecasting capabilities for a five-year period, on both a monthly and yearly basis

• The capability to tie various interest rates to user-specified driver rates

• The capacity to provide variance analysis between any two time periods

• A gap analysis function for maturity windows of 30 days, 60 days, 90 days, 180 days, 360 days, and over a year.

• Gap analysis and repricable funds gap analysis ratios

• Reports on interest rate spreads, net interest margins, breakeven yields, peer comparisons, and standard industry ratios

• The capability to store and compare various results so that alternative interest rate strategic planning scenarios can be produced

25

LOAN
PARTICIPATIONS

Since the Penn Square debacle in the early 1980s, loan participations have come under closer scrutiny. That was when a small Oklahoma bank was able to take advantage of the energy crisis to sell loans upstream to banks such as Continental Illinois and Seafirst without sufficient documentation. Loan participations can be good business for a bank. Unfortunately they also present potentially dangerous problems. The items in Chapter 25 are designed to keep loan participations on the right track.

THE FINE ART OF LOAN PARTICIPATIONS

Loan participations got a bad rap a few years ago when the Penn Square Bank problems hit the papers, not because loan participations were proven bad but because of the abuses in their use.

Participations are a valid and valued technique, particularly when a customer has grown to the point where its financial needs exceed the bank's legal lending limit.

All bankers, at one time or another, have had customers whose businesses have prospered and expanded to the point where their credit requirements exceed the bank's legal or comfort limit. Alert bankers will anticipate this development and take an active role in obtaining additional credit accommodations.

> **TIP:** Arranging a participation can allow you
> to meet your customer's needs *and* keep him or
> her with your bank.

From a banking perspective, participations spread the credit risk while maintaining a total relationship.

> **REMEMBER:** It is far better to share an
> account than to lose it altogether. The
> customer also gets the expanded borrowing
> capacity he or she needs while retaining ties
> with those who know, value, and understand
> his or her business.

An alternative that any enterprising businessperson should explore is to arrange credit facilities with several banks. Potential benefits:

• Wider possibilities for negotiating the best possible terms with respect to rate, collateral, and maturity
• Ability to pay off one bank by borrowing from another—in effect transforming debt into capital

Bankers naturally look askance at these practices but are often helpless to control them. Good exchange of credit information between banks with one bank acting as "lead" can help to curb abuses, but unfortunately, this level of cooperation is rarely achieved.

> **NOTE:** You should point out that such
> impersonal arrangements can result in the
> business being "shut off" in the event of tight
> credit.

In tight markets you will surely have more pull with regional correspondents than your customer.

Bankers originating participations need to provide accurate and timely information about the credit and originating (lead) bank.

CAUTION: Originating banks can be sued for substantial damages because of false or incomplete statements about the borrower or his or her operation or financial condition.

In addition, participants must be confident in the lead bank because correspondents may be considered unsecured creditors in the event of the lead bank's failure.

Participants must have the same knowledge about the credit as the lead bank and must reach fully independent credit decisions. This is a fundamental requirement for solid participant relations. The lead bank should send each potential participant a complete information package containing:

- Proposed loan and participation agreements
- Audited financial statements
- Interim financial statements (prepared by the company or its CPA)
- Projection
- Collateral valuation
- Disclosure of all existing or contemplated credit arrangements

This list is by no means all-inclusive, and the lead bank should readily supply any additional information requested by participants.

Correspondent banks, whose participation is being sought, will certainlly have questions about the credit. They may also have comments or suggestions to make, depending on their own expertise with the type of credit and their bank's policy requirements. This is not the time for oversensitivity; rather, it is a time to sit back, listen, and learn.

TIP: An independent judgment is a good check on your thinking and may disclose pitfalls overlooked in your bank's analysis.

Important Considerations in Drawing a Participation Agreement.   A participation agreement must clearly spell out all responsibilities of both originating and participating banks. It is a complex task, but a few of the many important considerations are:

- How will payments be shared?
- How will expenses and losses (if any) be divided?
- How will requests for loan agreement waivers, release or substitution of collateral, and other such requests be handled?

These and other questions must be discussed by all participants, and a final agreement must be drawn which reflects the consensus.

> **IMPORTANT:** Counsel's involvement in this process is essential.

Any correspondent bank worthy of the name works hard to develop its bank business and is not apt to jeopardize its reputation by directly contacting a respondent banker's customers. This important principle is usually violated by individual officers who ignore bank policy by calling directly on customers in their zeal for new business.

> **NOTE:** By using participations, a bank can expand its capacity to service the credit needs of customers, thus ensuring its ability to keep all their business.

LOAN PARTICIPATION GUIDELINES

When your loan business is not what you would like it to be, or when you simply want to diversify your loan portfolio, there is the possibility of buying into the loans originated by other banks.

Loan participation is a time-honored method by which a bank can increase its business rapidly and with little preparation costs. But should you go this route? This depends on several factors:

- How well the originating bank does its work.
- How creditworthy that bank is.
- The participating bank's ability to analyze the credit involved.
- How carefully the participation agreement is drawn.

A number of loan participation guidelines have been developed jointly by Robert Morris Associates and the American Bankers Association. Among the subjects dealt with in the guidelines are these:

1. *For Participants:*

- The need to obtain all available credit data, as though the borrower were a direct customer.
- The need to get copies of all relevant documentation.
- The analysis of the credit to make sure that it conforms to the bank's own standards.

2. *For Originating Banks:*

- Providing full credit data to participants.
- Being satisfied of the creditworthiness of each of the participants.

3. *For the Participation Agreement:*

- What should be spelled out in the specific transaction.
- What is required of each party—sharing of expenses, periodic reports, settling disputes, and other matters.

Each of the above topics, and many more not included here, are elaborated in some detail in the guidelines. As the RMA/ABA committee that wrote the guidelines has stated, the objective was to remove uncertainties and establish a set of principles upon which banks could operate. At the same time, the guidelines are not intended to intrude upon proprietary relationships between the parties to loan participation agreements.

> **NOTE:** The guidelines have only been touched upon in this section. For more

information on "Loan Participation Agreements: ABA/RMA Industry Guidelines," contact Robert Morris Associates, P.O. Box 8500, S-1140, Philadelphia, PA 19178.

THE ROLE OF PARTICIPANTS IN LOAN PARTICIPATIONS

When a loan participation goes wrong, it is usually the participants who go after the leader with claims of misrepresentation, mishandling, or other claims. However, sometimes it can be the other way around. Here is a case in point:

> **EXAMPLE:** An Indiana holding company's mortgage affiliate agreed to loan over $5 million for condominium construction. To this end it got commitments from two "family" affiliates along with the U. S. Steel Credit Corp. for a 100 percent participation. The project, unfortunately, faltered, making further advances essential. All parties agreed, except U. S. Steel Credit. The project went into default. The lead company worked out a settlement. With less than one-half of the units completed and the rest under construction no sales could be closed. In short, it was a mess. U. S. Steel Credit, in turn, was demanding that the lead mortgage company purchase its interest at an inflated price. Thus the mess was compounded further. The lead company's response was to disburse "...$734,929.59 from loan proceeds on behalf of the three loan participants," plus an additional $400,541.73 to preserve the project. The Indiana Company believed U. S. Steel Credit was responsible for its share (40 percent) of those disbursements (that is, $160,216.69). The money was not forthcoming. U. S. Steel Credit also did not

prove cooperative when it came to approving marketing plans. As a result, the prime selling season came and went. The project's value, in turn, declined. Plans were then made to unload the project "as is" at $1.7 million, and again U. S. Steel refused to go along unless claims against it were waived. As a result, even the sellout failed.

THE RESULT: A nasty lawsuit with damage claims running into six figures and punitive damage claims into the many millions.

Good-faith Dealing.   Just what were the participants' contractual obligations to the lead lender and the others? The language in the participation agreement required it to reimburse the mortgagee for all extraordinary costs and expenses incurred "for the protection and preservation of security, for the minimizing of loss...." There was also an implied requirement of good faith and fair dealing by U. S. Steel Credit. Those obligations in turn ran not only to the lead lender but to the other participants as well.

In the court's words, "Indiana law has long recognized the duty of a party engaged in a common enterprise to act in the utmost good faith toward its coventurers." In light of that, a full hearing on the allegations was in order. [See American Fletcher Mortgage Co. v. *U.S. Steel Credit,* Nos. 80-1485, 80-1719 (7th Cir.).]

NOTE: The typical loan participation consists of much more than a one-way flow of responsibility from the lead lender to its participants. Both sides have responsibilities.

26

SPECIAL LENDING CONCERNS

One major concern for a bank—and now more than ever as profit margins continue to be squeezed at most banking institutions—is pricing procedures. These procedures are covered in Chapter 26, along with items of particular concern such as tender offer financing, interest rate swaps, and lender liability.

SETTING PRICING GUIDELINES AND ENSURING PROFITABILITY

Consider the following example: A new customer comes to your bank for a line of credit. You put in some numbers, consider the firm's management, reputation, and prospects, and then make an offer: prime plus one, no commitment and no miscellaneous fees. The customer counters with prime plus three quarters, no balances nor fees. You finally agree on prime plus three quarters and balances only on the outstanding amount.

Although the relative profitability of these particular pricing alternatives to the bank is obvious, a banker can have difficulty determining the relative profitability of complex loans of long duration. For example: Revolving credits that convert into term loans with different balance requirements on the revolving credit and term loan portions, and that have different rates each year of the terms loan, can be difficult to negotiate and price. For this reason an example follows of one bank which developed a system that measures the pricing of its loans.

HOW TO DEVELOP A CONCEPT AND MAKE IT WORK

At this bank all unsecured loans to individuals exceeding $25,000, or corporate loans in excess of $100,000 must have their pricing measured. The concept behind the bank's loan pricing system is simple.

> **KEY POINT:** The actual pricing of a loan is compared to what the bank considers appropriate pricing for a loan of that level of risk.

For example: In the bank's system, a line of credit to a top customer is priced at prime with no commitment or miscellaneous fees. A line to the top customer priced in this fashion measures 100 percent.

Pricing changes, such as the elimination of balance requirements, which reduce the overall cost of the line to the customer, drop the loan's pricing below 100 percent. Changes that increase the cost of the loan raise its pricing above 100 percent. In addition, the bank's pricing system is arranged so that, as the risk of the loan increases, the bank's price standard rises. This system allows loan officers to determine whether their proposed rate and balance combinations are appropriate for the risk inherent to the loan.

How the System Works. The information fed into the computer varies according to the type of loan. For lines of credit, however, the following information is entered into the computer:

• Name of company, length of loan, frequency of interest payments

• Type of loan

- Credit rating (A,B,C, or D)
- Percent of usage expected
- Amortization schedule
- Rate
- Balances
- Commitment fee
- Miscellaneous fee

The computer then produces an analysis of the pricing arrangement. It gives the total cost to the customer in terms of spread over prime, and the overall pricing of the loan in terms of the bank's standard for the particular customer's credit rating. In addition, the computer breaks down the overall pricing of the loan into two components: the pricing on the facility (this includes commitment fees, miscellaneous fees, and balances maintained due to the availability of a line), and the pricing on the outstanding portion of the loan.

This pricing model helps the bank to determine what combination of balance and rate arrangements provides the most favorable pricing. In a market where prices are generally low, for instance, the proposed pricing on a particular loan can be compared to the current pricing of comparable loans to determine if the pricing reflects what the bank can get in its marketplace.

The breakdown of the pricing into its usage and facility components, can further help the banker to structure the loan in the bank's favor. If the banker feels a line of credit will not be used, for example, the loan officer may set up the loan so that the cost of the facility will be relatively high and charge somewhat less for line usage.

The bank in our example uses this model on all but its smallest loans.

> **TIP:** Although your bank may not have the facilities for such an elaborate system, you should develop pricing guidelines. Such guidelines will help you to arrive at more precise conclusions about your pricing policies.

FINANCING MANAGEMENT BUYOUTS

Consider the following situation: Company A has increased its sales by 50 percent in the last four years. It has enjoyed healthy pretax earnings over the same period. However, despite its solid status, the conglomerate that owns the company has to sell it. The U.S. Justice Department has filed suit charging that the conglomerate's ownership of the firm constitutes an anti-trust violation.

The manager of the company approaches you to discuss its purchase. You negotiate a package. The purchase price is $8 million. The manager puts up $200,000 and will then receive 20 percent of the business. Another $1.8 million comes from a group of small business investment companies (SBIC). In exchange for their funding, they receive stock and subordinated debentures entitling them to 80 percent of the business.

The remaining $6 million comes from a finance company and your bank. Exactly $4 million comes from revolving credit with the finance company, secured by receivables and inventory. The contract is for two years. The other $2 million comes from a ten-year term loan from your bank, secured by the company's plant.

Twenty years ago such buyouts were unusual. After all, managers seldom have enough capital to purchase their companies. Today, however, banks and finance companies will support these purchases.

This can be explained, in part, by a change in lending concepts. Today, finance companies will lend more than the liquidation value of collateral, provided they believe the borrower's cash flow can pay more than a term loan based on fixed assets. Banks are willing to participate because revolving loans made by finance companies are based on receivables and inventory and are not included in the borrower's debt–repayment schedules.

What to Look for in a Buyout. If you are approached by a manager who wants to buy out his or her company be sure to examine the following:

- The company's past financial statements

• The company's current products and markets

• The company's expected future cash flow, profits, and balance sheet

• The résumés of the managers who will stay on to ensure that these managers have satisfactory track records

• The company's established products that will maintain their market shares until the debt is paid off

Look closely at firms whose fortunes are cyclical. These firms may experience a bad season and have trouble paying interest. The best prospects have sales and profits that are in an upward trend or at least stable. Since you will have to rely on the company's financial reports, also check its financial controls carefully.

What a Bank Should Do. If a manager who wants to buy out his or her company approaches you for advice, you should:

• Tell the manager to make sure the owners are willing to sell. If this is the case, he or she should obtain a letter of intent. The letter should state the owners' desire to sell, indicate their price, and specify whether the deal will be for cash or cash plus notes. It should also make clear how much time the buyer has to arrange financing. The owners should be sure to ascertain the cash price. Because this is usually the lowest price, it can become the basis for negotiations.

• Advise the manager on negotiating the price. Only rarely should the price exceed five to eight times post-tax earnings; otherwise, difficulty may arise in meeting the interest payments and amortizing the debt within a period of time acceptable to lenders.

• Look carefully at any commercial finance company you hope will participate in the deal. Integrity is important, but the company should also be experienced in arranging similar financing. Do you think you will be able to work with this company? Will its executives recognize the needs of other parties in the transaction?

HOW TO KEEP INFORMATION CONFIDENTIAL IN TENDER OFFER FINANCING

In almost any situation, financing corporate takeovers can present ethical questions to a bank. This is particularly true when the bank has already indicated an interest in providing funds to consummate the acquisition—and then discovers the target is also a customer.

> **EXAMPLE:** There was a case in which Chemical Bank participated in a loan to the Washington Steel Corp. As part of the loan documentation, Chemical Bank received such nonpublic information as quarterly and year-end statements and projected earnings and cash flow figures for eight years.
> Three years before the end of the eight-year projections, another client of the bank asked for, and received, a loan commitment to finance a tender offer for the shares of the steel company. Washington Steel Corp. sought injunctive relief on the basis that Chemical Bank's possession of confidential information established a fiduciary relationship with Washington Steel Corp. that precluded financing takeover attempts. The district court enjoined the loan transaction (but not the tender offer itself), finding that Chemical Bank had violated "a common law fiduciary duty to Washington." On appeal, the lower court was reversed. The court believed that a contrary ruling would enable companies to thwart tender offers merely by spreading their business around with a number of large banks. The court observed: "To imply a common law fiduciary duty of banks not to deal with competitors of their borrowers, or even just potential acquirors of these borrowers, could

wreak havoc with the availability of funding
for capital ventures."

Chemical Bank was extremely careful to guard the use of
its confidential information about Washington Steel Corp. Not
only did it make sure not to divulge any information to the
potential acquiror, but it also sealed off the information from
the loan officers handling the contemplated tender offer loan.
In effect, the bank set up a wall within the loan department
sealing off the information in possession of the loan officer in
charge of the Washington Steel Corp. account from the loan
officer in charge of the contemplated tender offer loan.
[Washington Steel Corp. v. T.W. Corp., No.79-1217 (3d Cir.)]

The court's opinion left no doubt that the "invisible wall"
was not necessary. It noted that the commercial loan department must be free to make sure the information available to it
was correct. "If a competitor of a borrower seeks a loan for a
purpose which the loan department knows [from information
in its files supplied by the borrower] is preordained to failure,
it should hardly be permitted, let alone required, to ignore the
information, finance a foolhardy venture, and write off a bad
loan."

The court continued that a bank might very well violate
the law if it disseminated confidential information to a separate bank department such as the trust department, or, for that
matter, to the acquiring company itself. It concluded only that
"The use within that loan department of information received
from one borrower in evaluating the loan application of
another borrower does not state a cause of action against the
bank."

> **NOTE:** A bank can use all sources at its
> disposal to reach an informed credit decision.
> However the information must stay within the
> loan department.

UNDERSTANDING INTEREST RATE SWAPS

As financial techniques and procedures go, interest rate swaps
are relatively new—less than a decade old. However, they have

really only come into their own importance very recently.

Simply stated, an interest rate swap is an arrangement by which two entities exchange a fixed and variable interest rate, on an agreed upon amount of principal, and for a specified period of time.

Usually the swaps are used to modify the interest rate sensitivity of a bank's assets or liabilities. Let's take an example suggested by a partner with Ernst & Whinney:

> **EXAMPLE:** A U.S. bank with rate-sensitive liabilities in excess of assets agrees to make fixed-rate payments of an agreed upon amount to a European bank. In exchange, that European bank agrees to pay a variable rate tied to LIBOR. If the variable rate averages nine percent for a period and the fixed rate was eleven percent, the U.S. bank would owe the European bank the two percent difference. In subsequent periods, the variable rate could change based on the agreed index; the fixed rate, however, would remain constant.

> **NOTE:** Although a bank may enter into a swap for its own purposes (such as in the example above), it may also act as an intermediary for customers who may wish to enter such agreements. In addition, the bank may simply provide settlement services, accepting and paying interest differences to participating parties. Banks may also issue standby letters of credit, assuring the performance of one or both of the parties to the swap.

Accounting Concerns. Swaps involve some special accounting procedures. If the bank is a principal for its own benefit, the interest differential should be income/expense accrued periodically over the term of the agreement.

Fee rates, according to the partner at Ernst & Whinney should be determined through preferred accounting as follows:

• Brokerage or origination fees should be capitalized and treated as an adjustment to recorded interest difference

• Fees for acting as an intermediary should be recognized as services are performed

• Fees for settlement services are considered revenue when settlements are performed

• Fees for standby letters of credit should be deferred and amortized over the commitment period.

> **NOTE:** Banks that enter into interest rate
> swaps should pay particular attention to the
> credit risk associated with assets assumed or
> disposed of, as well as their obligation ratios of
> transactions that require the recognition of
> assets and liabilities.

HOW TO DEAL WITH LENDER LIABILITY

In recent years, a growing number of banks have found themselves being sued by disgruntled borrowers, who charge that banks have contributed to their problems.

Banks have been losing an alarmingly high number of these lawsuits for a variety of reasons. One lawyer, who represents banks, says, "If banks make fair dealing and good faith commonplace, they have nothing to worry about." Perhaps, but it is not that simple because many law firms enjoy a profitable business by suing banks for unhappy borrowers.

Lender liability is a problem that must be met head-on by banks if they are to stand a chance of being on the winning side. Here is a list of options published by *United States Banker* magazine*, which a bank should consider in order to reduce potential lawsuits based on lender liability.

* Used by permission of *United States Banker*. © Kalo Communications, Inc.

• Simplify loan documents. Onerous boilerplate terminology that serves no real purpose should be eliminated.

• Make certain that legal documents clearly reflect the understandings between the parties. Telling a borrower that provisions of the agreement "aren't really enforced" or "are just there for the lawyers" is a big mistake.

• Have a well-founded reason for terminating (or legally trying to collect) a loan. Make sure you can prove there has been a substantial change in the borrower's position. In court, the bank must be able to show it has exhaustively investigated the situation and can verify the changes.

• Don't suddenly terminate or try to collect. Good faith demands that you give the borrower timely notification.

• Have the borrower provide warranties and representations of creditworthiness and the condition of his or her business. Such documentation will enable the bank to show the borrower's change in status and could also prove the bank was mislead.

• Use committees to decide whether to terminate a loan. No one officer should have the authority to terminate a line of credit or call a loan.

• Keep the files clean. Banks have a tendency to put everything in writing—to stuff files with a variety of documents. It must be assumed that every file could be subpoenaed at any time.

• Be careful about how credit inquiries are handled. Statements made about credit policies should be consistent.

• Establish a solid training program for lending officers. Absent such training, a borrower can assert a lack of fair dealing, claiming the bank made no attempt to monitor lending officers.

• Have management policies in place for terminating or collecting loans. Without these, the bank is admitting to a lack of proper guidance and supervision.

• Develop a full understanding and knowledge of the borrower's business. You will be better able to justify your claim that a borrower is no longer creditworthy or that he or she can't repay.

• Avoid oral commitments. These are as important as a written agreement in the eyes of the jury.

• Make good faith a course of conduct. Good faith has to start the minute the borrower sets foot in the bank and should continue until the loan is repaid. That applies to everything said, every document signed, and every action taken.

• Don't overreach and take all possible collateral simply because it is available. Overreaching is something plaintiffs' attorneys consider preeminent.

• Make workouts symbiotic. Commercial borrowers aren't deadbeats; their businesses can be adversely affected by myriad economic considerations.

27

MORTGAGE LENDING

In recent years, commercial banks have been taking the control away from thrift institutions in this potentially lucrative lending business—something that is accelerating because of the ongoing savings and loan crisis.

The topics in this chapter are designed to help commercial banks make mortgage lending even more popular.

ADJUSTING TO ADJUSTABLE RATE MORTGAGES

In defiance of earlier predictions, the adjustable rate mortgage (ARM) has become a permanent part of the mortgage business. It has helped many mortgage lenders, particularly those who have been burned by mortgages written when interest rates were low. Just as important, borrowers have taken to ARMs, and not just when the rates on mortgages are rising. They realize that rates fluctuate and what goes up usually comes down—and vice versa.

Regardless of where interest rates may be at any given time, there are two developments a mortgage lender should consider when offering an adjustable rate mortgage program:

- A convertible feature
- Rates tied to the rate of inflation

Convertibles. A growing number of banks have found that making ARMS convertible—allowing borrowers to convert from ARMs to fixed rate mortgages (FRMs) for a nominal charge and after certain lengths of time—has attracted many borrowers who might not otherwise choose an ARM. The option, of course, can be exercised whether rates are going up or going down.

Inflation-Based ARMs.   These rates are sometimes called price level adjusted mortgages (PALMs). Although the idea is not new (they have been popular for decades in some South American countries such as Brazil) they are only recently finding favor in the U.S.

With a PALM, the rate is adjusted on a periodic basis, though usually no more often than once every twelve or eighteen months, to the rate of inflation or to some other indicator such as the consumer price index. Then the rate is adjusted on the basis of a percentage of the increase (or decrease).

> **NOTE:**   These two concepts certainly merit consideration. With more and more commercial banks getting into the mortgage lending business, they could provide major selling points.

UNDERSTANDING AND IMPLEMENTING REVERSE MORTGAGES

Reverse mortgages have been catching on in various parts of the country. One of the first financial companies to offer them was American Homestead Mortgage Corp. in New Jersey.

According to a spokesperson for the company, the success of American Homestead's individual retirement mortgage account (IRMA) program can be attributed to need. "The home is the largest single asset of the senior [citizen]," the spokesperson observed, pointing out that there are 30 million people aged 62 or older in the United States, and 70 percent of their net worth is tied up in real estate. Many of these people, however, are living on fixed incomes such as social security or small pensions, and cannot afford to stay in their homes. "The idea of the IRMA account is to allow older homeowners to free up to the equity of their homes." said the spokesperson.

To do this, the IRMA program allows older homeowners to borrow money based on the worth of their houses. Repayment of the loan is not due during the homeowner's lifetime. After the homeowner's death, the loan, plus interest, is repaid by his or her heirs or estate.

IRMA was modeled after the California reverse annuity mortgage program (otherwise known as RAM), which offers short-term reverse mortgages to homeowners. (RAM carries no age specifications and the terms are varied, from three to five to ten years, after which time the homeowner would have to pay back the loan plus interest. Most often homeowners would have to sell their homes in order to repay.)

The Reverse Mortgage Process. The first step in opening an IRMA with American Homestead involves a call to them inquiring about the program. After the homeowner gives his or her age and the market value of his or her house, the homeowner receives a quote from a retirement planner of what the monthly payments would be based on that information. If this amount is sufficient to meet the homeowner's needs, a representative of the company then pays a visit to the house, where the homeowner is given a full disclosure of what the payments would mean on a year-to-year basis—that is, what the payments would amount to each year and what interest payments would accrue, which would be paid back from the estate.

If, after discussing all this with American Homestead, the homeowner is still interested, he or she is asked to pay the company a $100 application fee (which is refunded at closing) and is given a list of the state-licensed appraisers in his area, from which he or she chooses one to appraise the house. The figure the appraiser comes up with is the one American Homestead uses in calculating the monthly payments. After the monthly payments are established, the company goes through the normal mortgage closing procedures and the payments to the homeowner begin.

Repayment (which, again, is due only after the homeowner dies) is based on whatever dollar amount has been paid out plus a fixed rate of interest on that dollar amount. The interest rate is now set at 11.5 percent, which is a below-market rate for typical reverse mortgages, set at 13 or 14 percent at this writing. Also figured into the repayment is the appreciation of the home. This can be any number up to 15 percent.

At the initiation of the loan, the homeowner has the option of negotiating the appreciation the bank will receive for repayment. Whatever the homeowner decides to give over to the bank and whatever he or she chooses to leave in his or her estate will have some bearing on the amount of the monthly payments during the homeowner's lifetime. *For example:* A homeowner that agrees to give the entire appreciation amount to the bank will be entitled to the maximum monthly payments.

In some cases, however, a homeowner might want to leave some money in an estate, thus his or her financial needs might be limited. The homeowner might therefore choose to negotiate a percentage of the value of his or her home and a percentage of the appreciation with the bank, thus reducing monthly payments while still being able to leave part of an estate to heirs.

> **KEY POINT:** The appreciation feature is key
> to the program's viability.

"What we're really doing is investing in pools of real estate—in that way we can be fairly sure that there will be a steady rate of appreciation," the spokesperson from American Homestead notes. "We're making a loan based on the fact that we believe the home will appreciate. In essence, we're letting them borrow money today, based on what the value of their home will be in the future."

> **CAUTION:** In some cases, the bank could
> end up not making any profit at all and not
> even getting its money back, when, for
> example, the homeowner outlives his or her
> life expectancy or the home depreciates.

The estate, however, will in no instance be responsible in the event of such an occurrence. "That's the risk we take," the

American Homestead spokesperson said, explaining that the fact that they are working with a pool of houses will more or less guarantee that everything will be balanced out in the end.

HOME EQUITY CREDIT GUIDELINES

One of the fastest-growing bank products is the home equity line of credit, particularly since the restrictions on interest deductibility in current tax laws. Generally speaking, home equity credit lines are open-end credit facilities secured by junior mortgages. These lines also have become immensely popular with consumers because of their variable rates, flexible repayment terms, and access by check, cash advance, credit card, telephone transfer, or ATM.

Concerned that banks might move too fast in this area and not institute adequate control procedures, the office of the Comptroller of the Currency suggests banks take some precautionary measures.

• Establish sound underwriting policies and procedures that emphasize the borrower's ability to service the loan from cash flow rather than from the sale of collateral and then set acceptable loan-to-value and debt-to-income ratios.

• Maintain proper credit and collateral documentation including current appraisals and evidence of lien priority status.

• Demonstrate an understanding of the interest rate risks created by the mandatory interest rate cap, crawdowns, and repayment options often offered in such plans.

• Adopt procedures and controls to ensure compliance with consumer credit protection rules such as Regulation Z (truth in lending) and Regulation B (equal credit opportunity).

• Establish a program to periodically review a borrower's financial condition, particularly in cases where the line has been inactive and is nearing maturity.

• Establish appropriate collection and charge-off procedures.

• Develop detailed and timely reports on equity line exposure that identify total commitments, outstanding amounts, account activity, maximum usage, delinquencies, nonaccurals, extensions, and renewals.

• Establish adequate training programs.

28

MARKETING IDEAS

For much of the history of banking in the United States, marketing was an aspect of banking that received little attention. Now, it has taken on increasing importance due to the selling of bank services that are essential to the success of any bank.

THE DIRECT SALES IMPERATIVE: ADVANTAGES AND DISADVANTAGES

Using direct sales as a major part of a bank's marketing effort has may advantages, particularly in highly fluid times. These factors have particular appeal when:

• The cost expended can produce measurable results. The best advertising campaign in the world cannot produce results that can be totally and substantively measured. This does not in any way imply that advertising is not effecdtive. It is only that its effects are hard to measure. Also, boards of directors faced with rising costs like measurable results.

• Prospects can be targeted in on. True, advertising media can and should be selected to fit the targets of the message. However, only with direct sales contact can the marketing officer be sure that prospects have heard the message he or she desires.

• Emphasis can be switched, instantly if necessary, to meet changing conditions. Thus, services can be targeted for promotion as situations dictate. Once a trained sales force exists, it is relatively easy to take advantage of new opportunities.

Direct sales, however, does have its downside, as well. The common problems facing a marketing officer who is interested in implementing a direct sales effort are:

• Selling requires constant training, supervision, and motivation. In advertising, an ad is designed and implemented. You can then sit back and let it work. Selling doesn't work that way. You must work at it constantly.

• Sales reluctance is bound to be a major obstacle. Many people who enter into banking deliberately do so to avoid having to sell.

• Sales responsibility will not normally be included in the typical job description, even for a public-contact person such as a teller. This leads employees to believe sales is an unpaid extra duty that they are free to perform or reject as they wish.

• Top management expects a sales effort to produce tangible results. Sometimes management expects too much. Invariably, it expects results much too fast. This realization makes marketing officers nervous about having to make a real or implied commitment to produce a level of sales they're not sure of attaining.

Here are the disadvantages related to direct sales that will be facing bank marketing officers in the years ahead:

1. A desire for results plus cost effectiveness will increase the importance of direct sales in the marketing mix.

2. There will be resistance from the staff in these efforts.

3. Management will probably expect too much in the way of results, and being nonmarketing oriented, will, at the same time, give little support.

> **KEY POINT:** Even with these hard realities in mind, direct selling offers unique opportunities to develop profitable new business and the best chance to keep profitable existing business on the books.

Combatting Staff Resistance. It is strange but true that bankers traditionally raise as much or more money for United Way than do representatives of any other industry. They can, in short, sell charity extremely well. Yet they are reluctant to sell bank services. Why? Because, as they will invariably say, "But I can't sell!"

There are two kinds of staff resistance to selling:

- Refusal to sell
- Reluctance to sell

The latter could also be called "buck fever" or "stage fright." With professional salespeople, the term is "call reluctance." In some cases, pros will actually get right outside a prospect's door, and, shaking, walk away.

Although it is not easy, something can be done about reluctance and/or timidity. Consider the following ideas:

1. *Concept of the concerned core.* This phrase was developed in the implementation of a sales training program for a savings bank in Troy, New York. In essence it means: If only a certain percentage of the public-contact people are career oriented enough to want to sell bank services, training and motivation should be concentrated on these people because, sooner or later, every prospect for cross-selling will come into contact with one of them. In other words, write off the disenchanted, the hangers-on, the uninterested and work to build a strong core group.

2. *Concept of expanded marketing.* This idea is apparently attributed to a bank in Vermont, where at least one person in each office *is* the marketing department representative for that branch. This person is responsible for feedback in both directions, for testing marketing concepts on the spot, and so on. This, of course, is in addition to his or her regular duties.

3. *Concept of reward.* "Money," goes the old cliche, "isn't everything. However, it is way ahead of whatever is in second place!" Thus, a bank in Massachusetts rewrote all tellers' job descriptions to include a marketing function—then backed this up with a substantial increase in pay grades.

> **TIP:** Another and even more effective tool is to openly take sales results into consideration at raise time.

> **NOTE:** The problem facing bank marketing officers isn't selling versus other marketing tools. It is using selling as an important implementation of the marketing strategy, which requires a three-way effort involving management, the staff, and the support of a hard-hitting advertising and public relations program.

DIRECT MAIL MARKETING IN BANKING

For the most part, banks market their services through account officers (wholesale services) or through branches (retail services). Nowadays, though, direct mail is fast becoming an important and effective bank marketing tool.

Remember the controversy Citibank created a few years ago when it unleashed an avalanche of direct mail offering its credit card to prospective customers throughout the Midwest and West? Since then other banks have followed suit using direct mail to penetrate markets beyond their own geographic boundaries and to target select customer segments in need of special services.

> **EXAMPLE:** One bank offered special lines of credit to out-of-state doctors just as they were facing the deadline for renewal of costly malpractice insurance. The campaign netted more than 400 new lines of credit worth over $5 million.

Growing Public Acceptance. At one time customers would have balked at such bank solicitation by mail. However, as the people become more accustomed to the barrage of direct mail received from a variety of sources, they have come to view it as a convenient way to do business and have responded accordingly.

Several studies show that consumers respond favorably to the quality of direct mail they receive from financial institutions in general.

How to Mount a Successful Direct-mail Campaign for Your Bank. A great deal of thought goes into putting a successful direct mail campaign together. The six key steps are:

1. *Map out a strategy.* A crucial element of strategy is identifying the target audience for the campaign. Some banks find that if they are trying to cross-sell services, the hottest list they can mail is to their current customer base. Specific campaigns, such as one directed to doctors and dentists, will have a well-defined purpose and prospect list.

2. *Test the central elements of the campaign.* These include the lists, the message, and any promotional tie-ins. Some banks prefer to test several alternative letters and premium offers to see which is the most effective.

3. *Plan an ongoing campaign* (in states, if possible, rather than a one-time mailing). Such ongoing, staggered mailings bring better results.

4. *Ensure adequate follow-up.* Once the direct mail materials are in the hands of the customer, the drive has only just begun. The success of any promotion depends heavily on the degree of follow-up that occurs. The type of follow-up will depend on the nature of the campaign and the size of the audience to be reached. In some cases telephone follow-up may be feasible.

5. *Closely manage the fulfillment process.* If a promotional gift was offered, make sure the respondent receives it promptly. More than a few direct mail campaigns have been ruined by sloppy fulfillment.

6. *Carefully monitor response.* The numbers will not only give you the data to measure the success of the current campaign but will also be important in planning the next one.

> **NOTE:** Make sure your bank is geared to handle the response. Slow response could hurt the entire sales effort and do more harm than good.

HOW TO MAKE MARKET SEGMENTATION WORK IN YOUR BANK'S MARKETING EFFORT

Market segmentation has taken hold on both the corporate and consumer banking fronts. Banks no longer treat all corporate and institutional customers the same. Banks distinguish between the services they offer the multinational and the domestic firm—for example, offering sophisticated foreign exchange advisory and trade services to the firms that require them.

On the consumer side, banks have begun to look at groups of customers based on such demographics as age, education and income level, profession, or other relevant characteristics. *Result:* the creation of special programs aimed at such groups as senior citizens, female executives, high net worth individuals, professionals, and others.

To date, many of these programs have been highly successful and brought thousands of new customers to a bank thereby generating millions in deposits and fees.

IDENTIFYING YOUR TARGET SEGMENT AND DESIGNING A PROGRAM

The first key to success is the proper identification of the market segment. The target segment must be valid, well-defined, understood, and substantial enough to constitute a profit opportunity. Conduct extensive market research to gather all the data you can because the more you know about the particular segment and its habits and needs, the more effectively you will be able to serve it.

Once you have dimensioned the segment and its needs, the next step is to design the program. For example, after reviewing both the business financial needs of law firms and the personal financial needs of partners, one bank came up with a program that offered the following services:

• Timely and regular distribution of profits to partners

• Short-term investment programs such as CDs and savings accounts, commercial paper, treasury bills, bankers' acceptances, municipal bonds, and money-market instruments

• Acquisition of assets such as law libraries, computer systems, word processing, and telephone systems through term financing

• Financing leasehold improvements

• Partnership capital contributions

• Financing tax payments, educational expenses, and other extraordinary living expenses between major distributions

• Acquisition of principal and vacation residences

• Loans for tax incentive investments, entrepreneurial investments, and security purchases

• Full-scale retail services

• Investment management, estate and trust planning and administration, escrow services

Another bank, aiming at the female executive market, launched a program including:

• A personal financial library: a series of six booklets on such subjects as budgeting, spending and saving, credit, investing, tax planning, and estate planning

• A referral service able to supply, on request, the names of accountants, attorneys, tax planners, and stockbrokers

• A hotline to get financial questions answered quickly

• Seminars on financial subjects and a reference collection housed at the program's headquarters

• Financial planning services and a counselor for personal financial guidance

• A periodic newsletter on financial topics

Segmentation Strategy. Program design is one component of overall strategy. Other important elements include:

• *Delivery system.* Will the services be offered through the regular bank network, through a special team of officers, or through a combination?

• *Pricing.* Will participation in the program be set by a fee or a required balance?

• *Publicity.* How will you reach the segment? What specialized media will you use? What precise message will you convey?

29

ADVERTISING YOUR BANK'S PRODUCTS AND SERVICES

Not too long ago, advertising was of little importance to banks. What little advertising was done was formal, usually unexciting, and rarely attracted much attention. This type of advertising has changed radically over the past ten years. As a result, advertising in banks is often quite innovative, and increasing in cost.

HOW TO MAKE AD DOLLARS COUNT

Banks cannot afford to spend freely on advertising. They must get the maximum return possible from all advertising expenditures. This requires the creation of clever concepts in advertising as well as wise media selection. Above all, it requires careful research, planning, and testing. Later, after the actual advertising begins, banks must make a realistic commitment to their goals and spend enough money in the right areas to obtain them.

Four Steps to Take in Planning Bank Advertising. A survey of banks conducted a few years ago revealed these interesting facts: 99 percent of the banks advertised; 98 percent had regular public relations programs; 89 percent were actively involved in the promotion of new business; 53 percent did market research.

> **DISASTROUS CONCLUSION:** 46 percent
> of the banks surveyed spent advertising dollars
> blindly, hoping to hit a target they had not
> defined, couldn't see, and weren't even sure
> existed!

Step 1. The first step in planning advertising is to determine your audience. Who's out there and might be receptive? Receptive to what? This is just the opposite of the all-too-common approach of bank marketing, which is to decide to sell a certain mix of services and then try to stir up an audience. Knowing who lives in your trading areas and what their needs and interests are, then selecting the service mix to best suit those needs, should be steps taken before any advertising program is even considered.

Steps 2, 3, 4. The second step is to determine the amount available for the advertising budget. Again, the approach here should not be the traditional "How much can we get appropriated?" but a realistic "How much do we need to do the job?" This, along with step 3, developing the message, and step 4, media selection, must out of necessity be integrated rather than be considered distinct steps, because creative development and media costs are obviously major factors in budgeting.

This approach to planning calls for absolute honesty. It may be necessary to put to rest past assumptions that have guided banks for years. For example: "People save where they get the highest rates," while the fact may be that, given a modest rate differential, they will opt for convenience instead.

> **THE KEY:** The salesperson's old adage,
> "Find a need and fill it," is the key, if you add
> the words, "then tell the right people in the
> right way that you have done so."

How to Create and Develop the Message. Generally speaking, a banker who writes his or her own ad copy can be likened to the person who acts as his or her own lawyer: He or she may have a fool for a client. Amateur copy usually tends to be sophomoric.

On the other hand, bankers who totally trust their agency to come up with concepts could become victims of a copywriter's dream to indulge in fantasy. Two real examples of headlines are:

> (Written by a banker) "The Bank Where the Bus Stops at the Door."
> (Written by a misguided copywriter) "It's Bigger Than the Moon!"

The creation of the message should start with the copy, not with the headline. Here are five steps to take in message development:

1. List all the benefits of the service to the person or persons you wish to reach.

2. Put those benefits into their order of impact, listing the best benefit first.

3. Write a simple description of each benefit, using short sentences and short paragraphs, with no more than one benefit included in each paragraph.

4. Eliminate any "weak" benefits.

5. Add on the action the prospect should take to obtain the benefit.

Now you have the outline of an ad, which can be easily adapted by a creative advertising team into newspaper, radio, magazine, TV, or other media copy.

After copy is written, write the headline next. The headline should make people want to read the ad by holding out a promise of benefits. Thus, the headline in our example about the bus stopping at the door could actually offer convenience, and instead of being bigger than the moon as written by the copywriter, a practical approach to savings could offer weary consumers a realistic hope for the future.

How to Test Your Ads. Testing ads can be a problem. Banks operating within tight regional areas simply do not have access to some of the sophisticated—and expensive—testing methods used by national advertisers. What can you do in this situation?

1. Run a lobby survey of your advertising. Use simple, check-off forms and ask tellers to have customers fill them in.

2. Ask new customers whether or not advertising brought them to the bank.

3. Conduct a simple survey in a good traffic location within the trading area, such as a shopping center.

4. Use the testing facilities offered by the local media. However, remember to allow for their biases.

Ad Production. National advertisers estimate 15 to 20 percent of the cost of advertising is attributed to production expenses, while local advertisers may find this figure runs as high as 50 percent. Obviously, the lower the production cost, the greater the amount that can be spent to gain actual exposure. However, do not sell production short. A poorly produced ad may run more often; however, it may not be noticed. Stick to these rules:

• Leave production to the pros—and that means your agency or someone it selects.

• Get production cost estimates spelled out in detail and in writing before you give the go-ahead. When ad specifications change, as they always do, also get updated estimates.

Three Tips on Selecting the Right Media. If you know your audience, the service mix you wish to sell to and what your budget will be, then given the defined trading area in which you have to work, your media choices will probably become apparent.

Here are some tips for media selection:

1. Choose media that zero in as much as possible on the target audience. For example, a rock and roll radio station that reaches teenagers is a waste of money for trying to sell trust services.

2. Allow enough money in your budget to achieve the degree of saturation and repetition of your message that will have the maximum effect.

3. Try for a media mix that will not only extend your reach but will overlap sufficiently to give you positive reinforcement with your target audience.

Following Up on Your Effort. Advertising creates the broad umbrella of consumer education and service identification under which a follow-up sales effort can be most effective. Two points can be concluded:

• Advertising should be designed with follow-up in mind. Who will sell the service? How? Do they need training? How much training? What kind? Who should conduct it?

• People who will do the selling should participate from the beginning. They should help to gather the initial research data and pretest the advertising. This means that, whenever possible, they must be kept informed of all steps along the way.

> **KEEP IN MIND:** "Fully half of what I spend on advertising is wasted," complained John Wanamaker. "Unfortunately, I don't know which half." You can't eliminate all wasted advertising dollars, but you can keep them to a minimum.

USING ENDORSEMENTS IN BANK ADS

Does your bank's ad campaign feature a popular person who endorses the services of the bank? Or is your ad agency considering a campaign where hidden cameras "surprise" shoppers to get their honest reactions for future commercials?

If either of these situations applies to you, you had better review the corporate ad materials in light of the Federal Trade Commission's *Guides Concerning the Use of Endorsements and Testimonials in Advertising.* These guides apply to each and every ad you run which features an endorsement or testimonial—from a famous athlete on T.V. to a homemaker at the branch office.

Three points advertisers should consider are:

• *Indirect product claims.* Endorsements may only reflect the honest views of the endorser and may not contain claims that cannot be supported if made directly by the advertiser.

• *Celebrity endorsements.* Endorsements cannot be presented in a manner that is out of context or distorts them. Celebrity endorsements or expert endorsements can be used only as long as the advertiser has good reason to believe the endorser continues to subscribe to the views presented in the advertisement.

• *Actual use requirement.* Where the advertisement represents the endorser as using the particular product, the endorser must indeed use it. The advertiser can use the endorsement only as long as it has good reason to believe that the endorser continues to use the product.

How to Use Consumer Endorsements Effectively. There are special considerations where second-component, consumer endorsements are used:

• *Average person rule.* Where an advertisement includes the endorsement of product performance by a consumer or group of consumers, there is an implication that the average person can expect to obtain comparable performance. Thus, advertisers will have to possess substantiation for this implicit claim. Or, the advertiser may "clearly and conspicuously" disclose what the generally expected performance of the product would be or "clearly and conspicuously" inform consumers of the limited applicability of the disclosed performance.

• *"Actual consumer" endorsements.* The new guidelines state that endorsements by so-called actual consumers should use actual consumers or disclose the fact that actors are appearing.

• *Support requirement.* Advertisers will have to provide adequate proof for consumers' endorsements of drugs. These endorsements must be consistent with any determinations about the drug made by the Food and Drug Administration.

Disclosure of Material Connection. The FTC guidelines also contain requirements affecting the disclosure of "materials connections." The advertiser must spell out any connection between the bank and the endorser that might materially affect the weight or credibility of the endorsement. The guidelines highlight two material connections that would require disclosure:

• Where the endorser is neither a celebrity nor an expert, any compensation paid prior to and in exchange for the endorsement must be disclosed.

• Where the endorser knew or had reason to know that he or she would "appear on television" if the "right things" were said, disclosure will be required.

TAKE CARE WITH COMPARATIVE ADVERTISING

One of the phenomena of the advertising business these days is the use of comparative advertising: one company mentioning (unfavorably) another firm's product or service. This type of advertising has led to all sorts of problems, including legal action. Unfortunately, some banks have already used comparative advertising while others are just now getting into the act.

Four Pitfalls to Avoid. Comparative advertising works sometimes, but not in all cases. Before launching a comparative advertising campaign, a bank should first consider the consequences: whether the benefit or service being promoted is important enough for the bank to name its competitors. Look at what can happen:

1. Comparative advertising provides a bank's competitors with free advertising. In effect, the ads will identify the other banks in the vicinity that offer competitive services with the advertiser. In doing so, the ads will tell disgruntled customers what banks to patronize if they want to close out accounts in the advertising bank and open them elsewhere.

2. There is also the burden of continuously monitoring the rates charged by those competitors named in the ads—and the competition for lower rates is increasing as restrictions continue to be lifted. If, for example, the competition lowers its rates, the comparative advertising campaign may have to be scrapped or at least adjusted to meet the new situation.

3. A bank can open itself to a charge of misleading advertising, unless all financing costs are revealed, exact quotes are provided, and financing restrictions are listed.

4. Comparative advertising makes waves.

> **NOTE:** A bank should consider this technique only if it is not concerned about ruffling the feathers of other banks in its market area.

WHY CAUTION IS NEEDED IN COMPARATIVE ADVERTISING: TWO EXAMPLES

The use of comparative advertising seems to be growing, with mixed results, as illustrated in the examples below.

• Not long ago, New York City's Manufacturers Hanover Trust Co. stated in an ad campaign that its competitor, Citibank, was caught napping. This was a knock against Citibank's claim that "the Citi never sleeps." The local press picked up on the ad and *Advertising Age* ran a first-page story on it.

• Also in New York City, Chase Manhattan Bank once ran a television ad pointing out that Chase has 250 branches in the area, but the largest savings bank (not named) had only eighteen. The unnamed savings bank started its own ad campaign, saying it was the bank in Chase Manhattan's ad and that it paid more on savings accounts and its checking was free.

30

BANK
BUSINESS DEVELOPMENT

There have always been business development undertakings in banking. In years past, however, this was often achieved through old school ties, contacts at the country club, some discreet advertising perhaps, and even some calling on potential customers by bank officers. Sales efforts were hardly mentioned; indeed, sales was not a word generally accepted in the banking business. Now, many banks have abandoned the old ways of developing business and recruit and hire sales personnel to drum up business, particularly since competition has heated up.

PLANNING AHEAD

Developing new business is not easy. With competition at such high levels, calling officers are under pressure to bring in profitable business. Focusing on the most effective techniques for the prospecting phase of the sales effort can help achieve this level of performance.

Developing a Prospect List. Before any calls can be made, a prospect list must be developed. Some of the resources available for developing the prospect list are:

• *Present customers.* Because a relationship is already established, these customers are usually receptive to cross-selling efforts. They also can be excellent information sources for new business leads.

• *Directories.* Business directories, chambers of commerce publications, Dun & Bradstreet, and the yellow pages are good sources. However, doublechecking information is essential because these sources have varying degrees of accuracy.

• *Published sources.* Trade magazines and newspapers often carry articles on specific companies, management changes, industry developments, and so on.

• *Other professionals.* Accountants, attorneys, management consultants, and others in the financial industry can be fertile sources for leads.

All information concerning a prospect should be carefully recorded and should include:

• Name, address, and telephone number of company
• Description of business activity
• Financial information—total assets and sales
• Number of employees
• Officers' names and areas of responsibility

How to Choose Prospects with Care.   The bank's sales goal is to achieve maximum benefit for the sales effort expended. Therefore, the prospect list should be screened with an eye to the potential profitability of the account and the amount of sales leverage you have with the prospect. Some possible considerations are:

• Your bank's competitive strength in the marketplace
• Estimated selling effort required
• Your knowledge of the business and its needs
• Knowledge of, and access to, decision-makers
• Your ability to use a third-party referral
• Estimated contribution to your bank's profitability

Perhaps the most common error calling officers make is to attempt a sale on the initial contact with the prospect.

The Objective of Prospecting: Not to sell the product, but to sell a sales interview. The interview is a time for establishing the calling officer's credibility, developing a feel for the prospect's needs, and relating those needs to the bank's services. As rapport grows and sales resistance decreases, the caller should request another meeting, at which time a complete sales presentation can be made.

> **NOTE:** There are times when cold calling is an appropriate prospecting technique, but, in most cases, particularly with larger companies, telephoning for an appointment is the wiser choice.

DEVELOPING NEW BUSINESS PROGRAMS

A continual flow of new business is essential to the success of a bank. Sometimes, however, new business development programs are too general to be effective. The following program, using elements from programs that have been working well at other banks, has three cornerstones as its base.

1. *Research.* Send members of your bank's credit department out into the bank's market area and copy (also photograph, if this is allowed) building registries. Secure information on the companies and their owners. Then establish prospect files, arranged according to industry and location. These files will then be the basis for a solicitation campaign.

One bank found that it was best to have a single officer oversee this research function; another used a committee with good results. It really depends on the organization and the people who may be available.

Whoever is responsible for the research should also be charged with maintaining the files of the program once the solicitation campaign gets going. This involves plenty of work, but it will all be justified when the extra preparation pays off with the increased success of the new business calls.

2. *Quotas on Calls.* Calling quotas should be assigned to teams when the team approach is used, and to individuals. The team approach might work best for certain kinds of businesses, with specialists sent to call on those prospects that might require special expertise. The senior member of a team should endeavor to include all members of the team in any solicitation effort. Teams, incidentally, probably should never have more than four or five members.

Seniority should govern all assignments. Smaller firms normally are assigned to junior officers. Large customers, and certainly those prospects that the bank has wanted to land over a period of years, should almost always be visited by senior lending officers with more experience.

Unannounced calls should be handled with care. When a bank representative who is unknown to the prospect calls unannounced, he or she may be shunted off to a lower level person than the company's treasurer or owner. This can be frustrating for the calling officer, and not productive for the bank. It is recommended that junior officers always call for appointments until a relationship has been established. If efforts to arrange appointments by phone fail, the officer can then visit the company and talk with a secretary or other company representative about the problem. It is possible that the prospect may have time to see the banker.

3. *Oversight.* Sheets summarizing the calling efforts made by the new business officers should be prepared and sent to the senior management of the bank on a regular basis, usually monthly.

These tally sheets will also compare the actual calls to the solicitation goals set for the individual officer or team. The goals provide targets for the calling officers and help to set the proper environment for the entire solicitation campaign—and usually prove to be excellent motivators. In addition, and not to be discounted, they provide a means for evaluating each calling officer.

NOTE: This program, of course, should be adapted and expanded by the individual bank, taking into account the goals of the organization, the marketplace, and the calling officers who are a part of the new business function.

HOW TO APPROACH THE NEW BUSINESS CALL

Sales professionals are unanimous in their conclusion that an effective opening is vital to the success of the prospect call. This transition from the initial greeting and introduction should be carefully planned to quickly capture the prospect's interest. Some of the proven ways of accomplishing this are:

• *Offer benefits.* Use this when your research has revealed a specific service that offers the prospect identifiable benefits.
• *Discuss prospect's business.* Any positive changes in the business—for instance, plant expansion, offer an opportunity to discuss the prospect's business in a complimentary way. Flattery may indeed get you somewhere.
• *Use third-party referrals.* This is a particularly strong opening because by associating yourself with someone known to the prospect your credibility is quickly established.

Do Not Sell the Product. Remember that your goal is to set an appointment, not to sell. As soon as you have identified a need, ask for an appointment to meet with the prospect to discuss how your bank can fill that need. It is very important for you to take the initiative and ask for a meeting. Offer two or three possible time slots. Doing this demonstrates your interest and puts the prospect on the defensive, making it more likely that he or she will agree to an appointment.

How to Avoid the Brush-off. Sales resistance may simply be the prospect's way of testing your interest and sincerity. If so, restating the needs your bank can satisfy will underscore your interest and probably gain you the appointment. In other cases you may have to scale down your goal by requesting a 15–20 minute meeting. Zeroing in on a limited meeting allows you to keep the conversation going while avoiding the selling trap. If the prospect asks you to send information to him or her, agree to do so, but still ask for the limited meeting by stressing the personal nature of the banking relationship.

Follow-up When Possible. If there is time before the appointment, it is a good practice to send a confirmation letter. Again, you want to create as much goodwill as possible. Also, if the prospect refuses to meet, it gives you the basis for follow-up later.

> **TIP:** The calling officer should limit the initial contact to arranging for a meeting and reserve selling until that time. By tailoring sales efforts to the personal nature of the banking relationship and carefully choosing prospects, it won't be long before those prospects will become profitable accounts for the bank.

SELLING YOUR BANK TO FINANCIAL OFFICERS

Most senior bankers make calls on new businesses. Furthermore, most banks tailor solicitation programs to the needs of the professionals or the specialized businesses in their area. To a considerable degree, how well these new business programs succeed depends on the effectiveness in addressing the financial needs and dealing with the mentality of corporate financial officers.

How to Deal Effectively with Corporate Financial Officers. There are corporate financial officers (CFOs) who are content (or reasonably so) with their existing banking relationships. Consequently, these CFOs complain that the persistent sales efforts of soliciting bankers only keeps them from doing their jobs. However, there are CFOs who believe they should extend their banking relationships beyond the beιιcr banks located near the headquarters of their firms. These CFOs often have had experience at companies that have been squeezed by a credit shortage or have had major (or important) loan requests turned down by their banks. In many cases, such CFOs enjoy the game of corporate finance; they like to pit their various bankers against one another to see who will offer the least expensive loan or the most interesting or innovative package of services. These CFOs understand that competition between their banks usually gets them the best service. At the same time, they like to meet and deal with bankers who are willing to fight for the edge in interbank competition.

Talk the Customer's Language. As a banker, you want a CFO to extend his or her banking relationships to include your bank. To accomplish this, you will have to humor the CFO's financial preoccupations and his or her notion of what is involved in prudent corporate financial management. This can be delicate work and means you must do the following:

• *Establish your loyalty.* Corporations pay their banks in balances or commitment fees for lines of credit. Top corporations may not need their credit lines often, but they want to know that their banks will support them should borrowing be necessary. Tell the CFO you offer your customers solid support through thick and thin, credit crunch, and recession. Tell the customer you will put your commitment in writing. If you can impress the CFO as being dependable in a crisis, you may well get his or her firm's balances.

• *Establish your competence.* Many corporations need large banks to properly handle their credit needs. Large banks know that their size can make them indispensable. However, this can sometimes make those banks complacent and somewhat sloppy and/or slow in servicing operational problems. Tell the CFO that his or her business is important to your bank; indicate that you cannot afford to give less than top service.

• *Establish your expertise.* A corporation may not need to borrow. But some may be in need of a good cash-management service. Others may need advice in specialized businesses. If your bank has a certain reputation or lending specialty, sell it to the CFO.

• *Stress your location.* A number of CFOs believe in geographic diversity. They believe credit shortages may occur regionally, thus, they spread their banking relationships to avoid geographic illiquidity. All CFOs recognize the value of working with local banks to assist noncentralized divisions with normal financial needs.

> **KEEP IN MIND:** Corporate financial officers will invariably want something in return for their business. They will expand their banking relationships with your bank only if they can be convinced they will get that return from you or others in the bank.

USING DIRECTORS TO BRING IN QUALITY BUSINESS

Attracting new business of good quality is always a problem for most banks. However, it must be pursued if a bank expects to grow and prosper. Yet too often one of the best possible resources readily available to a bank for bringing in new business is overlooked—its directors. Here is what we have found that a number of banks do to successfully develop profitable business utilizing the members of their boards.

A Senior Sales Person. First, use line officers to make regular, new business calls. Next, if the prospect looks good, have the head of the department join the calling officer for lunch with the prospect. Then marshall the bank's secret weapon to woo major corporate prospects by involving members of the board of directors, as described next.

Each fiscal quarter, have the head of each lending team or unit submit a business development memo to his or her superior. This memo should describe the lending team's recent solicitation efforts aimed at a major corporate prospect. The name and address of the company, the line of business, the firm's size (sales, profits, total assets, etc.).

Included in the memo should be the following information: the lending team (or individual) responsible for the solicitation, the names and titles of top management and the names and affiliations of the directors, and a summary of recent contacts with the company.

In conjunction with the superior receiving the memo (usually someone at the executive vice president level) and the bank directors, marketing specialists should determine whether or not any of the directors can assist in the business development effort. If it is decided that this is to be the case, a meeting with the company's top officers and the bank's director(s), along with senior bank officials, is arranged.

On the Plus Side. It is often difficult for another bank to break into a major corporation's banking arrangements. Although it can be frustrating, even time-consuming, the rewards can be great. A program that involves the directors of a bank, such as the one described above, will help keep new business officers on the train of major prospects. In addition, the program:

• Impresses prospects, even when it does not pay off with immediate business.

• Enhances regular solicitations. Calls by the directors help to consolidate the gains of new business calls.

• Broadens the contact base. A calling officer may know the corporation's treasurer, but a director may know the chairman or a major stockholder.

> **NOTE:** This program, or similar programs, underscores the interest of most directors of a bank in the new business efforts of business development officers. It also puts to use the clout directors may have in supporting the bank's solicitation efforts.

31

ESTABLISHING
AND MAINTAINING
GOOD CUSTOMER RELATIONS

Customers are important to a bank. They always have been, of course, although too often customers were taken for granted, or worse, as a necessary evil.

That attitude is gone forever, and banks are better for it. Some ideas on better relations with customers are included in this chapter.

COPING WITH CHANGING BANK–CUSTOMER RELATIONSHIPS: EIGHT STEPS TO TAKE

With competition rampant these days, it is too easy to lose customers. Without customers, a bank's future is not bright. Obviously steps must be taken to regain lost customers (or add new ones). Here are eight steps any bank can take.

1. Make sure the bank's entire staff—from board chairperson to custodian—is friendly and cooperative at all times to customers and potential customers.

2. See that loan officers are familiar with, or at least have a working knowledge of, each borrower's business. If the account is a substantial one, officers handling it should make a special study and dig into the structure of the business. Quite often this can make the difference between a safe and profitable loan and one turned down because of insufficient information.

3. Offer special services and programs. These might include loans on assignments of customers' accounts receivables, inventory field-warehousing agreement loans, discounts for trade acceptances, or loans based on assignment of money due on contracts.

There are other services a bank might perform such as act as custodian of voting trust records, act as dividend disbursing agent, guarantee signatures and give letters of credit and letters of introduction, handle withholding tax receipts, and so on.

4. Counsel customers on borrowing. Show your customers why it is necessary to have an adequate labor force, sufficient plant capacity, and a timely flow of raw materials if they are to profit from the funds advanced by the bank. For that matter, show them the importance of this assurance in convincing the bank to grant the loan in the first place.

5. Encourage meetings with the customer's accountant. In all likelihood, the accountant will be able to fill in bank personnel on vital details that the borrower doesn't know or understand, or is unable to assemble for the bank's consideration and analysis. This demonstrates to the customer your interest in him or her, and it could prove the difference between making and not making a profit for the bank.

6. Have the backup person to the account's loan officer meet with the borrower. Then, if the regular account executive is not available, the backup will be able to take up the slack and keep things running smoothly.

7. Require loan officers to visit a borrower's premises from time to time. These visits not only strengthen existing relationships, they also allow bank officials to discover improvements or deterioration in the borrower's operations.

8. If your bank does not have automated lending operations, do so as soon as possible. Chances are, the competition is automated and can provide the speed and accuracy necessary for proper handling of accounts.

CHECKLIST REVIEW OF CUSTOMER SERVICES

The following checklist will help to determine the quality and extent of services currently used by a bank's customers. The form is designed to be filled out by a customer account officer of the bank.

CUSTOMER'S REVIEW OF BANK'S SERVICES

Date .... Date of last call ....
Customer ....
Officer ....
  1. Return items procedure: ....
     ....
  2. Use of the branch night depository: ....
     Are agreements on file and up-to-date?
  3. Is the customer using our federal depository for taxes?
  4. Is the customer's coin and currency demand being met?
  5. Is the customer satisfied with his or her statement handling?
     ☐ Will call   ☐ Mailed
  6. Is the customer using our safe-deposit facilities?
  7. Service charge procedures:
     ☐ Regular   ☐ Analysis
  8. Encoding on checks and deposits: ....
     ....
  9. Interbranch service: ....
     ....
10. Local documentation: ....
     ....
11. Are fictitious firm name papers or corporate resolutions current?
12. City cash collections: ....
     ....
13. Items processed for collection:
     ☐ Incoming   ☐ Outgoing
14. The customer's evaluation of the service he or she is receiving:
     Branch service in general ....
     Particular individuals ....
15. Cover any additional services available to the customer that he or she may not be using.

GUIDE TO BETTER—AND SAFER—CHECK CASHING

Although each customer is not personally known by each teller, the teller can use bank records to verify each customer's identity. The identification of strangers, however, poses special problems for the teller.

When asked to cash checks of noncustomers, the teller does not have bank records to help determine that payment is being made to the right person. Failure to make proper identification can also result in a financial loss to your bank.

Seven Points to Consider. Alertness and good judgment on the part of your tellers will prevent most check-cashing losses. Among the special matters they must keep in mind to prevent check fraud are:

• All items must be endorsed exactly as drawn. This is particularly important in the case of government checks and insurance company drafts. Watch carefully for "and" payees. You must verify both endorsements on such checks.

• A check is not an effective order to pay if it is postdated. A check that is postdated one or two days and which is issued by a local utility or thriving major industrial concern, however, may be treated as an exception. These checks should be approved by an officer.

• Letters and other personal papers should not be treated as proof of identity. Once again, exceptions can be made, but only after the exercise of good judgment.

• Strangers who present themselves as friends of officers and employees who have just stepped out to lunch should be handled with caution.

• Treat any person gingerly who tries to establish an unprovable association with known responsible customers to get a check cashed.

• Occasionally, the endorsement of a check must be verified with a telephone call. In this situation, be sure to secure the number from the phone book and not from the person presenting the check.

• Beware of con-artist ploys. The con artist who uses the "fake deposit gambit," for example, makes deposits consisting of bad checks as he or she presents a large bad check for cashing. In the "small justifies large" ploy, the con artist cashes a number of small genuine checks and then presents a large check for cashing that is drawn on a closed or nonexistent account. These and other ploys can be combatted only if your tellers follow procedures carefully and handle each check as a separate transaction.

> **NOTE:** It is essential for your tellers to observe check-cashing guidelines. Most frauds occur during busy periods. It is much easier for tellers to follow guidelines if staffing is adequate and they are not inundated by shortcut-inducing pressure.

CUSTOMER COMPLAINTS: WHAT TO DO ABOUT THEM

Consider the following situations:

• A customer writes a letter protesting a delay and an error in posting a credit to his or her account.

• The assistant treasurer of a corporate customer calls to inform the bank that a money transfer was not processed correctly.

The operations area of a bank is often the hub for resolving such customer problems. How well operations responds can often determine the state of customer relations and will ultimately have a profound impact on the bank's bottom line.

The list of customer complaints is extensive. Whether serious or trivial, a complaint ignored or not satisfied could result in an ex-customer.

Seven Tips for Setting Up a System in Your Bank. Here are seven tips in setting up systems to handle customer inquiries and complaints:

• Establish a central unit or receiving point to handle calls and letters. Make sure each transaction is logged in appropriately.

• Set timeliness and quality standards. Make sure each inquiry or complaint is answered within a specified time period, usually 24 to 48 hours. If the matter will take longer to resolve, provide the customer with an acknowledgment and an interim reply during the set timeframe. Make sure each inquiry or complaint is answered accurately, completely, and courteously.

• Monitor and track calls and letters. Prepare analyses that will identify the key issues that surface and prepare corrective action to deal with any trends or patterns that develop.

• Provide reports and analyses to senior management. Senior management support is crucial to a successful customer service program.

• Follow-up to ensure customer satisfaction. (One bank sends a postcard to a randomly selected group of customers who have dealt with the customer service representatives and asks the customers to rate the services received.)

• Select and train well the personnel who staff the customer service function.

• Provide as much automated support as possible.

Customers are always impressed when the person who receives their call can quickly look up the information on a CRT and resolve the matter in a speedy, efficient manner.

> **NOTE:** You should also set up a system to acknowledge and respond to customer compliments. Also, notify employees when compliments concerning them are received.

HOW TO CUT THOSE TELLER LINES

Long lines at the teller's windows give a customer a good reason to move his or her account. Is there anything you can do to relieve the irritations of exasperated customers who, understandably, don't want to waste their time standing in a line?

Understanding the customer's point of view will help you to understand why offering seemingly reasonable explanation for delays to customers will usually fall on unsympathetic ears. *Example:* Only a few of the eight to ten teller windows are available for service at any one time, and the remaining are either empty or occupied by tellers engaged in nonservice activities. When lines are long and it takes 15 minutes to reach a window, customers will not accept any excuses because they see all the empty windows.

When managers attempt to solve this persistent problem, as they often do, they generally choose from among three alternatives:

• Hire more tellers and make certain they're available when needed.

• Rearrange the teller setup according to the various services offered—that is, check cashing, savings account transactions, and so forth.

• Remove responsibility for all difficult and time-consuming transactions and services from the windows and assign them to the manager's desk area.

Managers who have tried these alternatives agree they are all lacking in one way or another. First, as experience shows, long lines are not constant; they occur for parts of each day during periods of irregular demand. Unfortunately, the different times long lines form vary greatly. Therefore, managers who hire more tellers must be prepared to keep them busy with work throughout the day. Most cannot. Managers then are faced with a dilemma: Long lines that waste customers' time may send them elsewhere, but the cost of keeping customers satisfied by increasing service could outrun revenues.

Second, teller setups that segregate services force customers with multiple transactions to move from line to line. Because people generally have more than one type of banking transaction at any one time, this setup not only fails to cut down line time but actually adds to the confusion.

The Solution: Focus with Film. Your problem does not center on the length of the line but rather on the amount of time a customer must stand in it. Therefore, to solve the problem, you must pinpoint precisely when customers stand in the teller lines too long. This takes careful analysis and a time-lapse camera, which is a moving-picture technique that is the practical approach to resolving waiting line problems.

Time-lapse camera. The regular camera speed for a 16-mm film produces 16 frames per second. Therefore, a one-hour study requires a total of 57,600 frames, and, at the rate of 40 frames per foot, a total of 1,440 feet of film. The time-lapse technique, on the other hand, shoots 20 frames per minute (one frame every three seconds). A one-hour study adds up to 1,200 frames and only 130 feet of film is needed to do the job.

Played back frame by frame, the film gives you the ammunition for an in-depth analysis and appraisal. It records in detail interrelated events and focuses attention on the major movements taking place at the teller counters. Because it lets you study the situation more slowly, and therefore, more closely, the time-lapse technique is a far more accurate and effective means of analysis than on-the-spot observation.

Once you have established the use of the time-lapse camera as a tool for studying teller waiting lines, the true answers to your problem will reveal themselves.

> **TIP:** The astute manager will fit the pieces together and determine on what days and for what length of time additional help at the teller counters is needed so that lines are kept as short as possible.

32

PUBLIC RELATIONS
AND THE BANK

Much of what once was said about customers of banks could be said about relations with the public. This belief is changing. In fact, some of the larger banking institutions have as extensive and as professional public relations departments as can be generally found in business. That does not mean, however, that a bank's public relations efforts cannot be improved upon. The topics in this chapter will discuss improving public relations.

HOW TO IMPROVE YOUR BANK'S PR

There really is no mystery to the art of good public relations. Because every bank has public relations whether it wants to or not, it might just as well be good instead of bad.

Here are nine rules that can be applied to almost any bank:

1. Assign an officer as the bank's contact with the local press. All information for general public dissemination should be coordinated with and funneled through him or her.

2. The person charged with the PR function should quickly introduce him- or herself to the local media: newspapers, radio, and TV news staffs. The officer should learn which reporter is assigned to the kind of news his or her organization is likely to generate. The PR representative becomes both a name and a face and reporters will know whom to contact with inquiries. Similarly, the PR representative becomes the spokesperson for the bank, and has a personal working relationship with reporters. He or she thus stands a better chance of seeing the bank's news releases in print or hearing them broadcast.

3. News media, it should be remembered, are interested in news. You have a commodity basic to their operation—but only if it's news. Avoid trite material or deluging reporters with trivia that tends only to water down other, more legitimate news stories.

4. Supply local media with biographies and photos of the bank's top officer team. Be sure to periodically update both the background sheets and the pictures, perhaps every two years.

5. Forget dramatics and high-blown phrases in the bank's news releases. Keep them simple and to the point, with the most important information at the beginning. *Remember:* Most editors will chop out superlatives, so why waste time and space with them?

6. Don't forget to cover all bases of a news item. In other words, gain as much publicity mileage as possible with each release. Stories concerning bank promotions, for instance, should be covered by the local press where the bank's office is located. Also cover the promoted individual's hometown, college alumni publications, service organization newspapers and magazines, and the banking press.

7. Prepare media mailing lists in advance. Several directories and guides are available that offer breakdowns of publications on a geographical basis, topics of interest, contacts, and so on. Update these mailing lists frequently to ensure the right parties receive the releases.

8. Be alert to feature story possibilities. Reporters are always on the lookout for good story angles. Think out such stories, get upper-management approval, and then approach the reporter. Offer to cooperate by setting up interviews and photo sessions, and provide background material.

8. Know deadlines and provide releases in time. If you must rush to meet a deadline, call media people and alert them to what is coming and when.

A GUIDE TO BETTER PRESS RELATIONS

Every bank will have some kind of relationship with the press—that cannot be avoided and you really should not want to. However, you do have it within your power to help make press relations either good or bad. Better press relations, of course, is the way to go.

Here are some suggestions, based on experience and discussions with public relations people. These ideas are designed to help develop for your bank a positive image in the eyes of the members of the media with which you may have contact.

1. *Understand what the press wants.* The press is not in the public relations business; it wants news and/or interesting stories. Something you consider to be interesting about your bank and which would help business may be seen as too self-serving or commercial by the press. If you want publicity, you must supply material that appeals to the media's customers.

2. *Prepare material for the media's use.* Your material should be well thought out and written in journalistic style. Do not include a lot of extraneous information or present the material in overly descriptive terms.

3. *Supply material to meet media schedules.* Media people must meet deadlines. A hot news item should go to newspapers and broadcast media, not feature magazines. Try to find out when the deadlines are: what time of the day for newspapers and television, the day of the week for weekly papers and magazines, the day of the month for other magazines.

4. *Select the media carefully.* If you have a feature story, place it on an exclusive basis with one publication. If it's a news item, transmit it simultaneously to all media.

5. *Respond quickly to inquiries.* When a news publication or broadcast media people call with questions, get the answer to them as fast as possible. Editors appreciate prompt reactions and will be encouraged to contact your bank again. At the same time, never say "no comment." To much can be read into those two words. Do your best to provide an answer, even if it says little or nothing.

6. *Be honest.* Do not try to fool the press; it may work once, but you can create enemies. You can build credibility by being candid, straightforward, and leveling with your press contacts.

7. *Don't ask for favors.* This might be tempting when a potentially negative story develops. Asking for favors only puts the editor in a bad position. Treat the media fairly, and you will usually be treated fairly.

8. *Consider press needs.* If you are hosting an event, particularly if it extends over a period of time, have suitable refreshments, access to telephones, typewriters, and fax machines. Have informed people available for interviews and to answer questions.

9. *Be fair.* When you have good material, spread it around amongst the media without playing favorites.

SEVEN RULES FOR MORE EFFECTIVE PRESS RELEASES

The first contact most banks have with the media is through press releases—announcing a new service, personnel promotion, community relations activity, or other newsworthy event. Thus, it is important for the first contact to be effective.

By using the following generally accepted rules for the preparation of press releases, you can make the news editor's job easier, and thereby encourage maximum coverage of your bank's activities.

1. *Identify the organization sending the release.* The chances are fairly good that your release is one of many placed in editors' "in" boxes. If the editors are poring over several dozen or several hundred releases, they will want to know very quickly who the release is from. Having the name of the bank on the top of the first page is a good way of getting the job done.

2. *Identify the news contact.* Most editors usually want more information or have some questions about the copy. If the name and phone number of the person who can field questions is on the front of the release, obtaining additional information is not difficult. If journalists have to make two or three calls before getting to the appropriate person, that may be more trouble than the story is worth.

3. *Date the release.* Editors often file marginal releases in a separate drawer for possible use when there are holes to be filled. If, however, they go to the drawer and find an interesting but undated piece, they won't use it for fear that they're holding something of very ancient vintage.

4. *List a release date.* Editors have to know if the material is for immediate use or for release at a later date. State clearly at the top "For immediate release," "For release after 10 A.M., Tuesday, August 6," or whatever. Most releases are for immediate use, but if you find yourself listing times fairly frequently, try to be evenhanded in your treatment of morning and afternoon newspapers and news programs.

5. *Indicate the end of the release.* Releases of more than one page may be taken apart as they are routed through the editor's desk, to reporter, to copy desk, and beyond. It is important to indicate the end of the release so journalists needn't worry there is fantastic ending floating around somewhere in the office. A good way to indicate there is additional copy after a page is to write "more" at the bottom and "end" at the conclusion.

6. *Type copy in double-space.* Double-spacing allows for minor editorial changes and the space above the story and in the margins permits instructions and headlines. This is particularly important when dealing with weeklys, trade publications, and small radio and television stations not blessed with large newswriting staffs.

> **NOTE:** Single-spaced releases are immediately recognized and judged as the work of amateurs.

7. *Put a headline on the release.* The purpose of the headline is that it tells the editors, who have a mountain of mail in front of them, what the release is all about. Choose a headline that is straightforward—not cute or attention-getting.

TWO KINDS OF EFFECTIVE ANNUAL REPORTS

Not long after bank annual reports have been issued, the same statement can be heard: The reporting of results often fails to adequately meet the needs of the people who receive the report.

Traditionally this yearly report is viewed through the eyes of the owners of the bank, and all information is presented in a light that will be most pleasing to shareholders. The other readers of this material are often forgotten.

One Solution. Prepare two annual reports: one for shareholders, written from their viewpoint; the second for employees, written from their viewpoint.

The shareholder is concerned with profitability of his or her investment, how earnings have progressed (or regressed) in comparison with the year earlier. He or she is concerned with efficient operations as they solely influence profitability. The shareholder wants to take pride in your modern and profitable operation and is concerned with his or her share. The shareholder interests sum up to a need to confirm that he or she has made a prudent investment and that should continue to own a part of the bank.

The employee, on the other hand, is interested in the level of his or her employment. Is it secure? Are promotions available? How good is the benefit package? How does his or her employment package compare with the total package offered by other employers in the area? An employee will want to know if you have a promote-from-within policy, and he or she will identify with a report of a long-term staff member who started at an entry level and advanced to a high position. How do wages at the bank compare with those paid elsewhere? Most employees will want to receive some "psychic" wages and to be told that they are appreciated, that they are doing a good job, and that management is proud of them.

Actually, the information needs of these two groups at annual report time are not all that different. Both need to know that the bank is functioning well and that the outlook is favorable. Of course, good news should be passed along only if it is true. Falsehoods will inevitably be detected and will impair any future effort to report developments and believed.

Both groups—employees and shareholders—should be told that their loyalty and support are appreciated and are key elements in the bank's success.

> **TIP:** A bank that is operated along the theme of "we do it all for you" will go a long way toward developing loyal groups of customers, shareholders, and employees.

In addition to reading good numbers in an annual report, people need to read good things about themselves and their associates. It is no secret that a happy and secure person has a greater loyalty on all levels—shareholder, depositor, and employee.

> **NOTE:** Good news can be presented clearly and simply; also, clearly written material is more likely to be read and absorbed.

GUIDELINES FOR ANNUAL REPORT PREPARATION

The quality of bank annual reports ranges from poor to excellent. Unfortunately, there are more reports on the low end of the scale than on the high. This is true of all segments of business, of course, but perhaps more true in the banking industry.

Banks that score the highest in the quality of their annual reports usually can be found to have followed these points:

1. Begin with a meaningful or attention-getting front cover.

2. Develop a well-designed format, using modern and imaginative designs.

3. Provide complete, detailed, and accurate financial data, and present it in an attractive, yet understandable, manner.

4. Feature brief descriptions of the services offered by the bank.

5. Provide a full story of the bank's year—even if it covers topics covered in last year's report.

6. At some point, in the narrative or in a letter from the chairman and/or president, relate the bank to the banking industry—where the bank stands, the problems and opportunities in the industry, and their impact on the bank.

7. Don't ignore bad news. Present the facts, putting them in perspective, with an explanation of the bank's plans to correct the situation.

8. The writing throughout should be clear, but with style.

9. Discuss the bank's plans or expectations for the coming year.

10. Graphics should be understandable and provide a quick picture of the bank's current position and the trend of performance.

11. Artwork, whether drawings or photographs, should help move the report along. It is usually good to feature people—employees, customers—related to the bank and its facilities and services.

12. Keep in mind in the preparation of the report that it serves not only as a report to stockholders, but as a promotional piece to attract new stockholders, new customers, and new employees.

> **NOTE:** That last point should not be underestimated. Even the worst annual reports are costly to produce. A bank should make sure that it gets as much value for its money,

using the report to its fullest as a
communications tool.

CHOOSING A NEW NAME FOR YOUR BANK

Bank names seem to be changing faster than ever these days—
and not always for the better. The entire business of names and
symbols is now called corporate identity, and it has given birth
to a new kind of consultant who specializes in corporate
identification problems. It also is an important business because it is essential to have a name that is recognizable and an
identity that customers and potential customers can relate to.

With mergers and acquisitions, as well as the expansion of
the financial services industry, the identity of a bank can
become diffused and unclear.

> **KEY POINT:**   A corporate identity program
> that ties services together and enables both the
> public and the institution itself to focus in the
> organization is vital to its success.

Even if a bank is not involved in a merger or expanding
beyond its market area, it probably is a good idea for the
organization to examine its present identity—and what it
would like that identity to be. Actually, every bank is changing
to some extent by offering new services and fighting new
competitors. Therefore, it should use its existing acceptability
within the marketplace and combine that with any new image it
might wish to project.

However, a corporate identity program is not a cure for all
a bank's problems. John Young, the principal and co-founder
of Lee and Young Communications, says that an identity
program can "...only express what the bank is, what it wants to
be and then assist it to achieve the established perceptional
objectives." According to the head of this New-York-based
corporate identification and marketing communications firm,

a bank must "develop a game plan for change."* Part of that game plan may include a new name.

A Change in Name. Consider the case of a bank in the upper-midwest, a medium-size holding company with eight-member banks throughout the state. Because of different subsidiaries and no overall identity, the bank determined that a new name would better identify what the organization had become. Also, a different name would project the direction in which the organization was moving; in short, it would unify the group of banks. Not incidentally, a new name would make savings possible by pooling advertising, promotional activities, and public relations efforts.

The holding company called in Lee and Young which, after considerable study, came up with a name change. At the same time, it was decided that the local community identity should be preserved. Consequently, the new name was teamed with the individual bank's location.

The new name, according to Mr. Young, was selected to meet the needs of the organization. It also contained several important features that all banks should note. It was:

- Short
- Distinctive
- Had good recall
- Good phonetics
- Not limiting
- Provided considerable graphics potential
- Was legally available.

*Used by permission of Lee and Young Communications, New York, N.Y.

A FEW FINAL WORDS

This desk book has presented a great many ideas relating to the countless topics of concern to professional bankers. The material included is designed to provide you with useful tools that will assist you on the job. They are practical, workable suggestions and techniques and procedures that have helped other bankers in other banks address the problems that are part of the daily challenges of modern banking.

Of course, no desk book is ever complete, particularly when it is about an industry as dynamic as banking. However, this desk book does cover many of the current concerns now facing banking in the age of technology and ever-increasing competitive pressures.

The authors are already evaluating additional ideas and techniques to deal with some of the changes taking place in the industry. If you have a suggestion or procedure that has proven effective in your bank, and wish to share it with others in the industry, please let us know about it. We'll gladly consider it for a future edition.

If there are topics you feel should be covered, or if you have other suggestions that will help make the next edition more useful, please let us know that, as well. The objective of this book is to make it an important resource on the job.

In the meantime, we wish you continued success in banking, and we trust that *The Banker's Desk Book* will prove to be a handy—and useful—reference.

INDEX

Absenteeism, 70–72
Acquisitions/mergers, 131–45
   buyouts/takeovers, 136–38, 310–13
   and capital management, 35–37
   and data processing operations, 138–43
   and operations, 134–36
   pitfalls, 132–33
   and pooling vs. purchasing assets, 131–32
Adjustable rate mortgages (ARMs), 319–20
Advertising, 333–40. *See also* Marketing
   comparative, 339–40
   direct mail, 328–30
   planning campaigns, 333–37
   using endorsements, 337–39
Advisory boards, 29–31. *See also* Board of directors
Alarm systems, 233
American Fletcher Mortgage Co. v. *U.S. Steel Credit*, 305
American Homestead Mortgage Corporation, 320-23
Annual reports, 15, 364–67
Appraisals
   of equipment, 296–97
   and IRMAs, 321
Arthur D. Little, Inc., 109, 110
Arthur Young and Company, 102
Assets
   asset-based lending, 293–98, 314
   capital-to-asset ratio, 38–39
   and NIM, 52–54
   pooling vs. purchasing, 131–32
   and rate-mix analysis, 122
Assignment of rights, 100
Auctions, of stock, 6
Audits, 23, 243–46
   committees/departments for, 20, 233

of communications networks, 142
of insurance coverage, 229–32
Automatic teller machines (ATMs), 183, 191, 215–28, 241, 261
   and fraud, 179–80, 216
   network selection, 215–17
   network sharing, 217–19
   and POS terminals, 222–28
   security for, 216–17, 220–21
   site analysis, 219–20

Balance sheets
   off-balance sheet items, 44, 45, 55–56
   segregation (disaggregation) format, 53–55
   and strategic planning, 119–24
Bank holding companies, 7, 36–37
Bank Secrecy Act, 178
Benefits. *See* Compensation agreements; Fringe benefits
Bill paying, 265
Board of directors, 19–31. *See also* Directors
   and advisory boards, 29–31
   characteristics of, 19–21
   meetings, 22–23, 24
Bomb/riot security, 167
Bonding, of personnel, 174
Bonds. *See also* Stocks
   and bank investment portfolios, 59–60
   and liquidity, 58, 59–60
Borrowers. *See* Commercial loans; Customers
Branch banking, 183–93
   branch closings, 192–93
   branch consolidations, 190–92
   and fire insurance, 234–35
   profitability of, 186–88, 190

371